CAMBRIDGE
UNIVERSITY PRESS

Cambridge Grammar and Writing Skills

Teacher's Resource 1-3

Sarah Lindsay and Wendy Wren

University Printing House, Cambridge CB2 8BS, United Kingdom

One Liberty Plaza, 20th Floor, New York, NY 10006, USA

477 Williamstown Road, Port Melbourne, VIC 3207, Australia

314–321, 3rd Floor, Plot 3, Splendor Forum, Jasola District Centre, New Delhi – 110025, India

103 Penang Road, #05-06/07, Visioncrest Commercial, Singapore 238467

Cambridge University Press is part of the University of Cambridge.

It furthers the University's mission by disseminating knowledge in the pursuit of education, learning and research at the highest international levels of excellence.

www.cambridge.org
Information on this title: www.cambridge.org/9781108765466

© Sarah Lindsay and Wendy Wren 2019

20 19 18 17 16 15 14 13 12 11 10 9 8 7 6 5 4

Printed in Great Britain by Ashford Colour Press Ltd.

A catalogue record for this publication is available from the British Library

ISBN 978-1-108-76546-6 Paperback

Contents

Introduction

Cambridge Grammar and Writing Skills: Stages 1–6 is a six-level primary series that aims to help teachers in schools around the world deliver the critical English literacy skills of creative writing and writing for a purpose. It can be used directly to supplement Cambridge International Primary English courses, *Cambridge Global English* and *Cambridge Primary English*, as well as high-level ELT courses. It consists of six full-colour Learner's Books, which include a limited write-in aspect, and two Teacher's Resources. The Teacher's Resources are supplemented by a fully editable online version, which allows you to tailor the planning and amend activity sheets to fit the needs of your learners. The course also links with our new secondary *Grammar and Writing Skills* course, which covers Stages 7 to 9.

Writing is the final and most complex of the four main literacy skills. It is perceived as a key area of weakness in English medium and international schools, where learners often arrive at the school with limited or no English, and therefore need to spend much of their primary school education building up knowledge of usable vocabulary, as well as developing speaking and listening skills. This focus can conflict with the need later on in primary to develop the skill of writing for a purpose, which is a crucial foundation for learners to succeed in an English-medium secondary curriculum, where they will be expected to write in different forms, particularly non-fiction text types, such as explanations and recounts, for the various curriculum subjects.

Therefore, a further key purpose of this series is to help schools bridge the gap between high-performing learners who are currently being taught English as a second language and are looking to move across to the demands of a first-language English course. Alternatively, the series can be used to support children who are struggling with writing in a first-language course. The scheme works by providing the following features:

1 Specific units of work that deliver the teaching and learning objectives of creative writing and writing for a purpose.

2 A clear structure in each unit expressed clearly in the Learner's Books – modelled writing/stimulus and discussion/comprehension; grammar for writing; planning for writing; writing and checking/assessing writing.

3 Assessment and marking guidance for teachers – marking cribs and assessment advice. This assessment will also touch on the skill of choosing which type of writing is appropriate for a particular purpose.

4 Units of work which map to and share topics with the *Cambridge Global English* series, and are also mapped to *Cambridge Primary English*.

Cambridge Grammar and Writing Skills therefore will play a vital role in helping young international learners take the critical step of becoming proficient, practised and accomplished writers across an array of writing styles and purposes, which can only stand them in good stead to achieve success at IGCSE, IB Diploma and A Level.

How to use the Learner's Books

Unit walkthrough

Unit title

The unit title clearly states:
- the writing category
- the strand within the category that is the focus of the unit.

Let's read

Reading text: The reading text in each unit is an example of the required writing outcome for the unit.

It contains the grammar, stylistic points and appropriate layout of the writing style that learners are required to produce at the end of the unit.

Introduction box: This gives a simple explanation of what the writing type is and how it is used.

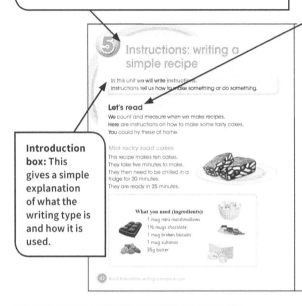

Let's talk

Class discussion: This section gives learners the opportunity to discuss the text in detail.

Let's learn

Activities: The reading and comprehension sections are followed by a series of activities designed to help learners focus on the appropriate features for the writing style, for example, style, grammar and layout.

Section A (Stages 1 and 2) / Section A and B (Stage 3):
Questions in this section tend to be literal, though occasionally they give the learners the opportunity to go deeper into the text to allow them to make inferences and deductions.

Section B (Stages 1 and 2) / Section C (Stage 3):
This section concentrates on the layout, style and grammar appropriate to the required writing outcome.

Stages 1 and 2

Let's practise

Writing practise: Here, teacher and learners collaborate in producing a piece of writing modelled on the reading text.

Writing activity: This clearly states what learners have to produce for the writing outcome.

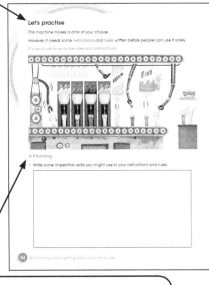

Stage 3

Let's practise

Writing practise: Here, teacher and learners collaborate in producing a piece of writing modelled on the reading text.

Writing: Based on the collaboration with the teacher, class discussion and note-making, learners now write their first draft.

Writing activity: This clearly states what learners have to produce for the writing outcome.

Planning: Learners are guided through the planning stage with questions, prompts and step-by-step guidance as a basis for planning notes.

Writer's Toolbox: Learners are given a 'toolbox' that consists of the grammar, stylistic points and layout guidance from the Let's learn section of the unit. This is to enable them to check, edit and proofread their work, before producing a final copy.

Teacher's Resource How to use the Learner's Books

© Sarah Lindsay and Wendy Wren 2019

Stages 1 and 2

Let's write

Independent writing: Learners are now asked to produce a piece of writing independently, using the grammar, style and layout skills they have learned in the unit.

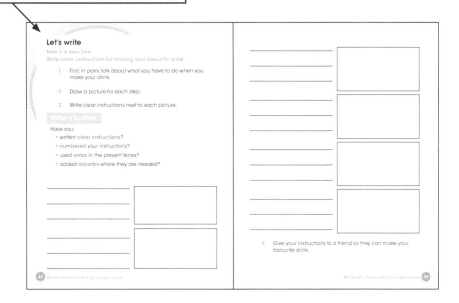

Stage 3

Let's write

Independent writing: Learners are now asked to produce a piece of writing independently, using the grammar, style and layout skills they have learned in the unit.

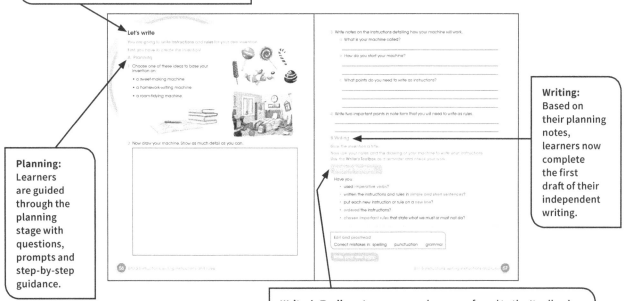

Planning: Learners are guided through the planning stage with questions, prompts and step-by-step guidance.

Writing: Based on their planning notes, learners now complete the first draft of their independent writing.

Writer's Toolbox: Learners are given, or referred to the 'toolbox', which consists of grammar, stylistic points and layout guidance from the Let's learn section of the unit. This is to enable them to check, edit and proofread their work before producing a final copy.

Teacher's Resource How to use the Learner's Books

Scope and sequence: Stage 1

Unit	Reading Let's read	Comprehension Let's talk	Writing features Let's learn	Teacher-guided writing Let's practise	Independent writing Let's write
1	**Narrative writing:** writing words, lists and captions *Off to school*	• What does the picture show? • What information does the list provide? • What extra information do captions provide?	• Naming words • Describing words	• Listing items found in a picture • Writing captions for some given items	• Writing a list of things that need to be done before going to bed
2	**Personal writing:** writing names and simple sentences *Meet the Patel family*	• What does the picture show? • Recognising small and capital letters • Discussing sentence structure	• Special naming words • Writing sentences	• Writing simple sentences	• Writing simple sentences
3	**Poetry:** writing poems *In the park*	• What does the picture show? • What is the poem about? • Find the rhyming words	• Doing words • Rhyming words	• Completing a poem with rhyming words	• Completing a poem with rhyming words
4	**Narrative writing:** writing sentences *A new kite*	• What happens in the story? • What are the characters in the story like?	• Describing words • Writing sentences • Joining sentences	• Writing sentences about a character	• Writing sentences about a character
5	**Explanatory writing:** writing labels and captions *City Farm*	• What is the poster about? • What do the photographs show? • What do the captions tell us?	• Naming words • More than one	• Adding labels and writing a caption	• Writing captions
6	**Factual writing:** alphabetic texts *The alphabet*	• Recognising letters in the alphabet • Discussing a simple dictionary page • Recognising alphabetical order	• The alphabet • Alphabetical order	• Writing a dictionary page – planning	• Writing a dictionary page
7	**Instructions:** writing instructions and rules *Let's go to the animal park*	• Following instructions • Discussing rules	• Full stops and capital letters • Doing words	• Writing instructions for the animal park	• Writing instructions for a given map • Writing rules for walking home from school
8	**Personal writing:** writing recounts *By the sea*	• What does the recount tell you? • Thinking about the personal recount • How is a personal recount written?	• Doing words • Describing words	• Recounting a visit by water	• Recounting an encounter with water
9	**Factual writing:** writing a fact file *Fact file: Cities*	• What does the fact file tell us? • What is a fact? • Which books give us facts not stories?	• Questions • Writing facts	• Writing a fact file about places you can visit in a city	• Writing a fact file about different types of transport you can find in a city

Resource sheets	Cross-curricular links	Critical thinking	Cambridge Global English links	Cambridge Primary English links
• Write a list • Write captions • Use naming and describing words	• Art (colouring pictures)	• Analysing and interpreting a picture and list • Self-organisation (working out jobs you need to do in the evening and making a list)	Stage 1: Unit 1: Welcome to school	Stage 1: Unit 2: Finding out and making
• Special naming words and writing sentences • Write about your family	• Social Studies (talking about family; identifying preferences)	• Analysing and interpreting pictures and texts • Planning writing of sentences (noting down words)	Stage 1: Unit 2: Family time	Stage 1: Unit 1: Playing with friends
• Rhyming words • Write a poem	• Literature (poetry and rhyme)	• Analysing and interpreting a picture and a poem • Identifying rhyme • Planning writing (noting down words) • Creating a poem	Stage 1: Unit 3: Fun and games	Stage 1: Unit 3: Rhyme time Stage 1: Unit 6: Rhyme time 2 Stage 1: Unit 9: Poems and rhymes on a theme
• Naming words and describing words • Write about a friend	• Science (flying a kite; the weather)	• Analysing and interpreting a story • Thinking about how to write longer sentences • Planning writing (noting down words) • Writing a description	Stage 1: Unit 4: Making things	Stage 1: Unit 1: Playing with friends Stage 1: Unit 7: Make-believe stories
• More than one • Write about a day out	• Science (caring for farm animals)	• Analysing and interpreting a poster • Looking closely at details in a photograph • Constructing captions for pictures	Stage 1: Unit 5: On the farm	Stage 1: Unit 4: Joining-in stories
• Alphabetical order • Plan a dictionary page • Write a dictionary page	• Science (the body and senses)	• Analysing and interpreting a dictionary page • Learning to use a dictionary • Sequencing words in alphabetical order • Writing a dictionary page	Stage 1: Unit 6: My five senses	Stage 1: Unit 5: Reading to find out
• Write sentences and look for doing words • Write instructions • Write rules	• Geography (reading a map) • Science (identifying zoo animals)	• Analysing and interpreting a map • Following instructions • Interpreting rules • Writing clear instructions and rules • Proofreading your writing	Stage 1: Unit 7: Let's go!	Stage 1: Unit 2: Finding out and making
• Doing words and describing words • Rewrite a recount	• Social studies (preferences for places)	• Analysing and interpreting a personal recount • Comparing experiences • Considering preferences • Writing a personal recount • Proofreading your writing	Stage 1: Unit 8: Wonderful water	Stage 1: Unit 8: Things that have happened
• Questions • Writing facts	• Social Studies (thinking about cities and transport)	• Analysing and interpreting a fact file • Describing pictures accurately • Considering the purpose of your writing • Creating a fact file	Stage 1: Unit 9: City places	

Teacher's Resource Scope and sequence: Stage 1

Scope and sequence: Stage 2

Unit	Reading Let's read	Comprehension Let's talk	Writing features Let's learn	Teacher-guided writing Let's practise	Independent writing Let's write
1	**Stories:** plot *Seagull*	• What happens in the story? • What happens in the beginning, middle and end of the story? • How does the main character feel?	• Exclamation marks • Ordering sentences	• Looking closely at what happened at the beginning, middle and end of a given story	• Writing a simple story using given picture prompts
2	**Stories:** dialogue in stories *Ben has lost his cat*	• What does the comic strip show? • Looking closely at who's talking	• Writing sentences • Speech bubbles	• Writing speech bubbles	• Writing speech bubbles
3	**Personal writing:** writing a recount *My race*	• What happens in the recount? • How do recounts differ from stories?	• Verbs • Adjectives	• Thinking about structuring a recount • Writing a recount	• Thinking about structuring a recount • Writing a recount
4	**Explanatory writing:** writing an explanation *Day and night*	• What does the information tell you? • How is the information written?	• Joining words	• Ordering sentences in an explanation • Completing a flow diagram	• Writing an explanation • Completing a flow diagram
5	**Instructions:** writing a simple recipde *Mini rocky road cakes*	• Following instructions • Discussing how instructions are organised	• Verbs • Adverbs	• Writing instructions on cleaning up	• Writing instructions on how to make a drink
6	**Writing poems:** rhyming poems and list poems *Bugs, bugs, everywhere*	• Discussing rhyming words • Discussing the poems • Personal preference	• Rhyming words • Contractions • Verbs	• Writing a list poem	• Writing a rhyming poem
7	**Factual writing:** writing notes and tables *Trees give us many things*	• What does the information tell you? • Discussing notes	• Nouns • Commas	• Highlighting important information • Writing notes • Completing a table	• Highlighting important information • Writing notes
8	**Writing to communicate:** interviews *Grandad, where did you live?*	• What does the interview tell you? • Discussing the questions and answers	• Past and present verbs • Questions	• An interview with a friend	• An interview with an older person
9	**Stories:** setting and characters *Sang Kancil and Crocodile*	• What does the story tell us? • Discussing the setting • Discussing the characters	• Writing sentences • Adjectives • Joining words	• Writing a setting • Writing about a character • Planning a story	• Writing a story

© Sarah Lindsay and Wendy Wren 2019

Resource sheets	Cross-curricular links	Critical thinking	Cambridge Global English links	Cambridge Primary English links
• Exclamation marks • Ordering a story	• Social/Environmental Studies (cleaning the beach and helping a seagull injured by oil and litter)	• Analysing and interpreting a story • Ordering sentences in a story for sense	Stage 2: Unit 1: Look in a book	Stage 1: Unit 1: Stories about things we know Stage 1: Unit 8: Things under the sea
• Speech bubbles • What happens next?	• Social Studies (supporting friends and neighbours) • Social Studies (conquering fears)	• Analysing a comic strip story and interpreting speech bubbles • Planning and creating a comic strip	Stage 2: Unit 2: Good neighbours	Stage 2: Unit 1: Stories about things we know
• Verbs and adjectives • Writing a recount	• Physical Education (running a race) • Social Studies (taking part in and enjoying competitive sport whatever the outcome)	• Analysing and interpreting a personal recount • Writing a recount, making it personal and interesting	Stage 2: Unit 3: Ready, steady, go!	
• Joining words • Writing an explanation	• Science (the Sun, the Earth and the sky; day and night)	• Analysing and interpreting a text and flow diagram • Thinking about how to write longer sentences • Creating a flow diagram • Writing a clear explanation	Stage 2: Unit 4: The big sky	Stage 2: Unit 4: What is my house made of?
• Verbs and adverbs • Ordering instructions	• Food Technology (reading and writing a recipe; cleaning up after cooking)	• Analysing, interpreting and following a recipe • Thinking about how to make a recipe clearer • Creating a recipe, with pictures and clear instructions	Stage 2: Unit 5: Let's count and measure	Stage 2: Unit 2: How to write instructions
• Rhyming words • Writing a poem	• Literature (poetry and rhyme) • Science (bugs and insects)	• Analysing, interpreting and comparing poems • Identifying rhyme • Planning and writing a rhyming poem	Stage 2: Unit 6: Bugs: fact and fiction	Stage 2: Unit 3: Rhymes about places and people we know Stage 2: Unit 6: Poems by famous poets Stage 2: Unit 9: All kinds of creatures
• Commas • Completing a table	• Science (trees and wood; cacao to chocolate)	• Analysing and interpreting notes and a table • Identifying important information in a text • Writing notes with important information • Using tables to describe things	Stage 2: Unit 7: Our green Earth	Stage 2: Unit 8: Things under the sea
• Verb tenses • An interview	• History (homes people used to live in; daily life for previous generations)	• Analysing and interpreting an interview • Finding out as much as you can when interviewing • Thinking about good interview questions • Carrying out a real interview	Stage 2: Unit 8: Home, sweet home	Stage 2: Unit 5: What is my house made of?
• A setting • A character	• Literature (reading, analysing and writing a story)	• Analysing and interpreting a story • Thinking about setting and characters • Thinking about how to make stories more interesting • Thinking about how to write longer sentences • Planning and writing a story, with an interesting setting and characters and clear plot development	Stage 2: Unit 9: Inside and outside cities	Stage 2: Unit 4: Tales from around the world

Teacher's Resource Scope and sequence: Stage 2

Scope and sequence: Stage 3

Unit	Reading Let's read	Comprehension Let's talk	Writing features Let's learn	Teacher-guided writing Let's practise	Independent writing Let's write
1	**Explanatory writing:** How is it done? *How do aeroplanes fly?*	• What happens in the explanation? • How is the explanation written?	• Writing sentences • Comparing words • Headings • Sequences • Pictures and diagrams	• Writing captions that plot the sequence of an explanation	• Writing an explanation
2	**Writing to communicate:** writing a letter	• Why is the letter written? • What happens in the letter? • Looking closely at how a letter is structured	• Pronouns • Address and date • Paragraphs • Letter endings	• Writing a letter	• Writing a letter
3	**Narrative writing:** dialogue in stories *What a race!*	• What happens in the story? • Looking at dialogue	• Dialogue • Contractions • Other words for 'said'	• Writing a conversation	• Writing a conversation
4	**Poems:** humorous poems *Catch a Little Rhyme*	• What is the poem about? • How is the poem written? • What do you think about the poem?	• Rhyme • Pronouns • Verbs • Prepositions	• Planning a humorous poem	• Writing a humorous poem
5	**Instructions:** writing instructions and rules	• What do instructions tell you? • Discussing how instructions are organised • Discussing how rules are organised	• Imperative verbs • Adjectives • Sentences	• Writing instructions • and rules for a given invention	• Writing instructions and rules for an imagined invention
6	**Writing to persuade:** posters and leaflets *Dinosaurs' Den*	• Discussing posters • Discussing leaflets	• Adjectives • Conjunctions • Sentences • Information • Layout	• Writing a poster	• Writing a leaflet
7	**Narrative writing:** play scripts *The Code of the Trees*	• What happens in the play? • What do we learn about the characters? • How is a play script written?	• Layout of play scripts • Dialogue in play scripts • Adverbs	• Writing a play script	• Continuing the play script
8	**Alphabetic texts:** a glossary	• What does the dictionary page tell you? • What does the glossary tell you? • Comparing dictionaries and glossaries	• Alphabetical order • Parts of speech • Definitions	• Writing a glossary for a given book	• Writing a glossary for a book of your own choice
9	**Narrative writing:** story settings and endings *Too small ... too big!*	• What does the story tell us? • Discussing the setting • Discussing the ending	• Past tenses • Adjectives • Story structure • Writing an opening • Writing an ending	• Writing a setting • Writing an ending	• Writing a setting • Writing an ending

Resource sheets	Cross-curricular links	Critical thinking	Cambridge Global English links	Cambridge Primary English links
• Sentences • Writing an explanation	• Science (how aeroplanes fly)	• Analysing and interpreting an explanation • Comparing things • Sequencing stages in chronological order • Editing and proofreading	Stage 3: Unit 1: Working together	Stage 2: Unit 5: What is my house made of?
• Pronouns • Writing a letter	• Social Studies (remembering the past)	• Analysing and interpreting a letter • Thinking about how formal or informal to be when writing a letter • Editing and proofreading	Stage 3: Unit 2: Family and memories	Stage 3: Unit 5: Letters
• Writing dialogue • Using speech bubbles	• Geography (the desert) • Science (desert animals)	• Analysing and interpreting narrative writing • Imagining and writing the next stage of a narrative story • Thinking about words to make writing more interesting • Editing and proofreading	Stage 3: Unit 3: The desert	Stage 3: Unit 8: Wonderful world
• Prepositions • Linking rhyming words	• Literature (poetry and rhyme)	• Analysing and interpreting a humorous poem • Identifying rhyme • Planning and writing a poem • Editing and proofreading	Stage 3: Unit 4: Look again	Stage 3: Unit 9: Laughing allowed Stage 3: Unit 3: See, hear, feel, enjoy Stage 3: Unit 6: Poems from around the world
• Imperative verbs • Writing instructions and rules	• Science (inventions)	• Analysing and interpreting instructions • Thinking about how to make instructions easy to understand • Imagining an invention • Planning and writing clear instructions • Editing and proofreading	Stage 3: Unit 5: Inventors and inventions	Stage 2: Unit 2: How to write instructions
• Adjectives • Planning the writing for a leaflet	• Social Studies (persuasive posters and leaflets) • Science (dinosaurs)	• Analysing and interpreting a persuasive poster and leaflet • Thinking about how to make writing persuasive and interesting • Planning and creating an interesting and attractive poster • Editing and proofreading	Stage 3: Unit 6: Dinosaurs	Stage 3: Unit 8: Wonderful world
• Adverbs • The layout of a play	• Literature and Drama (play scripts)	• Analysing and interpreting a play script • Imagining the next part of a play • Planning and writing the end of a play script • Editing and proofreading	Stage 3: Unit 7: Puzzles and codes	Stage 3: Unit 3: See, hear, feel, enjoy
• Alphabetical order • Writing a glossary	• Science (the human body)	• Analysing and interpreting a dictionary and a glossary • Sequencing words in alphabetical order • Distinguishing parts of speech • Planning and writing a glossary for a non-fiction book • Editing and proofreading	Stage 3: Unit 8: Our amazing body	Stage 3: Unit 8: Let's have a party! Stage 3: Unit 8: Wonderful world
• Verb tenses • Writing a story setting	• Physical Education (sports)	• Analysing and interpreting a story setting and ending • Thinking about the structure of stories (beginning, middle, end) • Viewing a situation from a different perspective • Planning and writing a story setting and ending • Editing and proofreading	Stage 3: Unit 9: Big and little	Stage 3: Unit 1: Ordinary days

13

Teacher's Resource Scope and sequence: Stage 3

Framework correlations: Stages 1–3

Learning objectives from Cambridge Assessment International Education's Primary English and Primary English as a Second Language frameworks have been correlated with *Cambridge Grammar and Writing Skills: Stages 1–3* in the tables below.

Stage 1: Cambridge Primary English curriculum framework

	Unit 1	Unit 2	Unit 3	Unit 4	Unit 5	Unit 6	Unit 7	Unit 8	Unit 9
Writing									
1Wo2 Form letters correctly						✔			
1Wa1 Write simple storybooks with sentences to caption pictures	✔								
1Wa3 Record answers to questions, e.g. as lists, charts					✔				
1Wa5 Write for a purpose using some basic features of text type									✔
1Wa6 Write simple information texts with labels, captions, lists, questions and instructions for a purpose					✔				
1Wt1 Write a sequence of sentences retelling a familiar story or recounting an experience								✔	
1Wp1 Mark some sentence endings with a full stop		✔		✔			✔	✔	✔
1Wp2 Compose and write a simple sentence with a capital letter and a full stop		✔		✔			✔	✔	
1Wp3 Write sentence-like structures which may be joined by *and*				✔					

Stage 1: Cambridge Primary English as a Second Language curriculum framework

	Unit 1	Unit 2	Unit 3	Unit 4	Unit 5	Unit 6	Unit 7	Unit 8	Unit 9
Writing									
1Wa2 Form upper and lower case letters of regular size and shape		✔				✔			
1Wa4 Copy letters and familiar high frequency words and phrases correctly		✔				✔			

Extracts from the curriculum frameworks are reproduced by permission of Cambridge Assessment International Education.

	Unit 1	Unit 2	Unit 3	Unit 4	Unit 5	Unit 6	Unit 7	Unit 8	Unit 9
1Wa5 Copy upper and lower case letters accurately when writing names and places		✔							
1Wa6 Write familiar words to identify people, places and objects	✔			✔				✔	
Use of English									
1Uf1 Use imperative forms of common verbs for basic commands and instructions							✔		
1Uf2 Use common present simple forms [positive, negative, question] to give basic personal information			✔						
1Uf3 Use common present continuous forms [positive, negative, question] to talk about what is happening now			✔						
1Ug1 Use common singular nouns, plural nouns [plural 's'] and proper names to say what things are	✔	✔			✔				
1Ug3 Use basic adjectives and colours to say what someone/something is or has	✔			✔				✔	
1Ut1 Use the questions: *What colour is it? What now?*	✔								
1Ut3 Use interrogative pronouns *which, what, where* to ask basic questions									✔
1Ut6 Use conjunction *and* to link words and phrases				✔					

Stage 2: Cambridge Primary English curriculum framework

	Unit 1	Unit 2	Unit 3	Unit 4	Unit 5	Unit 6	Unit 7	Unit 8	Unit 9
Writing									
2Wo3 Begin to reread own writing for sense and accuracy					✔	✔		✔	✔
2Wo4 Use simple non-fiction texts as a model for writing				✔	✔		✔	✔	
2Wo5 Use the structures of familiar poems and stories in developing own writing						✔			
2Wo7 Make simple notes from a section of non-fiction texts, e.g. listing key words							✔	✔	

Extracts from the curriculum frameworks are reproduced by permission of Cambridge Assessment International Education

	Unit 1	Unit 2	Unit 3	Unit 4	Unit 5	Unit 6	Unit 7	Unit 8	Unit 9
2Wa1 Develop stories with a setting, characters and a sequence of events	✔								✔
2Wa2 Choose interesting words and phrases, e.g. in describing people and places			✔						✔
2Wa4 Begin to use dialogue in stories		✔							
2Wa5 Use features of chosen text type				✔	✔		✔	✔	
2Wa6 Write instructions and recount events and experiences				✔	✔				
2Wt1 Structure a story with a beginning, middle and end	✔								✔
2Wt2 Use the language of time, e.g. *suddenly, after that*			✔						
2Wt3 Link ideas in sections, grouped by content									✔
2Wt4 Use a variety of simple organisational devices in non-fiction, e.g. headings, captions					✔		✔		
2Wp1 Write in clear sentences using capital letters, full stops and question marks	✔	✔					✔	✔	✔
2Wp2 Find alternatives to *and/then* in developing a narrative and connecting ideas									✔
2Wp3 Use mainly simple and compound sentences, with *and/but* to connect ideas. *Because* may begin to be used in a complex sentence				✔					✔
2Wp4 Use the past and present tenses accurately (if not always consistently)			✔		✔	✔		✔	
2Wp5 Begin to vary sentence openings, e.g. with simple adverbs					✔				
2Wp6 Write using a variety of sentence types		✔							✔

Extracts from the curriculum frameworks are reproduced by permission of Cambridge Assessment International Education

Stage 2: Cambridge Primary English as a Second Language curriculum framework

	Unit 1	Unit 2	Unit 3	Unit 4	Unit 5	Unit 6	Unit 7	Unit 8	Unit 9
Writing									
2Wa1 Plan, write and check, with support, short sentences on familiar topics	✔	✔							
2Wc1 Write, with support, short sentences which give basic personal information			✔						
2Wc2 Write short familiar instructions with support from their peers					✔				
2Wo1 Link with support words or phrases using basic coordinating connectors				✔					✔
2Wo2 Include a full stop and question mark during guided writing of short, familiar sentences	✔	✔						✔	✔
2Wo3 Use upper and lower case letters accurately when writing names, places and short sentences during guided writing activities	✔	✔					✔		
Use of English									
2Uf1 Use imperative forms [positive and negative] to give short instructions					✔				
2Uf2 Use common simple present forms, including short answer forms and contractions, to give personal information					✔	✔		✔	
2Uf3 Use common past simple forms [regular and irregular] to describe actions and narrate simple events including short answer forms and contractions			✔			✔		✔	
2Uf5 Use common present continuous forms, including short answers and **contractions,** to talk about what is happening now on personal and familiar topics								✔	
2Ug1 Use singular nouns, plural nouns – including some common irregular **plural** forms – and uncountable nouns, genitive 's/s' to name and label things							✔		
2Ug3 Use adjectives, including possessive adjectives, on familiar topics to give personal information and describe things			✔						✔

Extracts from the curriculum frameworks are reproduced by permission of Cambridge Assessment International Education

	Unit 1	Unit 2	Unit 3	Unit 4	Unit 5	Unit 6	Unit 7	Unit 8	Unit 9
2Ug6 Use common -ly adverbs to describe actions					✔				
2Ut2 Use who, what, where, how many to ask questions on familiar topics								✔	
2Ut8 Use conjunctions and, or, but to link words and phrases				✔					✔

Stage 3: Cambridge Primary English curriculum framework

	Unit 1	Unit 2	Unit 3	Unit 4	Unit 5	Unit 6	Unit 7	Unit 8	Unit 9
Writing									
3Wo6 Use reading as a model for writing dialogue			✔				✔		
3Wo8 Write simple playscripts based on reading							✔		
3Wa1 Develop descriptions of settings in stories									✔
3Wa1 Establish purpose for writing, using features and style based on model texts	✔	✔	✔	✔	✔	✔	✔	✔	✔
3Wa8 Write book reviews summarising what a book is about							✔		
3Wa9 Write and perform poems, attending to the sound of words				✔					
3Wa10 Write letters, notes and messages		✔							
3Wt1 Develop a range of adverbials to signal the relationship between events		✔	✔	✔					
3Wt2 Begin to organise writing in sections or paragraphs in extended stories									✔
3Wt3 Plan main points as a structure for story writing									✔
3Wp1 Maintain accurate use of capital letters and full stops in showing sentences	✔		✔			✔			
3Wp2 Use a wider variety of sentence types including simple, compound and some complex sentences					✔	✔		✔	
3Wp3 Continue to improve consistency in the use of tenses				✔	✔				✔

Extracts from the curriculum frameworks are reproduced by permission of
Cambridge Assessment International Education

	Unit 1	Unit 2	Unit 3	Unit 4	Unit 5	Unit 6	Unit 7	Unit 8	Unit 9
3Wp4 Vary sentence openings, e.g. with adverbs							✔		✔
3Wp6 Learn the basic conventions of speech punctuation and begin to use speech marks			✔						
3Wp7 Use question marks, exclamation marks, and commas in lists			✔			✔			
3Wp13 Ensure grammatical agreement of pronouns and verbs in using standard English		✔		✔					

Stage 3: Cambridge Primary English as a Second Language curriculum framework

	Unit 1	Unit 2	Unit 3	Unit 4	Unit 5	Unit 6	Unit 7	Unit 8	Unit 9
Writing									
3Wa1 Plan, write and check sentences, with support, on a limited range of general and curricular topics	✔	✔	✔	✔	✔	✔	✔	✔	✔
3Wa2 Write, with support, longer sentences on a limited range of general and curricular topics						✔			
3Wc1 Write, with support, short sentences which describe people, places and objects						✔			✔
3Wo1 Link, with some support, sentences using basic coordinating connectors						✔			
3Wo2 Use full stops, commas, question marks, and speech marks at sentence level with some accuracy when writing independently			✔			✔			
3Wo3 Use upper and lower case letters accurately when writing names, places and short sentences when writing independently	✔		✔						

Extracts from the curriculum frameworks are reproduced by permission of Cambridge Assessment International Education.

	Unit 1	Unit 2	Unit 3	Unit 4	Unit 5	Unit 6	Unit 7	Unit 8	Unit 9
Use of English									
3Uf1 Use numbers 1–100 to count; use basic quantifiers *many, much, not many, a lot of* on a limited range of general and curricular topics					✔				
3Uf4 Use imperative forms with direct and indirect object forms to give a short sequence of instructions					✔				
3Uf6 Use simple past regular and irregular forms to describe actions and narrate simple events on a limited range of general and curricular topics				✔					
3Ug6 Use common prepositions of location, position and direction: *at, above, below, behind, between, in, in front of, inside, near, next to, on, opposite, outside, to, under* on a limited range of general and curricular topics				✔					

Extracts from the curriculum frameworks are reproduced by permission of
Cambridge Assessment International Education

Cambridge Grammar and Writing Skills

Teacher's Resource 1-3

Stage 1

Unit guides: Stage 1

Unit 1: Narrative writing: writing words, lists and captions

Learner's Book unit focus

This unit introduces the **writing of words** in the form of **lists** and **extending writing words to writing simple captions**.

Progress table for Stage 1: Unit 1					
Category: Narrative writing					
Writing outcome: Writing lists and captions					
In this first stage of writing, the learners learn that writing words is a form of communication and that words can relate to things around them.					
Stage 1	**Stage 2**	**Stage 3**	**Stage 4**	**Stage 5**	**Stage 6**
• writing words • writing lists • writing captions					
Cambridge Global English link: Stage 1: Unit 1: Welcome to school **Cambridge Primary English link:** Stage 1: Unit 2: Finding out and making					

Unit teaching plan

Warm up

- Begin by talking to the learners about coming to school each day. Ask:
  - *Are there some things you need to remember?*
  - *Who reminds you about the things you must not forget?* [for example, teacher, parent, other family member]
  - *Can you think of another way you could remember things for yourselves?*
- Show the learners a list you wrote to remind yourself of the things you needed to bring to school today.
- Ask the learners to suggest things they needed to remember this morning. Write the class's suggestions on the board in the form of a list.

Let's read

The learners are introduced to Chad, who is getting ready for school. He has written himself a list of things he wants to remember. Some of the listed items are illustrated with captions that highlight colour words.

First, read the extract to the class, and then have learners read it to the class.

- Highlight why Chad has written a list. Discuss why people use lists (for example, as a reminder, as a way of grouping things, etc.).
- Be sure the learners all understand the extract and what it is showing.
- Discuss the different forms lists can take (for example, a list of items, a list of things to do, a list of names, a list of favourite things or places, etc.).
- Ask the learners what they notice about the captions (for example, they are made from more than one word, they describe a picture, they all have colour words).

Plenary

- Organise the learners into pairs. Ask each pair to write their own list of things they need to remember for school.
- Ask the learners, either in groups or individually, to list as many things as they can that they see around the classroom. Give them a time limit and the winning group or individual is the one with the most things on their list.

Let's talk

This section asks the learners questions that:

- give them a greater understanding of the text
- focus on the specific writing activity covered in the unit.

Activity A: This section is to ensure learners have understood what they have read.

Answers

A	1	To school	2	Green	3	Blue
	4	Shoes and ball	5	Yes		

Activity B: This section focuses the learners on what lists are and why we might use them. The learners should discuss the answers.

Answers

B *Example answers:*

1 There are five things on Chad's list.

2 Chad has written the list so he doesn't forget anything important he has to take to school.

3 *Open discussion on why lists can help us remember things and why this might be a good idea.*

4 The captions give us more information about the listed items. They tell us what colours they are.

Let's learn

This section:

- introduces work on naming words (*nouns*) and describing words (*adjectives*)
- gives learners the opportunity to practise what they have learned in a focused activity before incorporating it into their own writing.

Naming words

- Write a number of naming words on the board (for example, cat, jumper, rice, hat). Introduce the learners to the objects' 'names': cat, jumper, rice, hat).
- Hold up different objects. Ask the learners to give you the objects' names.
- Read the information box with the learners.
- Introduce the term *noun*. Mention that there are different types of noun, but that at the moment we are only interested in the nouns that are objects.
- Encourage the learners to work through each exercise individually or in pairs.

Activity A: The learners are asked to copy the naming words from the box next to the correct objects in the picture.

Activity B: There are three objects that still need labelling. Ask the learners to fill the labels correctly. Remind them that these objects were also on Chad's list; this might aid their spelling or give them a point of reference.

Answers

A and B

Describing words

- Write a number of colour words on the board (for example, red, yellow, blue, green). Explain to the learners that these are *describing words*; they describe the colour of something.
- Hold up different objects. Ask the learners what colours they are.
- Read the information box with the learners.
- Introduce the term *adjective*.
- Encourage the learners to work through each activity individually or in pairs.

Activity A: The learners are required to add the correct colour word from the box to each caption.

Answers

A	1	A blue book	2	A red cup
	3	A yellow flower	4	A green chair
	5	A blue cake	6	A green door

Activity B: The learners are asked to recognise the colour within the given captions and colour the pictures correctly.

Answers

B 1 A ball coloured blue

2 A cup coloured yellow

3 A door coloured red

Let's practise

This section allows you to model the required writing outcome with input from the learners.

Before writing

- Always encourage the learners to talk about what they are going to write. Discussing things can help them to organise their thoughts.
- Look at the picture with the learners. Ask them verbally to list objects they can see.

Shared writing activity

- Explain to the learners that they are going to write a list of things they can see in the playground picture.
- The listed words at the side of the picture will help focus their attention on items. The learners then circle the items they can see.
- Discuss which items cannot be found in the picture.
- Discuss other objects that can be found in the picture but are not listed. You could write these words on the board.
- Now ask the learners to write their own list of items found in the picture. Mention that lists are normally written vertically, down the page.
- The activity can be done individually, in pairs or in groups.
- Finally, look at individual items illustrated. Discuss the captions learners can write for these items describing their colours.
- Give the learners opportunities to discuss what they have written, either with you or with their peers.

Let's write

The learners are now required independently to produce a finished list, having worked through a similar exercise in the previous section. Encourage learners to share their work in progress with you so that, through discussion, they can improve it.

Before writing

- Remind the learners of Chad's list at the beginning of the unit, which reminded him of the things he needed to take to school.
- Encourage them to think about the different options and choose the best one.
- Ask them to write their list carefully and neatly.
- Help the learners with their spellings of words if necessary.

Marking criteria

Technical aspects
Look for correct use of: • list writing (normally vertically).
Content
• Does the list make sense?   • Has the learner considered actual things they might need to do when getting home from school and before going to bed?

After writing

- Read through the completed lists with the learners. Compare the different versions the learners will have written.
- Discuss the different things learners do when they get home from school.

Plenary

Discuss lists that use phrases rather than single words (for example, clean teeth, watch TV, eat lunch, etc.). Can the learners add more detail to the lists they have written?

Resource sheets

The resource sheets for Unit 1 provide differentiation for the writing outcome in this unit, as well as further practice on nouns and adjectives.

1 A resource sheet on writing a list.
2 A resource sheet on writing colour captions.
3 A resource sheet practising nouns and adjectives.

Resource sheet 1: Writing words, lists and captions: write a list

Resource sheet 1 covers another reason why we write lists. Learners are asked to write a list of items they would like to receive for their birthday. If they have recently had their birthday, it might be more appropriate to choose a different celebration during which they receive presents.

- Read through the sheet with the learners so they fully understand what is expected of them.
- Highlight that their list of present ideas can be in any order.
- Encourage the learners to write carefully and neatly.

- When the learner has completed their list, read through it with them to ensure it makes sense.
- To extend the activity, the learners can write a list of short phrases rather than single words, or they can give reasons for the objects they have chosen.
- With the class, compare the learners' lists – are there any objects that a number of the learners want? If so, why might that be?

Resource sheet 2: Writing words, lists and captions: write captions

Resource sheet 2 requires the learners to write captions. Learners are expected to colour given objects and then write a relevant caption describing the object and its colour.

- Explain the task and allow time for learners to ask questions so they fully understand what is required.
- Remind the learners what adjectives are and discuss why they are used.
- Ask them to use different colours to colour the objects.
- Help them with vocabulary they might want to use.
- Share their final captions with their peers. How many different colours did the group/class use?

Resource sheet 3: Writing words, lists and captions: use naming and describing words

Resource sheet 3 requires the learners to distinguish between naming and describing words. Learners are asked to look at the words in the word box and write them correctly in the given lists.

- Remind the learners what naming words (*nouns*) and describing words (*adjectives*) are.
- Explain that the box contains both naming and describing words. The learners need to sort these words into the correct lists.
- Explain the task and allow time for learners to ask questions so they fully understand what is required.
- Share their lists of naming and describing words. Have all the learners got the right words in the correct lists?

Assessment

The assessment sheet for this unit, 'Narrative writing: writing words, lists and captions', is on page 80 of Learner's Book 1. It provides learners with a picture stimulus to list four items Katie needs to remember to take swimming. The learners then write a caption for a close-up picture of a green towel.

- Read through the assessment sheet with the learners to ensure they have understood the writing task.
- Encourage the learners to spend some time looking carefully at the picture before writing their list.
- Remind the learners that the caption needs to include a colour word (a describing word).
- Do not penalise learners for spelling words incorrectly.

Marking criteria

Technical aspects
Look for correct use of:
• list writing (normally vertically).
Content
• Does the list make sense?   • Has the learner considered what is needed when someone goes swimming?   • Does the caption include a colour describing word?

Unit 2: Personal writing: writing names and simple sentences

Learner's Book unit focus

This unit introduces the writing of **special naming words** and the writing of **simple sentences**, highlighting the most common punctuation of a sentence (the initial capital letter and concluding full stop).

Progress table for Stage 1: Unit 2					
Category: Personal writing					
Writing outcome: Writing names and simple sentences					
The learners are introduced to proper nouns and the linking together of words to create sentences.					
Stage 1	**Stage 2**	**Stage 3**	**Stage 4**	**Stage 5**	**Stage 6**
• writing names • writing statements	• writing sentences • sequencing sentences • plot	• plot • story openings/ settings • continuing stories			
Cambridge Global English link:	Stage 1: Unit 2: Family time				
Cambridge Primary English link:	Stage 1: Unit 1: Playing with friends				

Unit teaching plan

Warm up

- Begin by talking to the learners about their families. Be very sensitive to the variety of home lives different children may have. Celebrate all forms of home life, whether it be single-parent families, children who live with grandparents, etc.

- Ask the learners: *Can you tell me the names of your siblings?* Write some of the names on the board. Ask the learners: *What do you notice about the first letter of each name?*

- Remind the learners what capital letters are. With the learners, write the capital letters of the alphabet either in the air or on paper.

- Discuss with the learners the things they enjoy doing with their families.

Let's read

The learners are introduced to the Patel family. There are four children of varying ages, approximately two, five, seven and ten. They are shown with their parents.

The picture highlights how special naming words are written. It then illustrates the family enjoying time by a river. Sentences highlight what the family members are doing.

- First, read the extract to the class and then nominate learners to read it to the class. Be sure the learners all understand the extract and what it is showing.

- Highlight the names of the children. Ask the learners what they notice about the first letter of each of the names. Introduce the term *special naming word* (used here rather than *proper noun*) to highlight why these words start with a capital letter and others do not.

- Remind the learners that *naming words* are nouns, as previously introduced in Unit 1.

- Discuss the picture of the Patel family by the river. Ask the learners questions (for example: *Are the family having fun? What are they doing? What would you do by the river?*)

- Ask the learners what they notice about the sentences (for example, they start with a capital letter and end with a full stop).

Plenary

- Put the learners into pairs. Ask each pair to write the names of people in their own families or ask them to write a list of their friends. Remind them that they need to start each special naming word with a capital letter.

- Ask the learners (arranged either in groups or pairs) to discuss other naming words that use capital letters (for example, days of the week, months of the year, names of people and animals, surnames, etc.).
- Introduce *special naming words* as *proper nouns* to those learners who are ready.

Let's talk

This section asks the learners questions that:

- give them a greater understanding of the text
- focus on the specific writing activity covered in the unit.

Introduce the term *special naming word*: A *naming word (noun)* that is particular to a person or animal (for example, 'Tom').

Introduce the term *sentence*: A unit of language that 'makes sense'. This can be a tricky concept for learners to understand, but over time they begin to recognise *sentences*.

Activity A: This section is to ensure learners have understood what they have read.

Answers

A **1** Asha   **2** Ali   **3** By a river
    4 Alya and Aadi   **5** A banana

Activity B: This section focuses the learners on where capital letters are used either in names or sentences and highlights the use of the full stop at the end of sentences.

Answers

B *Example answers:*
   1. There are six members of the Patel family; four children and two parents.
   2. Each name starts with a capital letter.
   3. The writing/sentences at the bottom of page 17 tell us more about what the Patel family are doing.
   4. Each line (sentence) starts with a capital letter.
   5. Each line (sentence) ends with a full stop.

Let's learn

This section:

- introduces work on *special naming words* (a type of noun) and *sentences*
- gives learners the opportunity to practise what they have learned in a focused activity before incorporating it into their own writing.

Special naming words

- Write a number of *naming words* on the board (for example, horse, cat, goat). Introduce the children to the animals' *special naming words* (for example, Mischa, Tilly, Matilda).
- Ask the learners to give you the *special naming words* of the Patel family.
- Read the information box with the learners.
- Remind the learners of the alphabet, specifically the alphabet in capital letters. Highlight the importance of using capital letters at the beginning of special naming words.
- Encourage the learners to work through each exercise individually or in pairs.

Activity A: The learners are asked to write their name, highlighting it as a *special naming word* as it is a naming word that belongs to them.

Answers

A *Learner's own name (with a capital letter)*

Activity B: The learners are asked to recognise and copy the special naming words in the word box.

Answers

B Meena, Lucas, Ranjit, Anna

Activity C: Finally, the learners are asked to write the *special naming words* of people in their family.

Answers

C *Learner's list of names of people in their own family*

Writing sentences

- Read the information box with the learners.
- Introduce the term *sentence*. Explain that a sentence is a unit of language that makes sense.
- Write examples that show sentences that 'make sense' (for example, *Tom rides a bike.*) and groups of words that do not (for example, *rides Tom bike a*).
- Encourage the learners to work through each exercise individually or in pairs.

Activity A: The learners are asked to recognise where the capital letter is needed in each sentence.

Answers

A **1** (a)sha   **2** (t)he   **3** (a)adi   **4** (t)he

Activity B: The learners are asked to recognise where the missing full stop is needed in each sentence.

Answers

B **1** Mum laughs at Ali.
  2 Alya eats a sweet.
  3 Dad clears up the food.
  4 The family walks home.

Activity C: The learners are required to sort muddled words to make sentences that match given pictures.

Answers

C **1** Ali is asleep.   **2** Aadi drops the ball.
  3 Asha sees a duck.

Let's practise

This section allows you to model the required writing outcome with input from the learners.

Before writing

- Always encourage the learners to talk about what they are going to write. Discussing things can help the learners organise their thoughts.
- Look at the picture with the learners. Ask them if they like the look of Alya. Explain they can make up who Alya is and what she likes.

Shared writing activity

- Explain to the learners that they are going to discuss in a group what Alya likes to do, what animals she likes, who her best friend is, whether she enjoys school and what food she enjoys eating.
- Encourage the children to build a clear picture of Alya, but remind them they can each make Alya who they want her to be; it is completely up to them.
- Help the learners to note down words they might find useful when writing sentences about Alya.
- Discuss what other things they might want to say about Alya.
- Now ask the learners to write four sentences about Alya. Remind them about the use of capital letters and full stops.
- The activity can be done individually, in pairs or in groups.

- Finally, share the learners' sentences about Alya with the class. Encourage the learners to read their sentences to the rest of the group or class.
- Give the learners opportunities to discuss what they have written, either with you or with their peers.

Let's write

The learners are now required to produce some sentences about Aadi independently, having worked through a similar exercise in the previous section. Encourage learners to share their work in progress with you so that, through discussion, they can improve their work.

Before writing

- Remind the learners of things they discussed about Alya in the Let's practise section.
- Encourage them to think about different options and choose the best ones.
- Ask them to write their sentences carefully and neatly.
- Help the learners with the spellings of words if necessary.

Marking criteria

Technical aspects
Look for correct use of:
• sentences that start with a capital letter
• sentences that end with a full stop
• special naming words with capital letters.
Content
• Do their sentences make sense?
• Has the learner considered what Aadi might really enjoy?

After writing

Read through the completed sentences with the learners. Encourage them to share their sentences with others.

Plenary

- Discuss different sentences the learners might write about themselves.
- You could create a display by taking pictures of the learners (or asking them to draw pictures of themselves) and arranging them on a board or around the room. Under the pictures, learners could write a sentence or two describing to others what they like/enjoy.

Resource sheets

The resource sheets for Unit 2 provide differentiation for the writing outcome in this unit as well as further practice on special naming words and writing sentences.

1 A resource sheet on special naming words and writing sentences.
2 A resource sheet on writing about their family.

Resource sheet 1: Special naming words and writing sentences

Resource sheet 1 covers further practice on special naming words and sentences. Learners are asked to copy four sentences. Each one requires a capital letter at the beginning and a full stop at the end. There are also missing capital letters for special naming words.

- Read through the resource sheet with the learners so they fully understand what is expected of them.
- Highlight that some sentences might also include names of people, so they will need to include capital letters for these words too.
- Encourage the learners to write the sentences carefully and neatly.
- When completed, read through the sentences with each learner to ensure they are correct.
- Look at the picture. Discuss with those learners who need the support what they might write about. Encourage those learners who are capable of writing sentences about the picture to do so without support or input.
- To extend the activity, the learners can write a few of their own short sentences on paper. These can then be cut up, the words muddled and given to a friend to rearrange so they make sense as a sentence.

Resource sheet 2: Writing names and simple sentences: write about your family

Resource sheet 2 asks each learner to choose a family member, draw and colour their picture and then write three sentences about them.

- Explain the task and allow time for learners to ask questions so they fully understand what is required.
- Discuss the different family members they might like to draw.

- Remind the learners that a sentence begins with a capital letter and usually ends with a full stop.
- Ask them to write interesting sentences about their family member.
- Help them with vocabulary they might want to use.
- Ask the learners to share their sentences with their peers.
- Display their artwork and sentences in the classroom.

Assessment

The assessment sheet for this unit, 'Personal writing: writing names and simple sentences', is on page 81 of Learner's Book 1. It provides the learners with pictures of three children doing different things. They write a name for each child and then write three sentences, one sentence about each child.

- Read through the assessment sheet with the learners to ensure that they have understood the writing task.
- Encourage the learners to spend some time looking at what each child is doing in the picture before writing their sentences.
- Remind the learners that they need to remember a capital letter for a special naming word and that a sentence starts with a capital letter and often ends with a full stop.
- Do not penalise the learners for spelling words incorrectly.

Marking criteria

Technical aspects
Look for correct use of:
• sentences that start with a capital letter • sentences that end with a full stop • special naming words with capital letters.
Content
• Do their sentences make sense? • Has the learner considered what is shown in the pictures of the three children?

© Sarah Lindsay and Wendy Wren 2019

Teacher's Resource Unit guide: Stage 1: Unit 2

29

Unit 3: Poetry: writing poems

Learner's Book unit focus

This unit introduces the writing of **rhyming words** within the context of a **'fun' poem**.

Progress table for Stage 1: Unit 3					
Category: Poetry					
Writing outcome: Writing poems					
Poems lend themselves to imaginative and expressive writing. Learners can enjoy exploring different vocabulary that creates rhyming poems.					
Stage 1	**Stage 2**	**Stage 3**	**Stage 4**	**Stage 5**	**Stage 6**
• identifying rhyming words • using rhyming words	• rhyming poems • formulaic poems • list poems	• rhyming poems • humorous poems • shape poems			
Cambridge Global English link: **Cambridge Primary English links:**	Stage 1: Unit 3: Fun and games Stage 1: Unit 3: Rhyme time Stage 1: Unit 6: Rhyme time 2 Stage 1: Unit 9: Poems and rhymes on a theme				

Unit teaching plan

Warm up

- Introduce this unit on poems to the learners. Ask:
  - *What poems do you know?*
  - *Do you enjoy listening to poems?*
  - *Are there poems you know that you might like to share with the group?*
- Remind the learners of action poems they might know or read a poem to them and ask them to add their own actions to it.
- Highlight rhyming words that appear in poems.

Let's read

The unit starts with an action-packed, interesting picture depicting children having fun in a park, alongside a simple poem. The poem is split into four short verses, highlighting things that are happening in the picture.

- First, read the poem to the class and then have learners read it to the class. Be sure the learners all follow the poem and what it is showing.
- Discuss the structure of the poem – how the poem is split into short verses that stand alone.
- Highlight the rhyming words. Ask the learners to say the rhyming words in each verse.

- Ask the learners what *naming words (nouns)* are. Remind them of previous work on naming words in Unit 1. Ask the learners to pick out the naming words in the poem (for example, children, slide).
- Ask the learners if they enjoy the poem. Can they find the children in the picture who are doing as the poem describes?

Plenary

- Put the learners into pairs. Ask each pair to read the poem and add actions to each verse. Then ask the learners to perform the action poem in front of others.
- Ask the learners, either in groups or pairs, to create another verse for the poem. Use the picture as a stimulus.
- Add all the additional verses of the poem together to create a new class poem.

Let's talk

This section asks the learners questions that:

- give them a greater understanding of the text
- focus on the specific writing activity covered in the unit.

The learners are required to look carefully at the picture. Remind them that pictures can often give further clues to passages of writing or poems.

Activity A: This section is to ensure learners have understood what they have read and fully appreciated all the picture shows.

Answers

A	**1**	yes	**2**	yes	**3**	no	**4**	yes
	5	yes	**6**	yes	**7**	yes	**8**	yes

Activity B: This section focuses the learners on rhyming words. Which words in the poem rhyme? It highlights that there is a pattern to where the rhyming words fall in each verse.

Answers

B	**1**	talk	**2**	race	**3**	slide	**4**	fun

5 The rhyming words appear at the end of each line.
Each verse has two words that rhyme.

Let's learn

This section:

- introduces work on *doing words* (verbs)
- gives learners the opportunity to recognise and practise what they have learned in a focused activity before incorporating it into their own writing.

Verbs are a complex part of speech for young children to fully understand because of their tenses (past, present and future) and their many forms.

This unit begins with the present simple tense, including the verb *to be*.

Doing words

- Write a number of *doing words* on the board (for example, write, walk, dance).
- Ask the learners to explain what they think a doing word might be.
- Read the information box with the learners. Highlight the term *verb* when discussing doing words.
- Ask the learners to suggest further doing words to add to the list on the board.
- Encourage the learners to work through each exercise individually or in pairs.

Activity A: The learners are asked to identify doing words from a mix of doing and naming words.

Answers

A run, jump, talk, hop

Activity B: The learners are asked to add the words *am*, *is* and *are* before verbs in sentences.

Activity C: Finally, the learners are required to underline the verb in each sentence.

Answers

B and C

1 He **is** talking to a friend.
2 They **are** running to the shop.
3 I **am** throwing a ball.

Rhyming words

- Introduce the term *rhyming words*. Explain that rhyming words have the same sounds. Often these sounds have the same letter pattern (for example, talk/walk), though not always (for example, chase/face).
- Explain that rhyming words can be found in poems.
- Read the information box with the learners.
- Encourage the learners to work through each exercise individually or in pairs.
- After completing the activities, you can ask the learners to identify *doing words* among the rhyming words.

Activity A: The learners are asked to recognise the rhyming word that links with the word in bold.

Answers

A	**1**	hall	**2**	day	**3**	see

Activity B: The learners are required to write a rhyming word to match each of the given words.

Answers

B *Example answers:*

	1	ball	**2**	pat	**3**	pan
	4	wish	**5**	sack	**6**	send

Let's practise

This section allows you to model the required writing outcome with input from the learners.

Before writing

- Always encourage the learners to talk about what they are going to write. Discussing things can help the learners organise their thoughts.
- Read through the poem 'Having fun' with the learner, highlighting the blanks they will be filling in.

Shared writing activity

- Explain to the learners that they are going to complete the poem with rhyming words.
- Encourage them to brainstorm rhyming words for each verse, settling on the word that works the best.
- Highlight that clues are provided at the beginning of the second line in each verse (for example, 'and count to…' suggests the rhyming word will be a number).
- The activity can be done individually, in pairs or in groups.
- Give the learners opportunities to discuss what they have written, either with you or with their peers.

Let's write

The learners are now required to independently produce a poem using the same structure as for the poem found in the Let's practise section. Encourage learners to share their work in progress with you so that, through discussion, they can improve their work.

Before writing

- Recap the different types of words the learners might use (for example, nouns and verbs).
- Highlight the structure of the verse (for example, they begin with a capital letter and end with a full stop).
- The poems can be amusing and fun.
- Encourage the learners to think about different options and choose the best ones. The rhyming words need to work together for the poem to make sense.
- Ask them to write their poems carefully and neatly.
- Help the learners with spellings if necessary.

Marking criteria

Technical aspects
Look for correct use of:
• verses that start with a capital letter
• verses that end with a full stop
• the correct use of rhyming words.
Content
• Does their poem, despite being amusing or fun, still make sense?
• Has the learner considered the overall poem when writing the verses?

After writing

Read through the completed poems with the learners. Encourage them to share their poems with others.

Plenary

- Discuss the different poems the learners have written. Which poems have the funniest verses?
- Encourage them to add actions to their poems and then perform them in front of a group or class.

Resource sheets

The resource sheets for Unit 3 provide differentiation for the writing outcome in this unit as well as further practice on rhyming words.

1. A resource sheet on rhyming words.
2. A resource sheet on writing a poem.

Resource sheet 1: Writing poems: rhyming words

Resource sheet 1 covers further practice on rhyming words. Learners are asked to link given rhyming words with a line. They then have to find their own four rhyming words for the words that are left. Finally, they are asked to write as many rhyming words as they can that go with the word *bat*.

- Read through the resource sheet with the learners so they fully understand what is expected of them.
- Encourage them to write their rhyming words carefully and neatly. Highlight the spelling-pattern link in the rhyming words.
- When completed, read through the rhyming words with each learner to ensure they are correct.

- To extend the activity, the learners can be given further words (for example, back, den, fun) and challenged to find as many rhyming words as they can to go with each one. They can work individually, in pairs or in groups.

Resource sheet 2: Write a poem

Resource sheet 2 supports the learners to complete the rhyming poem introduced in the Let's practice section. The learners are asked to choose the correct second line for each verse. Each line must rhyme with the line before. The resource sheet highlights the role of the rhyming words in the structure of the poem.

- Explain the task and allow time for learners to ask questions so they fully understand what is required.
- Read through the lines in the poem and those in the word box so the learners are familiar with them.
- Remind the learners that each verse begins with a capital letter and ends with a full stop.
- Ask the learners to share their poems with their peers.

Assessment

The assessment sheet for this unit, 'Poetry: writing poems', is on page 82 of Learner's Book 1. The assessment sheet provides the learners with the structure of a poem that requires them to add the correct rhyming weather words in the spaces. The pictures help guide the learners to the correct weather words and the words are provided in a box to aid the learners' spelling.

- Read through the assessment sheet with the learners to ensure they have understood the writing task.
- Encourage them to spend some time looking carefully at the picture and words provided before completing the poem.
- Remind them that the final word in each line in the verse must rhyme.
- Do not penalise the learners for spelling words incorrectly.

Marking criteria

Technical aspects
Look for correct use of:
• rhyming words.
Content
• Does their poem, despite being amusing or fun, still make sense?
• Has the learner considered the visual prompts?

© Sarah Lindsay and Wendy Wren 2019

Unit 4: Narrative writing: writing sentences

Learner's Book unit focus

This unit builds on the work previously introduced in Unit 2 on **sentences**. The writing of simple sentences builds on the addition of the **joining word *and*** to make longer, **compound sentences**. It also introduces more **describing words**, adding to the colour words that featured in Unit 1.

Progress table for Stage 1: Unit 4					
Category: Narrative writing					
Writing outcome: Writing sentences					
It helps learners to know, when writing a story, that there is a structure to it. This unit looks at story characters. The first stage of teaching learners about characters is asking them to describe what they see.					
Stage 1	**Stage 2**	**Stage 3**	**Stage 4**	**Stage 5**	**Stage 6**
• joining two sentences with *and* • characters	• sequencing sentences to form a narrative • characters	• plot • story openings/ settings • continuing stories			
Cambridge Global English link:		Stage 1: Unit 4: Making things			
Cambridge Primary English links:		Stage 1: Unit 1: Playing with friends			
		Stage 1: Unit 7: Make-believe stories			

Unit teaching plan

Warm up

- Begin by talking to the learners about things they have enjoyed making. Make a list of things people can make (for example, cakes, sweets, games, models, etc.).

- Ask the learners: *Have you ever made or flown a kite?* Discuss what might be tricky about making a kite.

Let's read

This unit starts with a short story. Two friends, Amul and Ella, begin by building a kite. They take the kite outside to fly it but are sadly unsuccessful. They try time and time again. Finally, they talk to Amul's mum and she explains why their kite won't fly.

The extract highlights simple sentences and also sentences joined by the word *and*. It also illustrates describing words (*adjectives*).

- First, read the story to the class and then nominate learners to read it to the class. Be sure the learners all understand the storyline.

- Discuss the pictures that are shown with the story. *How do the pictures help inform what we have read? Which picture do you like best? Why? Is it because it is associated with a 'nice' part in the story or a part of the story the learner might relate to?*

- Ask the learners to pick out simple sentences, as previously covered in Unit 2 (for example, *Amul and Ella make a kite*).

- What do the learners notice about the longer sentences? Guide them to the word 'and' and highlight how it joins two smaller sentences (for example, *Amul ties the wooden rods* and *Ella helps by holding them tight*).

- Remind the learners that *describing words* are *adjectives*, as previously introduced in Unit 1. Ask them for examples of the adjectives covered in Unit 1 (colour words).

- Remind the learners that sentences start with a capital letter and usually end with a full stop.

- Discuss whether the story ends as they would have expected.

Plenary

- Put the learners into pairs. Provide them with books. Ask each pair to find examples of simple sentences and examples of longer sentences that use the joining word *and*.
- Ask the learners what they think might happen next in the story. As a class or group, continue the story with you acting as scribe. The learners can then illustrate the story with their own pictures.

Let's talk

This section asks the learners questions that:

- give them a greater understanding of the text
- focus on the specific writing activity covered in the unit.

Activity A: This section is to ensure learners have understood what they have read.

Answers

A *Example answers:*

1 Amul and Ella are making a kite.
2 Amul and Ella fly their kite outside.
3 Amul holds the string.
4 When Ella throws the kite in the air it falls straight to the ground.
5 Amul and Ella feel sad and upset when the kite does not fly.
6 Amul's mum talks to them about the kite.
7 The kite doesn't fly because there is no wind.
8 Amul and Ella now find it funny that the kite does not fly. They think they should have realised!

Activity B: This section focuses the learners on Amul and Ella, the characters in the story.

Answers

B *Example answers:*

1 The story is about two children making a kite that doesn't fly.
2 Amul, Ella and Amul's mum are the characters in the story.
3 *A brief description of what Amul looks like and what his character is like*
4 *A brief description of what Ella looks like and what her character is like*

Let's learn

This section:

- introduces work on *describing words* (*adjectives*) and *sentences*. It recaps *simple sentences* and then introduces longer, compound sentences that use the joining word *and*
- gives learners the opportunity to practise what they have learned in a focused activity before incorporating it into their own writing.

Describing words

Revise the term *describing word* (*adjective*): A *describing word* (*adjective*) describes people, places and things.

- Write a number of *describing words* on the board (for example, red, yellow, green). Ask the learners if they can remember what these words are called. (Colour words, describing words, adjectives.)
- Look in detail at the story. Highlight where other types of describing words have been used (for example, *their new kite, the long string*).
- Read the information box with the learners.
- Encourage the learners, individually or in pairs, to find any further describing words in the story.
- Encourage them to work through each exercise individually or in pairs.

Activity A: The learners are asked to finish the given sentences by adding a describing word from the word box.

Answers

A 1 The snow is **cold**.
2 Meena has a **red** coat.
3 The **small** cat is sleeping.
4 Tom is **happy**.

Activity B: The learners are asked to recognise and underline the describing words in the given phrases.

Answers

B 1 The <u>big</u> lion
2 The <u>fast</u> car
3 A <u>green</u> bean
4 My <u>tall</u> brother

Activity C: Finally, the learners are asked to write a sentence that includes a describing word of their choice.

Answers

C *Learner's own sentence using a describing word*

Writing sentences

Answers

A 1 Amul and Ella like to make things.
   2 The kite is new.

B *Example answers:*
   1 A kite is flying in the sky.
   2 The kite flies away.

Joining sentences

Revise the term *sentence* – a unit of language that 'makes sense'. This can be a tricky concept for learners to understand but over time they begin to recognise *sentences*.

And is a joining word (*conjunction*). It can be used to join words, phrases and clauses together to make longer sentences.

- Read the information box with the learners.
- Revise the term *sentence*. Write examples that show sentences that 'make sense' (for example, *Amul and Ella make a kite*).
- Introduce *and* as a joining word (*conjunction*). Explain how using a joining word can help expand sentences and make them more interesting.
- Encourage the learners to work through each exercise individually or in pairs.

Activity A: The learners are asked to write two short sentences about the given pictures.

Answers

A *Example answers:*
   A boy makes some cakes.
   He gives a cake to his friend.

Activity B: The learners are then asked to join the sentences using the word *and*.

Answers

B *Example answers:*
   A boy makes some cakes **and** gives a cake to his friend.

Activity C: Finally, the learners are given two pictures and asked to write one longer sentence (including the joining word *and*) about them.

Answers

C *Example answers:*
   The friend eats the cake and asks for another one.

Let's practise

This section allows you to model the required writing outcome with input from the learners.

Before writing

- Always encourage the learners to talk about what they are going to write. Discussing things can help them organise their thoughts.
- The learners are asked to look in more detail at the characters in the story.
- Ask them who the main characters of the story are.

Shared writing activity

- Organise the learners into small groups or pairs. Explain that they are going to discuss what Amul looks like.
- Encourage the learners to imagine they are describing Amul to someone who has never seen him before. They need to paint a picture in words to enable the other person to clearly imagine what he looks like.
- Help them to note down describing words that they will find useful when writing sentences about Amul.
- Now ask them to write sentences about Amul. Remind them about the use of capital letters and full stops in their sentences.
- Discuss whether any of these sentences can be made into longer sentences by adding the joining word *and*.
- The activity can be done individually, in pairs or in groups.
- Finally, share the learners' sentences about Amul with the class. Encourage them to read their sentences to the rest of the group or class.
- Give the learners opportunities to discuss what they have written, either with you or with their peers.

Let's write

The learners are now required to produce some sentences about Ella independently, having worked through a similar exercise in the previous section. Encourage learners to share their work in progress with you so that, through discussion, they can improve their work.

Before writing

- Remind the learners of things they discussed about Amul in the Let's practise section.
- Encourage them to think about different describing words and choose the best ones.
- Ask them to write their sentences carefully and neatly. Encourage them to write longer sentences using the joining word *and*.
- Help the learners with spellings if necessary.

Marking criteria

Technical aspects
Look for correct use of:
• sentences that start with a capital letter
• sentences that end with a full stop
• sentences that include adjectives
• sentences that use the joining word *and*.
Content
• Do their sentences make sense?
• Has the learner provided a good description of what Ella looks like?

After writing

Read through the completed sentences with the learners. Encourage them to share their sentences with others.

Plenary

- Discuss different sentences they might write about themselves.
- Ask the learners to create a picture in their minds of Amul and Ella flying their kite with a friend. Talk about the fun they are having. Then ask the learners to write a description of Amul and Ella's friend. They will need to give the friend a name.

Resource sheets

The resource sheets for Unit 4 provide differentiation for the writing outcome in this unit as well as further practice on special naming words and writing sentences.

1 A resource sheet on naming words and describing words.
2 A resource sheet on describing a friend.

Resource sheet 1: Writing sentences: naming words and describing words

Resource sheet 1 covers further practice on naming words and describing words. Learners are asked to read four sentences and then copy the naming and describing words. They are then required to write three each of their own naming and describing words. Finally, they are asked to include naming and describing words in two sentences of their own.

- Read through the resource sheet with the learners so they fully understand what is expected of them.
- Revise naming words. Remind the learners of the activities they did in Unit 1.
- Encourage them to think carefully about which are naming words and which are describing words.
- When completed, read through the sentences in Activity C with each learner to ensure they are correct. Some learners may need more support than others for this activity.
- To extend the activity, the learners can share their sentences with their peers, asking them to highlight the naming and describing words in each other's work.

Resource sheet 2: Writing sentences: write about a friend

Resource sheet 2 asks the learners to select a friend and secretly write a description. This can then be read to their peers to guess who has been described. Learners are given, or are asked to choose, a peer; they are then required to write a detailed description of this person.

- Explain the task and allow time for learners to ask questions so they fully understand what is required.
- Discuss the importance of painting a picture in words.
- Remind the learners that the use of describing words is very important to make their description specific to the person they are describing.
- Ask them to write interesting sentences using the joining word *and*, if they are able.
- Help them with vocabulary they might want to use.
- Once the description is ready, ask them to read it out and see if anyone can guess who the person is that they are describing.

- Share their sentences with their peers.
- The descriptions can be displayed creatively in the classroom with the title 'Who do you think they are?' and the learners' names and/or photographs listed down the side of the display board.

Assessment

The assessment sheet for this unit, 'Narrative writing: writing sentences', is on page 83 of Learner's Book 1. The assessment sheet provides the learners with a picture stimulus to write two sentences. They then rewrite the sentences, joining them together using the joining word *and*.

- Read through the assessment sheet with the learners to ensure they have understood the writing task.
- Encourage them to spend some time looking carefully at the picture before writing their sentences.
- Remind the learners that the sentences need the joining word *and*.
- Ensure that they have added describing words to make their sentences more interesting.
- Do not penalise the learners for spelling words incorrectly.

Marking criteria

Technical aspects
Look for correct use of:
• sentences that start with a capital letter
• sentences that end with a full stop
• sentences that include adjectives
• sentences that use the joining word *and*.
Content
• Do their sentences make sense?
• Has the learner provided a good description of the picture?

Unit 5: Explanatory writing: writing labels and captions

Learner's Book unit focus

This unit introduces **writing labels** and builds on the work previously introduced on **captions** in Unit 1. It also introduces 'more than one' – **plural words** to support the vocabulary used in this unit.

Progress table for Stage 1: Unit 5					
Category: Explanatory writing					
Writing outcome: Writing labels and captions					
Explanatory writing in its simplest form explains something. An early stage in explanatory writing is to write labels and captions for pictures.					
Stage 1	**Stage 2**	**Stage 3**	**Stage 4**	**Stage 5**	**Stage 6**
• writing labels and captions	• sequencing events • making comparisons • flow diagrams • explaining how something happens	• writing labels and captions • making comparisons • flow diagrams			
Cambridge Global English link: Stage 1: Unit 5: On the farm					
Cambridge Primary English link: Stage 1: Unit 4: Joining-in stories					

Unit teaching plan

Warm up

- Ask the learners: *Have you ever been to a farm?* If they have, ask them to describe their experience – what they saw, smelled and did on the farm. If they have not visited a farm, ask them what they think a farm might be like.

- Discuss with the learners why we need farms and how farms vary in different parts of the world.

Let's read

This unit starts with a poster advertising visits to City Farm. It encourages people to come and meet the animals. The poster illustrates and labels the animals the visitors will see. It then details what can be done at the farm (for example, feeding animals, riding horses and eating ice creams). There are then four photographs showing children enjoying their time at City Farm. Each photograph has a caption.

The opening text highlights labels and captions.

- First, read the poster to the class and discuss it. Be sure the learners all understand the information it conveys.

- Ask: *What do you like about the poster?*

- Highlight how the labels emphasise the animals at the farm.

- Discuss where else labels can be found (for example, on diagrams, maps, etc.).

- Discuss the photographs that are shown with the poster. What do the photographs show? Discuss the captions with the learners.

- Highlight how captions provide information about pictures. Remind the learners of the captions they covered in Unit 1.

- Remind the learners that *naming words* are *nouns*, as previously introduced in Unit 1. Ask them for examples, of nouns from the poster.

Plenary

- Put the learners into pairs. Ask each pair to write different captions for the photographs.
- Ask: *Would you like to visit City Farm? Why?* Discuss how the poster encourages people to want to visit the farm. Ask learners to design a labelled poster for an attraction local to them.

Let's talk

This section asks the learners questions that:

- give them a greater understanding of the text
- focus on the specific writing activity covered in the unit.

Activity A: This section is to ensure learners have interpreted the poster correctly.

Answers

A 1 City Farm
2 You can feed the ducks and chickens.
3 You can stroke the goats and sheep.
4 You can ride the horses.
5 Six animals have labels.
6 You can buy ice creams at the farm.

Activity B: This section focuses the learners on the photographs and their captions and what they show. It also asks the learners for their opinions.

Answers

B *Example answers:*
1 The photographs show people having fun at City Farm.
2 The captions give us information about the photographs.
3 *Learner's own opinions on their favourite photograph and why they chose it*
4 *Learner's own caption for the photo chosen, for example, 'Children feeding chickens'*

Let's learn

This section:

- recaps work previously covered on naming words (*nouns*)
- introduces the term *more than one* (*plurals*)
- gives learners the opportunity to practise what they have learned in a focused activity before incorporating it into their own writing.

Naming words

Activity A: The learners are asked to list all the naming words they see.

Answers

A *Example answers:*
child, ducks, grass, T-shirt, stones, lollipop, tub, shoes

More than one

Nouns usually have a singular (one) and plural (more than one) form. Most plurals are formed by adding -s to the singular noun (for example, elephants, trees, etc.).

- Write a number of nouns on the board (for example, star, car). Ask learners what type of words these are. Link them to the naming words they have just covered.
- Now draw more than one of each of the nouns (for example, five stars, three cars). Ask the learners to say the noun aloud. Highlight the -s sound at the end of the plural nouns. Now label the pictures, adding the -s to make each noun plural.
- Read the information box with the learners.
- Encourage the learners, individually or in pairs, to find any plural words in the poster or the captions at the beginning of the unit.
- Encourage the learners to work through each exercise individually or in pairs.
- There might be an opportunity to mention that some nouns need -es added to make them plural. These nouns end in -ch, -sh, -s or -x (for example, bushes, matches, dresses, etc.).

Activity A: The learners are asked to match each noun from the word box with the correct picture and where necessary make it plural by adding an -s.

Answers

A	1	goats	2	tractor	3	horses
	4	farmer	5	ducks	6	cows

Activity B: The learners are asked to complete word sums, making nouns plural.

Answers

B	1	coats	2	boots	3	trees
	4	sweets	5	cats	6	doors

Let's practise

This section allows you to model the required writing outcome with input from the learners.

Before writing

- Always encourage the learners to talk about what they are going to write. Discussing things can help them to organise their thoughts.
- Introduce Kim. She is going to help on her uncle's farm.
- The learners are asked to label a picture of Kim.
- There is a picture of Kim arriving at her uncle's farm. The learners are asked to write a caption for the picture.

Shared writing activity

- Organise the learners into small groups or pairs. Explain that they are going to discuss what labels they can add to the picture of Kim showing the clothes she is wearing to work on the farm with her uncle.
- Discuss with the learners which words are *singular (one)*, and which words are *plural (more than one)* and thus require an -*s* to be added (for example, hat, boots).
- Now ask the learners to write a caption for the picture of Kim arriving at the farm. Discuss the different ideas the learners might have.
- The activity can be done individually, in pairs or in groups.
- Finally, share the learners' captions with the class. Encourage the learners to read their captions to the rest of the group or class.
- Give the learners opportunities to discuss what they have written, either with you or with their peers.

Let's write

The learners are now required to write captions for the pictures surrounding the map of Kim's uncle's farm. Encourage learners to share their work in progress with you so that, through discussion, they can improve their work.

Before writing

- Remind the learners of the details they discussed about adding labels and captions in the Let's practise section.
- Ask them to write their captions carefully and neatly. Remind them that some words will be singular and some plural.
- Help the learners with spellings if necessary.

Marking criteria

Technical aspects
Look for correct use of:
• nouns correctly written in their singular or plural form • sentences that start with a capital letter and end with a full stop.
Content
Look for correct use of:
• relevant captions.

After writing

Read through the completed captions with the learners. Encourage them to share their captions with others.

Plenary

- Ask the learners to bring in pictures of themselves on a day out. Ask them to write captions for the pictures. Display the pictures with the captions.
- Mix up the pictures and captions the learners have written and challenge them to match the correct captions and pictures together.

Resource sheets

The resource sheets for Unit 5 provide differentiation for the writing outcome in this unit as well as further practice on plural words.

1 A resource sheet on plural words.
2 A resource sheet on writing captions from their own experience.

Resource sheet 1: Writing labels and captions: more than one

Resource sheet 1 covers further practice of plural words. Learners are asked to organise the singular and plural words into the table provided. They are then given singular words to make plural and finally asked to use plural words in sentences of their own.

- Read through the resource sheet with the learners so they fully understand what is expected of them.
- Revise plural words, reminding them that in most cases an -*s* is added to the singular word to make it plural.

- When completed, read through the sentences in Activity C with each learner to ensure they are correct. Some learners may need more support than others for this activity.
- To extend the activity, ask the learners to write further sentences adding their own plural words. They can then share their sentences with their peers, highlighting the plural words in each other's work.

Resource sheet 2: Writing labels and captions: write about a day out

Resource sheet 2 asks the learners to think about a day out they have had. The day out can be a visit to an organised event or to a friend or relative's house. They are then asked to draw four pictures of things that they did during the day and write captions for them.

- Explain the task and allow time for learners to ask questions so they fully understand what is required.
- Discuss the importance of making their pictures clear and simple.
- Remind the learners that their captions should describe what is happening in the picture – but only briefly.
- Help them with vocabulary they might want to use.
- Once they have written the captions, ask them to share them with a peer.
- Do any of the learners describe the same day out? Compare their memories/ captions.

Assessment

The assessment sheet for this unit, 'Explanatory writing: writing labels and captions', is on page 84 of Learner's Book 1. It provides the learners with a picture stimulus and asks them to label the farm animals. The learners then write a caption for a photograph showing a child feeding chickens.

- Read through the assessment sheet with the learners to ensure they have understood the writing task.
- Encourage the learners to spend some time looking carefully at the picture before writing the labels.
- Remind the learners to write the nouns correctly in their singular or plural form.
- Talk with them about what the photograph shows before they write the caption.
- Do not penalise the learners for spelling words incorrectly.

Marking criteria

Technical aspects
Look for correct use of:
• a clearly labelled poster
• nouns correctly written in their singular or plural form
• sentences that start with a capital letter and end with a full stop.

Content
Look for correct use of:
• relevant labels
• a relevant caption.

Unit 6: Factual writing: alphabetic texts

Learner's Book unit focus

This unit looks in detail at **alphabetical order**, linking it to the **writing of a simple dictionary page**.

Progress table for Stage 1: Unit 6					
Category: Factual writing					
Writing outcome: Alphabetic texts					
There are a number of alphabetic texts the learners will be introduced to during the course. In this unit, they are introduced to a simple dictionary. In Stage 3, the learners revisit a more sophisticated dictionary, which links the information needed in a dictionary with that provided in a glossary.					
Stage 1	**Stage 2**	**Stage 3**	**Stage 4**	**Stage 5**	**Stage 6**
• alphabetic texts (simple dictionary)		• alphabetic texts (dictionary, glossary, index)			
Cambridge Global English link: Stage 1: Unit 6: My five senses					
Cambridge Primary English link: Stage 1: Unit 5: Reading to find out					

Unit teaching plan

Warm up

- Recite the alphabet with the learners, either singing the alphabet song or just calling the letters aloud.
- Ask the learners questions about the alphabet (for example: *How many letters are in the alphabet? Why are a, e, i, o and u special letters?*)
- Hold up a dictionary, preferably one that shows pictures of the items, and ask the learners if they know what it is and what it can be used for.

Let's read

This unit starts by highlighting the alphabet. It then introduces the role of a dictionary and details how a dictionary is set out. It guides the learners through why words are put in the particular order in which they are found in the dictionary, linking it closely to the alphabet. Finally, the learners are given a sample dictionary page on the theme of the senses.

- Read through the alphabet with the learners. They can point to the letters as they read them.
- Discuss the importance of the order of the letters in the alphabet. Introduce the term *alphabetical order*.

- Work through the information carefully. Make sure all learners are able to appreciate why words are found in the order they are in dictionaries.
- Discuss in detail the layout of the dictionary page.
- Discuss the role of a dictionary.

Plenary

- Organise the learners into small groups. Ask the members of each group to line up in alphabetical order using the first letter of their given name.
- If the learners enjoy doing this activity, challenge all of the class to stand in alphabetical order of their given name. Ask the learners how they will organise themselves if they have a name that is the same as someone else's or starts with the same letter (as a suggestion, they could stand one behind another).
- Look at a dictionary with the learners in small groups. Do some exercises that will familiarise them with the dictionary, for example, ask them to find a word in it to tell the rest of the group about; ask them to find specific words on a page.

Let's talk

This section asks the learners questions that:

- give them a greater understanding of the text
- focus on the specific writing activity covered in the unit.

Activity A: This section is to ensure learners have interpreted the information correctly.

Answers

A *Example answers:*
1 a
2 z
3 We hear with our ears.
4 We smell with our nose.
5 All the words are linked with our senses.
6 Eyes – the sense of sight.

Activity B: This section focuses the learners on the structure of a dictionary.

Answers

B *Example answers:*
1 Alphabetical order is the order in which the letters are found in the alphabet.
2 The word *mouth* comes after *hands* because the letter *m* comes after *h* in the alphabet.
3 A dictionary tells us how to spell words and a bit about what each word means. It can show you a picture of the item too.
4 *Learner's own body word beginning with 'a', for example, ankle, arm*
5 The word would go at the top of the dictionary page as *a* is the first letter in the alphabet.

Let's learn

This section:

- introduces the terms alphabet and alphabetical order
- gives learners the opportunity to practise what they have learned in a focused activity before incorporating it into their own writing.

The alphabet

There are 26 letters in the English alphabet. These can be written in *upper case* (*capital letters*) or *lower case* (*small letters*). All English words are formed from these letters.

- The more familiar the learners become with the order of the alphabet, the better. They should be encouraged to say or sing the alphabet until they know the order easily.
- Read the information box with the learners. Highlight that the alphabet can be written in both upper and lower case. Give the learners random letters and ask them to write them in either upper- or lower-case letters.
- The learners can work individually or in pairs.
- Ask the learners to look carefully at the alphabet and answer the questions. Challenge the learners to ask similar questions of their partners.
- Hold up different items from around the classroom and ask the learners to write down the first letter of each one as quickly as possible.

Activity A: The learners are asked questions about where letters are found in the alphabet.

Answers

A 1 l **2** c **3** T **4** Y

Activity B: The learners are required to identify the first letter in given words.

Answers

B 1 d **2** p **3** t **4** f **5** c **6** b

Alphabetical order

Alphabetical order is the order in which the letters are placed in the alphabet.

- Read the information box with the learners. Remind them that the alphabet can be written in both upper and lower case.
- Encourage the learners, individually, to order the given letters. More able learners should be able to do this without referring to the listed alphabet.
- Encourage the learners to work through the following exercises individually, or in pairs if they need the support.
- Remind them that when they order words alphabetically they need to use the first letter of the words.
- The final activity can be done as a challenge for a partner: learners write three words and then ask a partner to order the words alphabetically.
- Place three items in front of a group and ask them to rearrange them in alphabetical order, according to their first letter, as quickly as possible.

Activity A: The learners are asked to order random letters alphabetically.

Answers

A 1 d e f   2 q r s   3 c h t
   4 G N U   5 B K Y   6 H O V

Activity B: The learners are required to order words alphabetically.

Answers

B 1 kite monkey nut
  2 book lion sock
  3 sack van wind

Activity C: Finally, the learners are asked to write three words, each starting with a different letter, in alphabetical order.

Answers

C *Three of the learner's own words, each starting with a different letter*
The three words then written in alphabetical order

Let's practise

This section allows you to model the required writing outcome with input from the learners.

Before writing
- Always encourage the learners to talk about what they are going to write. Discussing things can help the learners to organise their thoughts.
- While the learners are working through the given activities, highlight that eventually they are going to write their own dictionary page.
- Look again at the dictionary page at the beginning of the unit.

Shared writing activity
- Organise the learners into pairs. Explain that they can discuss each activity with their partner, though the final dictionary page will be their own work.
- Carefully work through each activity with the learners, clearly illustrating how each one builds towards the final outcome.
- Discuss the different subjects from which the learners might choose words. Encourage the more able learners to choose their own subjects, should they wish.

- Talk to the learners about writing a sentence for each word. They need to convey the essence of the word in one sentence. They may well need support with this, either from you or from their peers.
- Remind them that sentences start with a capital letter and often end with a full stop.

Let's write

The learners are now required to write their dictionary page independently. Encourage them to share their work in progress with you so that, through discussion, they can improve their work.

Before writing
- Look again at the dictionary page at the beginning of the unit. Highlight the three aspects to each entry: the word, the picture and the sentence.
- The learners will need to use the details they produced in the Let's practise section to build their dictionary page.
- Ask them to write their dictionary entries carefully and neatly.
- Help them with spellings if necessary.

Marking criteria

Technical aspects
Look for correct use of: • words written in alphabetical order • sentences that start with a capital letter and end with a full stop.
Content
Look for correct use of: • appropriately chosen words that relate to a subject • a clear picture of the word • a relevant sentence explaining the word clearly.

After writing
Read through the completed dictionary page with each learner. Encourage them to share their dictionary page with others.

Plenary
- Choose a subject and ask the learners to write an entry for it. Add all the entries together to create a class dictionary for display.
- Discuss what problems would occur if the entries in a dictionary were not in alphabetical order.

© Sarah Lindsay and Wendy Wren 2019

Resource sheets

The resource sheets for Unit 6 provide differentiation for the writing outcome in this unit as well as further practice.

1 A resource sheet on alphabetical order.
2 A resource sheet on planning a dictionary page.
3 A resource sheet on writing a dictionary page.

Resource sheet 1: Alphabetic texts: alphabetical order

This resource sheet covers further practice on alphabetical order. Learners are asked to copy the alphabet. They are then asked to correctly order given letters. Finally, they are asked to choose three words relating to the given subjects to list in alphabetical order.

- Read through the resource sheet with the learners so they fully understand what is expected of them.
- Revise the alphabet.
- Encourage the learners to think carefully about the order in which letters are found in the alphabet.
- When completed, check the order of the words in Activity C with each learner to ensure they are correct. Some learners may need more support than others for this activity.
- To extend the activity, give the learners five letters instead of three to list in alphabetical order. Then do the same with five words instead of three words.

Resource sheet 2: Alphabetic texts: plan a dictionary page, and resource sheet 3: Alphabetic texts: write a dictionary page

These resource sheets support the writing activity in the Learner's Book. Initially, the learners are asked to think of four words that are body parts, place them in alphabetical order and write a sentence about each one. They are then expected to write up these words as a dictionary page.

These resource sheets can be used independently or worked on in tandem.

- Explain the task and allow time for the learners to ask questions so they fully understand what is required for each resource sheet.

- Discuss the importance of working with care and consideration so the words are put in alphabetical order correctly and the sentences are clear.
- Help them with vocabulary they might want to use.
- The learners can either work individually or in pairs. If two learners work together, they can take it in turns to produce the word and the picture or the sentence about the word.
- As an extension to the activities, learners could read out their sentences and their peers guess the word they are referring to.
- Build a class dictionary on the human body, using entries from the work the learners have created for the resource sheet.

Assessment

The assessment sheet for this unit, 'Factual writing: alphabetic texts', is on page 85 of Learner's Book 1. It provides the learners with three words for them to list alphabetically in the dictionary blank provided. The learners then draw a picture and write a sentence about each word.

- Read through the assessment sheet with the learners to ensure they have understood the writing task.
- If needed, provide them with an alphabet to help them list the words alphabetically.
- Remind them of the purpose of a dictionary.
- Do not penalise the learners for spelling words in their sentences incorrectly.

Marking criteria

Technical aspects
Look for correct use of:
• words written in alphabetical order
• sentences that start with a capital letter and end with a full stop.
Content
Look for correct use of:
• a clear picture of the word
• a relevant sentence explaining the word clearly.

46

Unit 7: Instructions: writing instructions and rules

Learner's Book unit focus

This unit introduces **writing instructions and rules**. It also recaps previous work on **full stops, capital letters** and **verbs**.

<table>
<tr><td colspan="6">Progress table for Stage 1: Unit 7

Category: Instructions/Advice/Guidance

Writing outcome: Instructions and rules

In this unit, the learners write very simple instructions on how to get somewhere. It is a good example of instructions for learners of this age, introducing them to sequences, clear sentences, imperative verbs, precise language and layout. They are then required to write simple rules they need to consider in certain circumstances.</td></tr>
<tr><th>Stage 1</th><th>Stage 2</th><th>Stage 3</th><th>Stage 4</th><th>Stage 5</th><th>Stage 6</th></tr>
<tr>
<td>• writing simple instructions
• writing rules</td>
<td>• writing simple instructions
• writing clues
• explaining how something happens</td>
<td>• writing simple instructions for making something</td>
<td>• writing simple instructions for making something
• writing simple instructions for mending something
• directions</td>
<td>• writing instructions for using something</td>
<td></td>
</tr>
<tr><td colspan="6">Cambridge Global English link: Stage 1: Unit 7: Let's go!
Cambridge Primary English link: Stage 1: Unit 2: Finding out and making</td></tr>
</table>

Resource list

A variety of example instructions and rules (for example, school rules or board game instructions).

Unit teaching plan

Warm up

- Ask the learners how they got from the school entrance into their classroom this morning: *When you walked through the school entrance, which way did you turn first? Then where did you go? What next?*

- Ask them to explain the exact instructions for someone who does not know the school: *What instructions would you give to someone coming to our school for the first time?*

- Act as scribe for the learners' instructions. If appropriate, take the class to follow them.

- Discuss with the learners what instructions are. Can the instructions the class or group wrote be improved?

- List the school rules the learners are aware of. Ask:
  - *What rules do we have at school?*
  - *Do you agree with these rules?*
  - *Can you think of any more school rules we need?*

- Discuss why we have rules.

Let's read

This unit starts with a map illustrating an animal park. On the following page there are clear instructions detailing how someone would get from the entrance of the park to the playground. The rules of the animal park then follow.

          Teacher's Resource Unit guide: Stage 1: Unit 7

The opening text highlights instructions and rules.

- First, read and discuss the map with the class. Be sure the learners all understand the information it conveys.
- Ask the learners questions about the animal park. Ask:
  - *Would you like to visit the animal park?*
  - *Which animals would you like to visit?*
  - *Would you enjoy going to the playground?*
- Remind the learners how labels emphasise different points on the map.
- Discuss whether the labels help the learners interpret the map. Ask:
  - *Do you find the labels useful?*
  - *Would the map be as clear without the labels?*
- Discuss the instructions with the learners. Ask:
  - *How easy are the instructions to follow?*
  - *What makes the instructions easy to follow?*
  - *Would it matter if you changed the order of the instructions?*
- Read the rules with the learners. Discuss why rules are important. Ask:
  - *Why does the animal park have rules?*
  - *Do you think these rules are sensible?*
  - *Are there any other rules you think the animal park should have?*

Plenary

- Put the learners into pairs. Ask each pair to follow the instructions carefully. *Where do the instructions take you?*

Let's talk

This section asks the learners questions that:

- give them a greater understanding of the text
- focus on the specific writing activity covered in the unit.

Activity A: This section ensures the learners have interpreted the map and instructions correctly.

Answers

A *Example answers:*
1 The map shows an animal park.
2 The animals that are close to the goats are the rhinos and wolves.
3 The animals furthest away from the entrance are the lions and tiger.

4 The instructions take you from the entrance to the playground.
5 If you follow the instructions you don't walk past the rhinos, the lions, the antelopes or the giraffes.
6 Instructions tell us how to do things.
7 *Learner's own suggestions of different ways they might go from the entrance to the playground*

Activity B: This section focuses the learners on the rules. It also asks them for their opinions.

Answers

B *Example answers:*
1 The rules clearly tell you what you should and shouldn't do at the animal park.
2 The animal park needs rules to keep the visitors and the animals safe.
3 *Learner's own opinions on which is the most important rule and why*
4 *Learner's own suggestions for rules*

Let's learn

This section:

- recaps work previously covered on full stops and capital letters
- recaps work previously covered on doing words (verbs)
- gives learners the opportunity to practise what they have learned in a focused activity before incorporating it into their own writing.

Full stops and capital letters

Answers

A 1 **O**n Saturday we are going to the animal park.
  2 **W**e quickly get ready.
  3 **T**he car is packed and off we go.
B 1 **W**e arrive at the animal park**.**
  2 **D**ad parks the car**.**
C *Learner's own sentence about what they might do next; the sentence should start with a capital letter and end with a full stop*

Doing words

Answers

A <u>Go</u> into the animal park.   <u>Walk</u> to the monkeys.
  <u>Walk</u> to the tiger.   <u>Eat</u> at the café.

B Do not **walk** on the grass.

Talk quietly near the animals.

Never **run** near the animals.

Only **eat** in the café area.

C *Learner's own rule with verb circled*

Let's practise

This section allows you to model the required writing outcome with input from the learners.

Before writing

- Always encourage the learners to talk about what they are going to write. Discuss things that can help the learners organise their thoughts.

- Look again at the map of the animal park on page 56. The learners are going to write instructions for a friend who wants to visit the giraffes at the animal park. Their instructions need to begin at the entrance of the park.

- Remind the learners that their instructions need to be numbered, and also need to be as simple and straightforward as possible.

- Give the learners examples of long-winded instructions and compare them with short and simple ones. Ask them which instructions were easier to follow.

- Remind the learners to refer to the map constantly to help make their instructions accurate.

Shared writing activity

- Organise the learners into small groups or pairs. They are going to discuss the instructions they are going to write.

- Remind the learners all sentences need a capital letter and full stop.

- Give them opportunities to discuss what they have written, either with you or with their peers.

- The activity can be done individually, in pairs or in groups. They can swap around their instructions and test them out.

- Finally, share the learners' instructions with the class. Encourage them to read their instructions to the rest of the group or class. Do they all get to the giraffes?

- More able learners could give instructions to get to other places in the animal park, starting and ending in different places.

Let's write

The learners are required to produce instructions independently for Jake's journey home from school.

They are also asked to write rules of the road to consider. Encourage learners to share their work in progress with you so that, through discussion, they can improve their work.

Before writing

- Remind the learners of the details they discussed about writing instructions in the Let's practise section.

- Encourage them to keep their instructions and rules simple.

- Remind them to use capital letters and full stops and recognise when they are using verbs.

- Discuss how to walk home from school safely (for example, take care when crossing a road, do not talk to strangers, do not play with a ball near a road, walk carefully near busy roads).

- Ask them to write their instructions and rules carefully and neatly.

- Help the learners with spellings if necessary.

Marking criteria

Technical aspects
Look for correct use of:
• clear, simple instructions and rules that are numbered • verbs written in their present tense • sentences that start with a capital letter and end with a full stop.
Content
Look for correct use of:
• relevant instructions that start at the school and end at Jake's house • relevant rules that consider road safety.

After writing

- Read through the completed instructions and rules with the learners. Encourage them to share their instructions with others.

- Consider what would happen if there were no rules in this situation.

Plenary

- Discuss with the learners other times that instructions are important (for example, for a game, using equipment, following a recipe).

- Ask the learners to bring in other examples of instructions and display them.

- Discuss the importance of rules, highlighting what would happen in certain situations if there were no rules (for example, playground rules).

Resource sheets

The resource sheets for Unit 7 provide differentiation for the writing outcome in this unit as well as further practice on full stops, capital letters and verbs.

1   A resource sheet on full stops, capital letters and verbs.
2   A resource sheet on writing instructions.
3   A resource sheet on writing rules.

Resource sheet 1: Writing instructions and rules: write sentences and look for doing words

Resource sheet 1 covers further practice of writing sentences using capital letters and full stops correctly. It also covers identifying *doing words* (*verbs*). Learners are given a noun and a verb and asked to write a sentence (using capital letters and full stops correctly). They are then asked to identify the verbs in the sentences they have written, before writing two sentences of their own.

- Read through the resource sheet with the learners so they fully understand what is expected of them.
- Revise what elements a correct sentence needs (for example, a capital letter, full stop and verb).
- When completed, read through the sentences in Activity A with the learners to ensure they are correct. Some learners may need more support than others for this activity.
- To extend the activity, ask the learners to write longer sentences that might include two verbs. They can then share their sentences with their peers, asking them to highlight the verbs.

Resource sheet 2: Writing instructions and rules: write instructions

Resource sheet 2 covers writing instructions. Learners are asked to think about the journey they make from home to school. They are then asked to write instructions for this journey.

- Explain the task and allow time for learners to ask questions so they fully understand what is required.
- Discuss the importance of making their instructions clear, simple and numbered.
- Help them with vocabulary they might want to use.
- Once learners have written their instructions, ask them to share them with a peer. Are the instructions easy to follow?

Resource sheet 3: Writing instructions and rules: write rules

Resource sheet 3 covers writing rules. Learners are asked to consider the things they need to think about when crossing a road. They are then asked to write four rules that need to be followed when crossing a road. Picture prompts are provided to help.

- Read through the resource sheet with the learners so they fully understand what is expected of them.
- Revise what makes a good rule (for example, it should be short and clear).
- Discuss the key safety aspects of crossing roads, encouraging input from the learners.
- Help them with vocabulary they might want to use.
- Once the learners have written their rules, ask them to share them with a peer. Are their rules clear? Are the rules relevant?

Assessment

The assessment sheet for this unit, 'Instructions: writing instructions and rules', is on page 86 of Learner's Book 1. The learners write instructions for their journey to school each day and then write any rules that might make their journey safer.

- Read through the assessment sheet with the learners to ensure they have understood the writing task.
- Remind the learners that instructions need to be clearly written and numbered.
- Remind them to write verbs in the present tense.
- Remind them that rules are things we must or must not do. They need to be short and simple so that they are easily understood.
- Do not penalise the learners for spelling words incorrectly.

Marking criteria

Technical aspects
Look for correct use of:
• clear, simple instructions and rules that are numbered
• verbs written in their present tense
• sentences that start with a capital letter and end with a full stop.
Content
Look for correct use of:
• relevant instructions that start at the learner's home and end at school
• relevant rules that consider road safety and possibly stranger danger.

Unit 8: Personal writing: writing recounts

Learner's Book unit focus

This unit introduces the writing of **recounts**, personal writing on something that has already happened, focusing on things the writer likes and dislikes. It highlights verbs written in the **past tense** and how **adjectives** can make the learners' writing more interesting.

Progress table for Stage 1: Unit 8					
Category: Personal writing					
Writing outcome: Writing recounts					
A personal experience is when a writer relates an experience that they have had. This could be a visit, an event they have taken part in, such as sports, or somewhere the writer has been invited to, such as a party. Personal recounts are written in past tenses and use first person pronouns.					
Stage 1	**Stage 2**	**Stage 3**	**Stage 4**	**Stage 5**	**Stage 6**
• writing a simple recount • writing about likes and dislikes	• writing a simple recount	• writing a recount • writing about likes and dislikes	• writing a recount	• writing a recount • writing about likes and dislikes	• writing a recount
Cambridge Global English link: Stage 1: Unit 8: Wonderful water					
Cambridge Primary English link: Stage 1: Unit 8: Things that have happened					

Unit teaching plan

Warm up

- Ask the learners if they have ever read a postcard from someone who is on holiday. If possible, have some postcards available. Read them together and discuss how the writer is telling the reader what they have been doing. The writer is recounting things that have happened on their holiday.
- Ask the learners to tell you about things they did at the weekend. Ask:
  - *What did you do at the weekend?*
  - *Did you meet friends or family?*
  - *Did you have fun?*
  - *What did you like about your weekend?*
  - *What did you not like about your weekend?*
- List some of the things on the board. Be sure to write the verbs in the past tense to show they have already happened (for example, *Ben walked to his nan's house*).
- Remind the learners that in this unit they will be writing in sentences. Sentences need to start with a capital letter and end with a full stop.
- Discuss with the learners the things they enjoy doing with their family, then introduce the Let's read text, a recount of something Aslam and Rabia enjoy doing with their family.

Let's read

The learners are introduced to Aslam and Rabia. They are visiting the beach with their mother and father. Aslam then writes about his visit to the beach.

- Read the introduction and recount to the class, then ask nominated learners to do the same. Be sure the learners all understand the recount and what it is describing.
- Highlight the names of the children, Aslam and Rabia. Ask the learners what they notice about the first letter in each of the names. Remind the learners of the term *special naming word* (used here rather than *proper noun*). Highlight why these words start with a capital letter and others do not.
- Discuss the picture of the children playing on the beach. Ask the learners questions:
  - *Are the children having fun?*
  - *What are they doing?*
  - *Would you enjoy jumping the waves?*
  - *Have you ever been to a beach?*
- Highlight to the learners that the *doing words* (*verbs*) are written in the past tense. Ask the learners to look at the word *splashed*:
  - *What do you notice about the ending of the word?*

- Explain that adding -ed changes the meaning of the verb to something that has happened in the past.
- Discuss the details of Aslam's recount.
- Remind the learners that sentences start with a capital letter and end with a full stop. Illustrate this in Aslam's recount.

Plenary

Put the learners into pairs. Ask each learner in the pair to tell the other about a trip they have had, recounting what they did, with whom and where.

Let's talk

This section asks the learners questions that:

- give them a greater understanding of the text
- focus on the specific writing activity covered in the unit.

Introduce the term *personal recount*. This is the detailing of something that has happened from a personal perspective. It is written in the past tense.

Activity A: This section is to ensure learners have understood what they have read.

Answers

A *Example answers:*
1   Aslam and Rabia visited a beach.
2   Their mother and father went with them.
3   Yes, they do live near the beach as the text says they live near the water.
4   Aslam enjoys jumping in the small waves and being splashed by his sister.
5   Rabia made Aslam laugh by splashing him.
6   Aslam and Rabia were sad when they had to go home.

Activity B: This section focuses the learners on the details of the recount, including the language used and Aslam's likes and dislikes. It also asks the learners to look at the trip from the perspective of Aslam's mother.

Answers

B *Example answers:*
1   Aslam wrote about his visit to the beach.
2   Aslam used the words *I* and *we* in his writing because it was written from his point of view, not about someone else.
3   Aslam did write about what he liked and did not like. He liked playing in the water; he did not like it when he had to go home.

4   *Learner's own interpretation of the mother's perspective of the visit to the beach*

Let's learn

This section:

- introduces work on *doing words* (*verbs*) in the past tense
- reminds learners how the use of *describing words* (*adjectives*) can improve their writing
- gives learners the opportunity to practise what they have learned in a focused activity before incorporating it into their own writing.

Doing words

- Write a number of *doing words* on the board (for example, walk, talk, howl).
- Ask the learners to give you further present tense *doing words*.
- Read the information box with the learners.
- Explain to the learners that if something has already happened it has been done in the past. To make verbs in the past tense we often add -ed to the verb (for example, *splash – splashed*).
- Encourage the learners to work through each exercise individually or in pairs.

Activity A: The learners rewrite the verbs in the past tense.

Answers

A	1	helped	2	jumped	3	kicked
	4	talked	5	lifted	6	watched

Activity B: The learners recognise and underline the verb in each sentence.

Answers

B 1   Aslam <u>walked</u> into the sea.
2   Rabia <u>followed</u> him.
3   They <u>splashed</u> in the water.
4   They <u>watched</u> some fish.

Activity C: Finally, the learners write a sentence with a verb in the past tense.

Answers

C *Learner's own sentence with verb written in the past tense*

Describing words

- Read the information box with the learners.
- Remind the learners of the term *describing words*. Explain that *describing words* (*adjectives*) tell us more about *naming words* (*nouns*).
- Using describing words makes our writing more interesting (for example, *the cold water* is more interesting than *the water*).
- Ask the learners for more examples of adjectives that can be added to *the water* (for example, *the fast water*, *the hot water*, *the still water*, *the sparkly water*).
- Encourage the learners to work through each exercise individually or in pairs.

Activity A: The learners write the adjective that best suits the pictures of the cat.

Answers

A *Example answers:*

1	a wet cat	**2**	a fat cat
3	a black cat	**4**	a stripy cat

Activity B: The learners add an adjective to each sentence.

Answers

B *Example answers:*

1 It was a <u>long</u> walk to the beach.
2 Aslam ran to the <u>cold</u> water.
3 Rabia jumped over the <u>small</u> waves.
4 A <u>big</u> wave splashed them.
5 Rabia and Aslam had very <u>wet</u> clothes.

Let's practise

This section allows you to model the required writing outcome with input from the learners.

Before writing

- Always encourage the learners to talk about what they are going to write. Discussing things can help them to organise their thoughts.
- Remind the learners what a personal recount is.
- Discuss different scenarios where the learners may have had a fun time at a location where water featured.

Shared writing activity

- Explain to the learners that they are going to write a recount, but first it is a good idea to help them organise their thoughts.
- They can discuss their experiences in pairs to aid them in clarifying their ideas.

- Encourage the learners to list the things they liked on their visit and the things they did not like. Introduce the words *likes* and *dislikes*.
- Remind the learners of the roles of doing words and describing words in their recount.
- Now ask the learners to write at least four sentences of their recount. Remind them about the use of capital letters and full stops.
- The activity can be done either individually or, if individuals need extra support, in pairs.
- Introduce the learners to the concept of improving what they have written. Ask them to check they have correctly used capital letters and full stops, they have used the correct tense for the verbs and they have included at least two describing words.
- Finally, share the learners' recounts with the class. Encourage them to read their recounts to the rest of the group or class.
- Give the learners opportunities to discuss what they have written, either with you or with their peers.

Let's write

The learners are now required independently to produce a recount of their own, having worked through a similar exercise in the previous section. Encourage learners to share their work in progress with you so that, through discussion, they can improve it.

Before writing

- Remind the learners of things they discussed in the Let's practise section.
- Encourage them to think about different options and choose the best ones.
- Ask them to write their sentences carefully and neatly.
- Help the learners with spellings if necessary.
- Encourage the learners to look back at the recount once it has been written and check they have included capital letters and full stops, they have used the correct tense for the verbs and they have included at least two describing words.

Marking criteria

Technical aspects
Look for correct use of:
• sentences that start with a capital letter
• sentences that end with a full stop
• doing words written in the past tense
• describing words.

After writing

Read through the completed recounts with the learners. Encourage them to share their recounts with others.

Plenary

- Discuss other recounts they might write.
- Ask the learners to write a recount of their choice for homework, if they are able.
- You could create a display entitled 'Having fun by the water'. You can ask the learners to bring in or draw pictures to go with their recounts, that you can then display.

Resource sheets

The resource sheets for Unit 8 provide differentiation for the writing outcome in this unit as well as further practice on special naming words and writing sentences.

1 A resource sheet revising doing words and describing words.

2 A resource sheet on rewriting a recount.

Resource sheet 1: Writing recounts: doing words and describing words

Resource sheet 1 covers further practice on identifying doing words and describing words. Learners carefully read the recount and then identify the doing words and the describing words.

- Read through the resource sheet with the learners so they fully understand what is expected of them.
- Encourage the learners to read the recount carefully.
- The learners can work in pairs or individually on this activity.
- Check through the learners' answers to be sure they fully understand both doing and describing words before proceeding to resource sheet 2.

Resource sheet 2: Writing recounts: rewrite a recount

Resource sheet 2 asks the learners to rewrite a recount, improve it and correct its punctuation. Learners copy the recount, improving it by writing the

correct verb tenses, including some describing words, and adding missing capital letters and full stops.

- Explain the task and allow time for learners to ask questions so they fully understand what is required.
- Encourage the learners to read the recount carefully.
- Remind them that a sentence begins with a capital letter and usually ends with a full stop.
- Ask them to make the recount as interesting as possible with the addition of describing words.
- Help them with vocabulary they might want to use.
- Ask them to share the new, improved recount. Discuss the improvements different learners have made.

Assessment

The assessment sheet for this unit, 'Personal writing: writing recounts', is on page 87 of Learner's Book 1. The learners write a short recount of what they did yesterday.

- Read through the assessment sheet with the learners to ensure they have understood the writing task.
- Remind the learners of the things they need to include in their recount:
  - correct sentence punctuation
  - doing words in the past tense
  - describing words to make their writing more interesting.
- Remind them to include likes and dislikes in their recount.
- Do not penalise the learners for spelling words incorrectly.
- Ask them to read through their recount. Are there any corrections or additions they could make?

Marking criteria

Technical aspects
Look for correct use of:
• sentences that start with a capital letter
• sentences that end with a full stop
• doing words written in the past tense
• describing words.
Content
• Do their sentences make sense?
• Has their recount included likes and dislikes?
• Is the content interesting/engaging for the reader?
• Is the material ordered in a logical way?

Unit 9: Factual writing: writing a fact file

Learner's Book unit focus

This unit introduces the writing of **questions** and **facts** through the use of a fact file. The questions, used as subtitles, begin each section and facts answer the questions provided.

Progress table for Stage 1: Unit 9					
Category: Factual writing					
Writing outcome: Writing a fact file					
Organising information into a fact file is the first step for a writer when making decisions about what to include and what not to include. This is an important skill for factual writing.					
Stage 1	**Stage 2**	**Stage 3**	**Stage 4**	**Stage 5**	**Stage 6**
• writing questions and facts • writing simple non-fiction texts • writing a fact file	• writing simple non-fiction texts		• writing a fact file		
Cambridge Global English link: Stage 1: Unit 9: City places					
Cambridge Primary English link: –					

Unit teaching plan

Warm up

- Ask the learners some questions about cities:
  - *What is a city?*
  - *Do you live in a city?*
  - *Have you ever visited a city?*
- Inform them that this unit will look into writing questions and facts, on the subject of cities.
- Ask the learners, in pairs, to think of two questions to share with the rest of the class or group.
- Write a few of the learners' suggestions on the board. Highlight the question mark at the end of each sentence. Ask:
  - *When is the ? sign used?* [To show a question is being asked.]
  - *What do we normally add to the end of a sentence?* [full stop]
- Introduce the fact file: *We are now going to read some information on cities.*

Let's read

A fact file on cities is the stimulus for this unit. The subheadings are questions and the questions are answered with facts about cities.

- First, read the extract to the class, then ask nominated learners to read it again to the class. Be sure the learners all understand what has been read to them.
- Highlight the questions in the fact file to the learners. Ask:
  - *Who can read aloud a question in the fact file to me?*
  - *How do we know which of the sentences are questions?* [They ask something; they end with a question mark.]
- Remind the learners that sentences start with a capital letter and often end with a full stop but they can end with a question mark (?).
- Discuss the answers given to the questions in the fact file.
- Highlight that the answers are facts. They tell us information about cities.
- Discuss the difference between fact and fiction. Fact is actual information; fiction is made up.

Plenary

- Put the learners into pairs. Ask them to tell each other about a fact file they might like to read:
  - *Would you like to read a fact file on your favourite animal or sport?*
  - *Would you like to read a fact file on somewhere you are going to visit?*

Let's talk

This section asks the learners questions that:

- give them a greater understanding of the text
- focus on the specific writing activity covered in the unit.

Activity A: This section is to ensure learners have understood what they have read.

Answers

A 1 The fact file is about cities.

2 A city is a place where many people live and work.

3 Eight different types of transport are listed.

4 *Learner's own suggestions of other types of transport, for example, mopeds, trams*

5 *Learner's own suggestions of what might happen in the tall buildings in a city, for example, people work in offices, shops sell items, etc.*

6 *Learner's own suggestions of other places people might visit in cities, for example, art galleries, sports centres, historical buildings*

Activity B: This section focuses the learners on the structure of a fact file, highlighting what facts are and in which types of book we find facts.

Answers

B *Example answers:*

1 Each section of the fact file begins with a question.

2 A fact tells us information about something.

3 For example: *Are there many schools in cities? Is there a football or cricket club in the city?*

4 Non-fiction books, for example, information books, dictionaries

Let's learn

This section:

- introduces work on *questions*
- introduces work on *facts*

- gives learners the opportunity to practise what they have learned in a focused activity before incorporating it into their own writing.

Questions

- Ask the learners a question: *What time is it?* Write the question on the board.
- Discuss with the learners how questions ask us something. Tell them to ask the person next to them a question.
- Read the information box with the learners.
- Highlight the question mark at the end of each question sentence.
- With the learners, practise writing a question mark in the air.

Activity A: The learners read aloud the questions in the fact file at the beginning of the unit.

Answers

A There are four questions:

What is a city?

How do people move around?

What are the buildings like?

What places do people visit?

Activity B: The learners add full stops or question marks correctly to given sentences.

Answers

B 1 Do you live in a city?

2 Would you like to go to the shops?

3 I live close to a city.

4 What time shall we meet?

5 I will catch the train to the city.

6 I'll meet you at 11 o'clock.

Activity C: Finally, the learners write three questions of their own.

Answers

C *Each learner writes three questions; check each one ends with a question mark*

Writing facts

- Read the information box with the learners.
- Give the learners a topic (for example, school). Ask them for examples of facts, such as *School starts at 8:45am. We have five lessons a day.*
- Look at the first picture with the learners. Discuss the facts they can write about the motorbike (for example, *A motorbike has two wheels*).

- What other examples of facts can they give?
- Encourage them to work through each picture individually or in pairs.
- Check the learners' facts are written with a capital letter and full stop.

Activity A: Learners write a fact about each transport picture.

Answers

A *Example answers:*

1 A motorbike has two wheels.
2 A car can carry more people than a motorbike.
3 A plane travels a long distance.
4 A train can travel quickly between towns and cities.
5 A bus is a cheap way to travel.
6 A taxi picks you up from one place and takes you to another.

Let's practise

This section allows you to model the required writing outcome with input from the learners.

Before writing

- Always encourage the learners to talk about what they are going to write. Discussing things can help the learners organise their thoughts.
- Remind the learners that fact files provide information about something.
- Ask the learners for examples of situations when fact files might be used.

Shared writing activity

- The learners are going to write a fact file, but first it is a good idea to help them to organise their thoughts.
- Encourage the learners to list the different places they might go to when visiting a city.
- In pairs they can discuss the possible questions they might use to aid them in clarifying their ideas.
- Remind them of the difference between fact and fiction.
- The activity can either be done individually or, if individuals need extra support, in pairs.
- Finally, share the learners' fact files with the class. Encourage them to read their fact files to the rest of the group or class.
- Give the learners opportunities to discuss what they have written, either with you or with their peers.

Let's write

The learners are now required to produce a fact file of their own independently, having worked through a similar exercise in the previous section. Encourage learners to share their work in progress with you so that, through discussion, they can improve it.

Before writing

- The learners can either write their final fact file on a blank sheet of paper, possibly folded in half, or you can give them resource sheet 2 to use as a structure for their fact file.
- Remind the learners of things they discussed in the Let's practise section.
- Encourage them to think about different questions they might use as subsections and choose the best ones.
- Ask them to write their sentences carefully and neatly.
- Remind them of the punctuation needed at the end of a question and a fact.
- Help them with spellings if necessary.
- Encourage the learners to look back at the fact file once they have written it and to check they have included capital letters, full stops and question marks and that they have used the correct tenses for the verbs.

Marking criteria

Technical aspects
Look for correct use of:
• sentences that start with a capital letter
• sentences that end with a full stop
• questions that end with a question mark.
Content
• Do their sentences make sense?
• Are their questions relevant?
• Have they included facts that appropriately answer their questions?
• Do the pictures they have drawn support the material they have written?

After writing

- Read through the completed fact files with the learners.
- Display the fact files so all learners and visitors to the class can access them.

Teacher's Resource Unit guide: Stage 1: Unit 9

Plenary

Fact files are an ideal way of asking the learners to focus on the details they are learning about a topic. Use fact files during other class topics as a way of assessing their understanding of a topic covered. The learners could be given this task as a project to work on at home, if they are able.

Resource sheets

The resource sheets for Unit 9 provide differentiation for the writing outcome in this unit as well as further practice on writing questions.

1 A resource sheet on writing questions.
2 A resource sheet on the fact file layout.

Resource sheet 1: Writing a fact file: writing questions

Resource sheet 1 covers further practice on writing questions, with a focus on question words. The learners identify question words, highlighting that they start with *wh-*. They then complete questions using the words given and finally write questions of their own.

- Read through the resource sheet with the learners so they fully understand what is expected of them.
- Carefully read the information box with the learners.
- They then read the question words aloud.
- They identify that each question word begins with *wh-*.
- They complete questions using the given question words.
- The learners write four of their own questions.
- Encourage them to read carefully the questions they have written. Have they ended each question with a question mark?
- They can work in pairs or individually on this activity.
- Check through their answers to be sure they fully understand how to write questions.

Resource sheet 2: Writing a fact file: fact file layout

Resource sheet 2 provides the learners with a suggested layout that can be used when writing a fact file. Learners are provided with the scaffolding on which to base their own fact file. Some learners may need support when completing the different sections; others will be able to work independently.

- Use this resource sheet in conjunction with the Let's write section.
- Explain the layout of the fact file.
- Help the learners with vocabulary they might want to use.
- Encourage them to work carefully and neatly.
- Ask them to share their completed fact files.

Assessment

The assessment sheet for this unit, 'Factual writing: writing a fact file', is on page 88 of Learner's Book 1. It provides the learners with a structure on which to base a fact file about their school.

- Read through the assessment sheet with the learners to ensure they have understood the writing task.
- Encourage the learners to spend some time thinking of appropriate questions they might answer about their school (for example, *Where is … School? How many children go to the school? What sports do the children play?*
- Remind the learners of the correct structure for the fact file.
- Remind them that questions always end with a question mark.
- Do not penalise learners for spelling words incorrectly.

Marking criteria

Technical aspects
Look for correct use of:
• sentences that start with a capital letter
• sentences that end with a full stop
• questions that end with a question mark.
Content
• Do their sentences make sense?
• Are their questions relevant?
• Have they included facts that appropriately answer their questions?

Cambridge Grammar and Writing Skills

Teacher's Resource 1-3

Stage 2

Unit guides: Stage 2

Unit 1: Stories: plot

Learner's Book unit focus

This unit introduces the structure of writing a **simple narrative**. It focuses the learner on the basic structure of the **beginning, middle** and **end** of stories.

Progress table for Stage 2: Unit 1

Category: Narrative writing

Writing outcome: Writing a story

When learners are writing a story, it helps them to know that there is a structure to it. The first stage of teaching learners about plot is highlighting the beginning, middle and end of stories.

Stage 1	Stage 2	Stage 3	Stage 4	Stage 5	Stage 6
• joining two sentences with *and* • characters	• sequencing sentences to form a narrative • plot – beginning, middle and end • characters • setting	• plot • story openings/ settings • continuing stories	• characters – physical appearance – personality	• stories teaching lessons	• story endings

Cambridge Global English link:	Stage 2: Unit 1: Look in a book
Cambridge Primary English links:	Stage 1: Unit 1: Stories about things we know
	Stage 1: Unit 8: Things under the sea

Unit teaching plan

Warm up

- Discuss the differences between fact and fiction. Fact is actual information; fiction is imaginary, made up.
- Talk to the learners about books. Ask:
  - *What do we find in books?* [information/stories/ poems]
  - *Do you have a favourite story?*
- Inform them that this unit, on the subject of 'Look in a book', will look at stories.
- Ask the learners, in pairs, to talk about a story they have read in a book. Ask:
  - *What happened in the story?*
  - *What happened at the beginning of the story?*
  - *What happened in the middle of the story?*
  - *What happened at the end of the story?*
- Introduce Seagull, the main character of the story in the Learner's Book.
  - *We are now going to read a story about a seagull who is called Seagull.*

Let's read

The story *Seagull* by Kathryn Harper (ISBN: 978-1-316-50310-2) is the stimulus for this unit. Seagull meets various things that pollute our world. Pep and Lin, two children, find Seagull and help clean him up. They then all set about cleaning up the beach.

- Introduce the story to the class.
  - *In this story, a seagull gets very dirty. Two children, Pep and Lin, help Seagull. Shall we find out how the children help?*
- First, read the story to the class, then ask nominated learners to read it again to the class. Be sure the learners all understand what has been read to them.
- Highlight the artwork to the learners. Ask:
  - *Do you like the pictures?*
  - *Do they help tell us what is happening in the story?*
- Remind the learners that sentences always start with a capital letter. Ask:
  - *How do we know which of the sentences are questions?* [They ask something; they end with a question mark.]

Plenary

- Despite being a tricky topic for this age, this story can be a way of introducing pollution and how it affects wildlife.
- Highlight the pollutants Seagull comes across and the effect they have on him.
- Ask the learners what pollution they are aware of (for example, litter in the street or around the school).
- Discuss why it is not good to have litter in our environment.

Let's talk

This section asks the learners questions that:

- give them a greater understanding of the text
- focus on the specific writing activity covered in the unit.

Activity A: This section is to ensure learners have understood what they have read.

Answers

A *Example answers:*

1 Seagull flies up into the clouds first.
2 When Seagull landed on the water he got covered in a sticky mess.
3 Seagull asked for help because litter had become stuck to him and he couldn't fly.
4 Pep and Lin helped Seagull by taking off the litter and washing off the sticky mess.
5 Pep, Lin and Seagull cleaned the beach to make it nice for everyone and safe for other seagulls.

Activity B: This section focuses the learners on the structure of a simple narrative, highlighting that stories are written with a beginning, a middle and an end.

Answers

B *Example answers:*

1 At the beginning of the story Seagull got caught in a sticky mess and litter stuck to him.
2 Seagull might have felt frightened.
3 In the middle of the story Seagull was helped by Pep and Lin, who cleaned him up.
4 Seagull probably felt relieved and grateful.
5 At the end of the story Seagull, Pep and Lin cleaned all the litter from the beach so it would be clean and safe for everyone.
6 Seagull might have felt happy that the beach was being cleaned.

Let's learn

This section:

- introduces work on *exclamation marks*
- revises previous work on *full stops* and *question marks*
- introduces work on *ordering sentences*.

Exclamation marks

- The learners have previously covered work on sentences ending with full stops and question marks. Now they are introduced to exclamation marks.
- Revise the terms *capital letters*, *full stops* and *question marks* with the learners.
- Ask the learners:
  - *What type of sentence ends with a full stop?* [a telling sentence]
  - *What type of sentence ends with a question mark?* [an asking sentence]
- Ask the learners for examples of the different types of sentence.
- Read the information box with the learners. Introduce the term *exclamation*. With the learners, draw an exclamation mark in the air, on the board or on paper.
- Highlight that sometimes telling sentences can end with an exclamation mark. Adding an exclamation mark allows expression in the written word (for example, compare *Quick, we must go.* with *Quick, we must go!*).

Activity A: The learners add a full stop, question mark or exclamation mark to each of the sentences.

Answers

A 1 Seagull flew up into the clouds**.**
2 Where am I**?**
3 Help, I am lost**!**
4 Shall I fly down to the water**?**
5 Oh no, litter is stuck on my wings**!**

Activity B: The learners write three sentences of their own, one with a full stop, one with a question mark and one with an exclamation mark.

Answers

B *Each learner writes three sentences: a telling sentence, a question and an exclamation. Check each sentence ends with the correct punctuation.*

Ordering sentences

- Reread the story *Seagull* with the learners.
- This activity concentrates on narrative sequence, that is, the order in which the events happen in a story.
- Read the information box with the learners.
- Give the learners an example of a well-known story. First, discuss the order in which things actually happen, then change some of the events around, illustrating the importance of order.
- Look at the first picture with the learners. Discuss which sentence should begin the story and then allow the learners to complete the rest of the activity.
- Encourage the learners to work through each picture individually or in pairs.
- Check the learners' sentences are written with a capital letter and full stop.

Activity A: Sentences to be written in the correct order, reflecting the pictures.

Answers

A Seagull went into the clouds.

Seagull went into the water.

Seagull went onto the beach.

Seagull needed help to clean his wings.

Seagull helped clean the beach.

Let's practise

This section allows you to model the required writing outcome with input from the learners.

Before writing

- Always encourage the learners to talk about what they are going to write. Discussing things can help the learners to organise their thoughts.
- Remind the learners that stories have a beginning, middle and end to help order the story. Discuss what happens at the beginning, middle and end of the story *Seagull*.
- Remind the learners of the difference between fact and fiction.

Shared writing activity

- The learners are going to write, from memory, what happened at the beginning, the middle and the end of the story *Seagull*.
- Encourage the learners to write what happened in their own words.

- The activity can either be done individually or, if individuals need extra support, in pairs.
- Finally, share the learners' sentences with the class. Do they all agree about what happened in the beginning, the middle and the end?
- Give the learners opportunities to discuss what they have written, either with you or with their peers.

Let's write

The learners now independently produce a story of their own, having worked through the familiar story in the previous section. Encourage learners to share their work in progress with you so that, through discussion, they can improve their work.

Before writing

- The learners are expected to write another Seagull story based on the artwork prompts provided.
- Remind the learners of the story structure they discussed in the Let's practise section.
- Ask them to write their sentences carefully and neatly.
- Remind the learners of the different types of punctuation needed at the end of a telling sentence, a question and an exclamation.
- Help the learners with spellings if necessary.

Marking criteria

Technical aspects
Look for correct use of:
• sentences that start with a capital letter
• sentences that end with a full stop
• questions that end with a question mark
• sentences that end with an exclamation mark.
Content
• Do their sentences make sense?
• Are the sentences written in order?
• Does their story have a beginning, a middle and an end?

After writing

- Read through the completed story with the learners.
- In pairs, ask the learners to read their stories to each other.

Plenary

- Find the beginning, middle and end of stories that are familiar to the learners.
- Give the learners sentences from a familiar story and, in groups, ask them to order the story.

Resource sheets

The resource sheets for Unit 1 provide differentiation for the writing outcome in this unit as well as further practice on writing questions.

1 A resource sheet on exclamation marks.
2 A resource sheet on finding the beginning, the middle and the end of a story.

Resource sheet 1: Plot: exclamation marks

Resource sheet 1 covers further practice on recognising exclamation marks. The learners identify the different forms of exclamation (for example, surprise, anger and shouting). They organise the exclamations into a table and then write an exclamation of their own.

- Read through the resource sheet with the learners so they fully understand what is expected of them.
- Carefully read the information box with the learners.
- Ask the learners for other examples.
- They complete the table of exclamations, writing the exclamations from the word box in the correct columns.
- They write an exclamation of their own.
- Encourage them to read carefully the exclamation they have written. Have they ended it with an exclamation mark?
- They can work in pairs or individually on this activity.
- Check through the learners' answers to be sure they fully understand the use of exclamation marks.

Resource sheet 2: Plot: ordering a story

Resource sheet 2 provides the learners with support for the Let's write activity. Learners are provided with the sentences that make up the story illustrated in the unit. Some learners may need support when completing the different stages; others will be able to work independently.

- Use this resource sheet in conjunction with the Let's write section.
- Explain the beginning, middle and end structure of stories.
- Discuss the artwork before the learners read and organise the sentences into the correct order.
- Encourage the learners to work carefully and neatly.
- Ask them to share their completed stories.

Assessment

The assessment sheet for this unit, 'Stories: plot', is on page 87 of Learner's Book 2. The learners are provided with a picture stimulus and guided to write a story with a beginning, a middle and an end.

- Read through the assessment sheet with the learners to ensure they have understood the writing task.
- Encourage them to spend some time looking carefully at the pictures before writing their story.
- Remind them that they could also include an exclamation in their writing.
- Do not penalise learners for spelling words incorrectly.

Marking criteria

Technical aspects
Look for correct use of:
• sentences that start with a capital letter
• sentences that end with a full stop
• questions that end with a question mark
• sentences that end with an exclamation mark.
Content
• Do their sentences make sense?
• Are the sentences written in order?
• Does their story have a beginning, a middle and an end?

Unit 2: Stories: dialogue in stories

Learner's Book unit focus

This unit introduces **direct speech** within the context of **comic-strip stories** and **speech bubbles**.

Progress table for Stage 2: Unit 2

Category: Narrative writing: stories

Writing outcome: Using speech bubbles

Learners are first introduced to speech in writing via the use of speech bubbles. This helps the learner to visualise what is actually being said. In Stage 3, the learners are introduced to speech marks and other associated punctuation.

Stage 1	Stage 2	Stage 3	Stage 4	Stage 5	Stage 6
	• speech bubbles • capital letter for first word spoken	• adding speech marks when speaker is at the end • dividing spoken words from non-spoken words by a comma, question mark and exclamation mark	• paragraphing in dialogue • contractions • synonyms for *said* • split direct speech		

Cambridge Global English link:	Stage 2: Unit 2: Good neighbours
Cambridge Primary English link:	Stage 2: Unit 1: Stories about things we know

Unit teaching plan

Warm up

- Explain to the learners that they are going to look at a comic strip. Ask:
  - *Where might you find comic strips?*
  - *Who are your favourite comic-strip characters?*
- Show the learners examples of comic strips.
- Draw two children walking together, each with a speech bubble coming from their mouth. Ask:
  - *What might these two children be saying to each other?*
- Write example conversations in the speech bubbles (for example, the children could be talking about what they are going to have for lunch, where they are going on holiday, who their best friend is, etc.). Ask two learners to act out the children: *what else could they say?* Write the class's suggestions on the board.

Let's read

In this comic strip, Tia and Ben, who live next door to each other, are having a conversation. Ben has lost his cat, Spot. He is worried about his cat and what his mum will say. The extract is an example of speech bubbles within a comic strip.

- First, read the extract to the class, then ask nominated learners to read it again to the class.
- Highlight the use of the speech bubbles and how they aid the understanding of what is happening in the comic strip.
- Be sure the learners all understand the extract and what has happened in it.
- Discuss what makes a 'good' neighbour.
  - *Is Tia a good neighbour to Ben?*

Plenary

- Ask the learners for examples they might have of 'good neighbours'.
- Discuss what they think would make a good neighbour. Ask:
  - *Imagine your neighbour was locked out of their home; what would you do?*
  - *Imagine your neighbour had dropped all their shopping on the ground or lost a favourite toy; what would you do?*
  - *Why is it important to be a good neighbour?*

- Put the learners into pairs, with one taking on the role of Ben and the other Tia from the comic strip.
- Ask the learners to act out what has happened so far and to continue the conversation the children might go on to have.
- Bring the learners back into a larger group and discuss what else the children might say. Record some of the learners' ideas in further speech bubbles, highlighting to them how to capture the conversation.
- This activity highlights conversations between children and how they can be recognised in speech bubbles.

Let's talk

This section asks the learners questions that:

- give them a greater understanding of the text
- focus on the specific writing activity covered in the unit.

Activity A: This section is to ensure learners have understood what they have read.

Answers

A *Example answers:*
1 Ben is looking for his cat.
2 The cat is called Spot.
3 The cat ran into the bushes.
4 Ben is upset.
5 Tia is a good neighbour because she is going to help Ben.
6 Ben is worried about what his mother will say.

Activity B: This section focuses the learners on the use of speech bubbles. The learners should discuss the answers.

Answers

B *Example answers:*
1 The speech bubbles show the children are talking to each other.
2 The speech bubbles come directly from the child who is talking.
3 Tia says 'Hi Ben!' in the first picture.
4 Ben says 'My mum will be cross if I can't find him' in the last picture.

Let's learn

This section:

- recaps work previously covered on writing sentences
- introduces work on speech bubbles and how they represent what is being said
- gives learners the opportunity to practise what they have learned in a focused activity, before incorporating it into their own writing.

Writing sentences

The information box recaps the basic layout of sentences that the learners have met earlier in the course.

- Read the information box with the learners.
- Go through the list, asking the learners to point to an example in the extract of:
  - a sentence beginning with a capital letter
  - a sentence ending in a full stop
  - a sentence ending in a question mark
  - a sentence ending in an exclamation mark.

Activity A: Learners should work individually so you can assess their knowledge. The learners pick out the sentences that have a capital letter at the beginning and are punctuated correctly.

Answers

A 1 Written incorrectly – missing capital W for We
   2 Written correctly
   3 Written correctly
   4 Written incorrectly – missing question mark at end

Activity B: Again, learners should work individually. They copy out simple sentences correctly, including all capital letters and punctuation.

Answers

B 1 Shall I look in the shed?
   2 I will get his food.
   3 Quick, I can see him!

Speech bubbles

- Draw a large speech bubble on the board, next to a picture of a child's head.
- Write something in the speech bubble and ask the learners what the child is saying. Do this several times.

- Read the information box with the learners.
- Highlight that all spoken sentences begin with a capital letter.
- Encourage the learners to work through each exercise individually or in pairs.

Activity A: The learners recognise and copy what each person is saying.

Answers

A 1 The child is asking… What is his name?

2 The man is saying… No, I have not.

3 The old lady is asking… Can I help you?

4 Tia is asking… Have you found Spot?

Activity B: In this activity the learners choose the correct sentence to write into each speech bubble. The pictures will give them clues.

Answers

B 1 Have you seen Spot?

2 Look, is that Spot?

3 I missed you!

Activity C: Finally, the learners write in given speech bubbles what they think the children would say to Ben's mum.

Answers

C *Example answers:*

Ben: I'm really sorry I'm late back.

Ben's mum: Where have you been?

Tia: Spot ran off but we found him.

Let's practise

This section allows you to model the required writing outcome with input from the learners.

Before writing

- Ask the learners to retell the comic-strip extract. Ask:
  - *Can you name the characters?*
  - *What is the cat called?*
  - *Did Tia help Ben?*

Shared writing activity

- Explain to the learners that they are going to complete a comic-strip story. They have to add the conversation.

- Look at the pictures with the learners. Discuss what happens.
- The activity can be done individually, in pairs or in groups.
- Look at the first picture. What might the children say? Ask the learners for their suggestions.
- Write the suggestions on the board or on a photocopy of the comic strip.
- Work through each picture in the same way, reminding the learners of what has come before and what is coming up.
- Encourage the learners to write their own ideas of what the children are saying in the boxes provided.

Let's write

The learners now produce a finished comic strip independently, having worked through a similar exercise in the previous section. Encourage them to share their work in progress with you so that, through discussion, they can improve their work.

Before writing

- Remind the learners of the suggestions they made in the previous section.
- Encourage them to think about the different options and choose the best ones.
- Ask them to write carefully and neatly in the speech bubbles.

Marking criteria

Technical aspects
Look for correct use of:
• speech bubbles
• capital letters
• full stops
• question marks
• exclamation marks.
Content
• Does the dialogue make sense?
• Has the learner considered the pictures as prompts for the dialogue?
• Does the dialogue flow, as a conversation might?

After writing

Read through the completed comic strips with the learners. Compare the different versions they have written.

Plenary

- Discuss what might happen next. How might the conversation continue?
- In small groups, the learners could now act out the whole comic strip from both the Let's practise and the Let's write sections.

Resource sheets

The resource sheets for Unit 2 provide differentiation for the writing outcome in this unit.

1   A resource sheet supporting those learners who might find the writing activity challenging.
2   A resource sheet that will further extend learners.

Resource sheet 1: Dialogue in stories: speech bubbles

Resource sheet 1 covers identifying relevant spoken words and adding missing dialogue. Learners are expected to copy given sentences into a reproduction of the Let's write writing activity. They need to order them correctly before adding them to the pictures.

- Read through the resource sheet with the learners so they fully understand what is expected of them.
- Highlight that the sentences need to be in the correct order before the learners add them to the pictures.
- Encourage the learners to write carefully and neatly.
- When completed, read through the comic strip with each learner to ensure it makes sense.

Resource sheet 2: Dialogue in stories: what happens next?

Resource sheet 2 allows the learners to create their own comic strip. Learners are expected to continue the story from the independent writing activity, though this time they have to draw the pictures as well as adding dialogue. They can do this activity independently or in pairs.

- Encourage the learners to read through the conversation they wrote for the Let's write activity.
- Explain the task and allow time for learners to ask questions so they fully understand what is required.

- Ask them to plan what might happen next.
- Help them with vocabulary they might want to use.
- Suggest they write notes and draw rough sketches before producing the final comic strip in the space available.
- Encourage learners to share their final comic strip with their peers.

Assessment

The assessment sheet for this unit, 'Stories: dialogue in stories', is on page 88 of Learner's Book 2. The learners are provided with a picture of Tia and Ben looking up a tree at Spot, who is at the top of the tree looking down on them. The learners write what Tia and Ben are saying in the speech bubbles provided.

- Read through the assessment sheet with the learners to ensure they have understood the writing task.
- Encourage them to spend some time looking at what the picture shows. Ask them to think about what Tia and Ben might be thinking and saying before they write anything.
- Remind them that they need to remember a capital letter for special naming words. Also remind them that a sentence starts with a capital letter and ends with a full stop, question mark or exclamation mark.
- Do not penalise learners for spelling words incorrectly.

Marking criteria

Technical aspects
Look for correct use of:
• speech bubbles
• capital letters
• full stops
• question marks
• exclamation marks.
Content
• Does the dialogue make sense?
• Has the learner considered the pictures as prompts for the dialogue?
• Does the dialogue flow, as a conversation might?

Unit 3: Personal writing: writing a recount

Learner's Book unit focus

This unit introduces the writing of **recounts**, personal writing recalling something that has happened in the past. It highlights verbs written in the **past tenses** and how **adjectives** can make the learners' writing more interesting, as well as considering the use of the **pronouns** *I* and *we* in recount writing.

Progress table for Stage 2: Unit 3

Category: Personal writing

Writing outcome: Writing recounts

A personal experience is when a writer relates an experience that they have had. This could be a visit, an event they have taken part in, such as sports, or somewhere the writer has been invited to, such as a party. Personal recounts are written in past tenses and use first person pronouns.

Stage 1	Stage 2	Stage 3	Stage 4	Stage 5	Stage 6
• writing a simple recount • writing about likes and dislikes	• writing a simple recount	• writing a recount • writing about likes and dislikes	• writing a recount	• writing a recount • writing about likes and dislikes	• writing a recount

Cambridge Global English link:	Stage 2: Unit 3: Ready, steady, go!
Cambridge Primary English link:	—

Unit teaching plan

Warm up

- Ask the learners if they have ever read a postcard, letter or email from someone who is on holiday. If possible, have some examples available. Read them together and discuss how the writer is telling the reader what they have been doing. The writer is recounting things that have happened on their holiday.

- Ask the learners to tell you about things they did during their last holiday:
  - *What did you do on holiday?*
  - *Did you meet friends or family?*
  - *Did you have fun?*
  - *What did you like about your holiday?*
  - *Was there anything you did not like about your holiday?*

- List some of the things on the board. Be sure to write the verb in the past tense to show it has already happened (for example, 'Tuhil *played* on the beach.').

- Remind the learners that in this unit they will write in sentences. Sentences need to start with a capital letter and end with a full stop, question mark or exclamation mark.

- Ask the learners if they have ever run in a race. Remind them of races they might have run at school, then introduce the Let's read text, Tuhil's recount of a race he ran in at school.

Let's read

The learners are introduced to Tuhil. He ran in a race at school with his friends. He wrote a recount about what happened and how he felt.

- Read the introduction and recount to the class and then ask nominated learners to do the same. Be sure the learners all understand the recount and what it is describing.

- Discuss the picture that shows the race taking place. Ask the learners questions:
  - *What are the children doing?*
  - *Are the children having fun?*
  - *Which child do you think is Tuhil?*
  - *Would you like to have a race?*
  - *Does it matter if you do not win?*

- Highlight to the learners that the doing words (verbs) are written in the past tense. Ask the learners to look at the word *cheered*:
  - *What do you notice about the ending of the word?*
- Explain that adding *-ed* changes the meaning of the verb to something that has happened in the past.
- Discuss the details of Tuhil's recount. Ask:
  - *Does Tuhil's recount build a picture in your mind of what happened?*
  - *Does Tuhil write about how he feels?*
  - *Does adding his feelings make his recount more interesting?*
- Ask the learners why there is an exclamation mark after Ready, steady, go! Refer to the work on exclamation marks they did in Unit 1.

Plenary

Put the learners into pairs. Ask each learner to tell their partner about a race they have been in. It might be a running race, but it could also be a race to get into bed first; a race to eat a meal quickly; a race to finish a game first. Ask them to recount what they did, with whom and where.

Let's talk

This section asks the learners questions that:

- give them a greater understanding of the text
- focus on the specific writing activity covered in the unit.

Introduce the term *personal recount*: writing that describes something that has happened from a personal perspective. It is written in the past tense.

Activity A: This section is to ensure learners have understood what they have read.

Answers

A *Example answers:*
1 Tuhil's teacher was kind because she said they were going to stop work and go outside to run some races.
2 The children cheered.
3 Six children ran in each race.
4 Tuhil felt excited about the race.
5 Three of Tuhil's friends cheered as he ran by.
6 No, Tuhil didn't win the race.

Activity B: This section focuses the learners on the details of the recount, including looking at the difference between stories and recounts.

Answers

B *Example answers:*
1 Tuhil has written a recount.
2 Stories are made up. Recounts actually happened.
3 Tuhil wrote about a race he was in.
4 Yes, Tuhil wrote about how he felt. He used these phrases to describe how he felt: I felt excited; I felt very nervous; I really enjoyed it.
5 The other children in the race would have written similar recounts but not the same: they would have described how they felt and what they saw.

Let's learn

This section:

- introduces work on *verbs (doing words) in the past tense*
- reminds learners how the use of *adjectives (describing words)* can improve their writing
- gives learners the opportunity to practise what they have learned in a focused activity before incorporating it into their own writing.

Verbs

- First, ask the learners if they remember what a doing word is. Ask:
  - *What is a different name for a doing word?* [verb]
- Remind them of the work they previously covered in Learner's Book 1 Units 3, 7 and 8 on doing words.
- Write a number of verbs on the board (for example, cheer, scream, wave).
- Ask the learners to give you further present tense verbs.
- Read the information box with the learners.
- Explain to the learners that if something has already happened it has been done in the past. To make verbs in the past tense we often add *-ed* to the verb (for example, cheer – cheered). However, if the verb family name ends in *-e* we just add *-d* (for example, wave – waved).
- Encourage the learners to work through each exercise individually or in pairs.
- Ask the learners to look back at Tuhil's recount. How many past tense verbs can they find ending in *-ed* or *-d*?

Activity A: The learners add the correct ending (*-ed* or *-d*) to the verbs, changing them into the past tense.

Answers

A
1	scratch**ed**	**2**	like**d**	**3**	push**ed**
4	live**d**	**5**	dive**d**	**6**	scream**ed**
7	finish**ed**	**8**	brush**ed**	**9**	smile**d**

Activity B: The learners add a past tense verb to each given sentence.

Answers

B *Example answers:*

1 Tuhil <u>watched</u> his friend in his race.
2 He <u>cheered</u> when his friend won his race.
3 Tuhil <u>talked</u> to his friend after the race.
4 Tuhil and his friends were tired when they <u>went</u> home.

Adjectives

- First, ask the learners if they remember what a *describing word* is. Ask:
  - *What is a different name for a describing word?* [adjective]
- Remind them of the work they previously covered in Learner's Book 1 Units 1, 4 and 8 on *describing words*.
- Read the information box with the learners.
- Remind them of the term *adjective*. Explain that adjectives tell us more about nouns (naming words).
- Using adjectives makes our writing more interesting (for example, *our kind teacher* is more interesting than *our teacher*).
- Ask the learners for more examples of adjectives that can be added to *the teacher* (for example, *the grumpy teacher*, *the happy teacher*, *the quiet teacher*, *the tall teacher*, etc.).
- Ask the learners to look back at the recount and pick out other adjectives that Tuhil has used.
- Illustrate *comparative adjectives* by asking a small child and a tall child to stand in front of the group or class. State: [name] *is smaller than* [name]. Write the sentence on the board. Highlight how the adjective is used to compare the two children. Make further comparisons between different children, or ask the learners for their suggestions.
- Encourage the learners to work through each exercise individually or in pairs.

Activity A: The learners add an interesting adjective to complete each phrase.

Answers

A *Example answers:*
1	a **fast** race	**2**	a **brave** girl
3	my **bossy** sister	**4**	the **sleepy** cat

Activity B: The learners add a comparative adjective to each sentence.

Answers

B
1 He is **smaller** than his friends.
2 He is **taller** than Tuhil.
3 He is **faster** than the others.
4 They were **louder** than everyone else.

Let's practise

This section allows you to model the required writing outcome with input from the learners.

Before writing

- Always encourage the learners to talk about what they are going to write. Discussing things can help the learners to organise their thoughts.
- Remind the learners what a personal recount is.
- Read the information box with them.
- Discuss the different types of race the learners might have had or seen (for example, races at school, races at home with friends and family, races on the television at the Olympics or other big race meets).

Shared writing activity

- Explain to the learners that they are going to write a recount, but first it is a good idea to help them to organise their thoughts.
- They can discuss their experiences in pairs, to aid them in clarifying their ideas.
- If they are able to make the distinction, encourage them to answer the questions in note form rather than full sentences.
- Remind them of the roles of doing words (*verbs*) and describing words (*adjectives*) in their recount.
- Now ask them to write at least six sentences for their recount. Remind them about the use of sentence punctuation.

- The activity should be done individually, though some learners may need more one-to-one support.
- Ask the learners to check they have correctly used capital letters and full stops, they have used the correct tense for the verbs and they have included adjectives.
- Finally, share some of the recounts with the class. Encourage some learners to read their recounts to the rest of the group or class.
- Give the learners opportunities to discuss what they have written, either with you or with their peers.

Let's write

The learners now independently produce a recount of their own, having worked through a similar exercise in the previous section. Encourage them to share their work in progress with you so that, through discussion, they can improve their work.

Before writing

- Remind the learners of things they discussed in the Let's practise section.
- Encourage them to think about different options and choose the best ones.
- Ask them to write notes or word prompts about the exciting event to organise their thoughts. You might suggest less able learners write three prompts and more able learners write six.
- The learners can use resource sheet 2 to structure their recount, and either include a photo or draw a picture.
- Ask the learners to write their sentences carefully and neatly.
- Encourage them to write about how they felt during the event.
- Help them with spellings if necessary.
- Encourage them to look back at the recount once they have written it and check that they have included capital letters and full stops, they have used the correct tense for the verbs and they have included adjectives.

Marking criteria

Technical aspects
Look for:
• correct use of capital letters
• correct use of full stops, question marks and exclamation marks
• verbs written in the past tense
• the addition of adjectives.

Content
• Do their sentences make sense?
• Has their recount included how they felt?
• Is the content interesting/engaging for the reader?
• Is the material ordered in a logical way?

After writing

Read through the completed recounts with the learners. Encourage them to share their recounts with others.

Plenary

- Discuss other recounts they might write.
- You could create a display entitled 'Exciting times', where their recounts are displayed.

Resource sheets

The resource sheets for Unit 3 provide differentiation for the writing outcome in this unit as well as further practice on verbs and adjectives.

1   A resource sheet revising verbs and adjectives.

2   A resource sheet on writing a recount.

Resource sheet 1: Writing a recount: verbs and adjectives

Resource sheet 1 covers extension work on identifying the different types of verbs and adjectives. Learners need to identify both past and present verbs as well as adjectives and comparative adjectives.

- Revise past and present verb tenses.
- Revise the distinction between adjectives and comparative adjectives.
- Read through the resource sheet with the learners so they fully understand what is expected of them.
- The learners can work in pairs or individually on this activity.
- Check through their answers to be sure they fully understand both verb tenses and adjectives.

Resource sheet 2: Writing a recount

Resource sheet 2 provides the learner with a recount template for the Let's write activity.

- Explain the task and allow time for learners to ask questions so they fully understand what is required.

- Ask them to make the recount as interesting as possible with the addition of describing words.
- Encourage them to read their recount carefully.
- Remind them that a sentence begins with a capital letter and usually ends with a full stop.
- Help them with vocabulary they might want to use.
- Ask them to share their recount. Discuss the different improvements they could make.
- You could set this task as homework if the learner is capable of writing the recount independently.

Assessment

The assessment sheet for this unit, 'Personal writing: writing a recount', is on page 89 of Learner's Book 2. The learners write a recount of what they did yesterday. They are provided with reminders of what makes a good recount.

- Discuss with the learners what a recount is.
- Read through the assessment sheet with the learners to ensure they have understood the writing task.
- Encourage them to spend some time thinking about what they did yesterday and to pick out something that happened, rather than recounting the whole day.
- Remind them to take care while writing and to make their recount interesting, adding feelings as well as facts.
- Do not penalise learners for spelling words incorrectly.

Marking criteria

Technical aspects
Look for:
• correct use of capital letters
• correct use of full stops, question marks and exclamation marks
• verbs written in the past tense
• the addition of adjectives.
Content
• Do their sentences make sense?
• Has their recount included how they felt?
• Is the content interesting/engaging for the reader?
• Is the material ordered in a logical way?

Unit 4: Explanatory writing: writing an explanation

Learner's Book unit focus

This unit looks at **explanatory writing**. The learners are introduced to a **flow diagram**, which can aid explanation.

Progress table for Stage 2: Unit 4					
Category: Explanatory writing					
Writing outcome: Writing to explain					
Explanatory writing explains a process. Processes that happened in the past are written in past tenses. Processes that still happen today are written in present tenses.					
Stage 1	**Stage 2**	**Stage 3**	**Stage 4**	**Stage 5**	**Stage 6**
• writing captions/labels	• sequencing events • explaining how something happens • flow diagrams	• writing captions/labels • making comparisons • flow diagrams	• explaining how something happens • explaining how something was done • explaining how something works	• explaining how something happens • explaining how something works	• explaining how something happens • flow diagrams • explaining how something works
Cambridge Global English link: Stage 2: Unit 4: The big sky					
Cambridge Primary English link: Stage 2: Unit 4: What is my house made of?					

Resource list

A selection of non-fiction books.

Unit teaching plan

Warm up

- Ask the learners:
  - *What do you see when you look up into the sky in the daytime?*
  - *Do you see the same things during the night?*
  - *What do you see when you look up into the sky in the night-time?*
- Inform them that this unit, on the subject of the sky, will explain why we have night and day and the differences between them.
- Ask the learners what they know about why we have daytime and night-time. Write a few of their suggestions on the board.
- Introduce the information:
  - *We are now going to read some information about day and night.*
  - *This information is facts about day and night. What is the difference between facts and fiction?* [Fact is actual information; fiction is made up.]
- Introduce the term non-fiction.

Let's read

Information about day and night is the stimulus for this unit. The Let's read section also introduces a very simple flow diagram for the learners to interpret.

- First, read the extract to the class, then ask nominated learners to read it again to the class. Be sure the learners all understand what has been read to them.
- Highlight the pictures and diagram to the learners. Be sure they interpret them correctly. Ask:

– *What do the pictures show us?*

– *Why are there arrows between the pictures?*

– *Can you describe how one picture leads on to the next?*

• Remind the learners that sentences start with a capital letter and often end with a full stop, but they can also end with a question mark or exclamation mark. Ask the learners for an example of a statement and of a question found in the extract.

• Discuss the difference between fact and fiction.

Plenary

Put the learners into pairs. Give them non-fiction books to look through. Ask each pair to tell another pair about an explanation they have read.

Let's talk

This section asks the learners questions that:

• give them a greater understanding of the text

• focus on the specific writing activity covered in the unit.

Activity A: This section is to ensure learners have understood what they have read.

Answers

A *Example answers:*

1 The information tells us about why we have day and night.

2 The four pictures show how the Sun comes up in the morning and then goes down at night.

3 Earth is a planet.

4 The Sun is a star.

5 If it is light outside, our country is on the side of the Earth that is facing the Sun.

6 If it is dark outside, our country is on the side of the Earth that is facing away from the Sun.

Activity B: This section looks at the role of the flow diagram and the order in which information is written.

B *Example answers:*

1 The information explains how the Sun creates day and night.

2 A flow diagram is information in picture form that shows you the cycle of something. The information flows from one picture to the next.

3 The flow diagram is showing how the Sun creates daylight and that when it goes, there is darkness.

4 The order in which information is written can be very important because it helps to explain the sequence of events.

Let's learn

This section:

• reinforces previous work on *joining words (conjunctions)*

• gives learners the opportunity to practise what they have learned in a focused activity before incorporating it into their own writing.

Joining words

• Ask the learners:

– *Who remembers what a joining word does?*

– *Who can name a joining word?* [and]

• Joining words were previously covered in Learner's Book 1 Unit 4.

• Introduce the word *conjunction* as a term used for joining words.

• Discuss with the learners that other words can join sentences. Ask them if they can suggest any.

• Read the information box with the learners.

• Highlight the words that join the sentences in the examples.

• Put the learners in pairs and ask them to create further examples of sentences that use joining words. Ask them to share their examples in groups or with the class.

Activity A: The learners identify the conjunctions in the given sentences.

Answers

A 1 Kim liked looking into the sky <u>but</u> sometimes it hurt his neck.

2 The stars were very bright <u>because</u> the lights were turned off.

3 The Sun was high in the sky <u>and</u> it was very hot.

Activities B–D: The learners write their own sentences using the words *and*, *but* and *because* as conjunctions.

Answers

B–D *Learner's own three sentences using the given conjunctions (and, but and because)*

Let's practise

This section allows you to model the required writing outcome with input from the learners.

Before writing

- Ask the learners:
  - *Do you think it is important to write information in order?*
- Explain how writing things in order can help them make sense.
- Always encourage the learners to talk about what they are going to write. Discussing things can help them to organise their thoughts.

Shared writing activity

- The learners are going to write a list of given sentences in order so they flow and make sense.
- Start by reading the sentences in the order in which they are given. Highlight how the order is disjointed and that it makes little sense.
- Encourage the learners in pairs to discuss the order in which these sentences would best be written.
- This activity can be done individually if this is preferred and if the learner is able.
- Finally, share the learners' sentence order. Discuss the possible differences in sentence order that still give a valid order.
- The learners draw pictures in the form of a flow diagram, reflecting the order of the sentences.
- Discuss the role of flow diagrams, and that they show a sequence of events visually.
- Give the learners opportunities to discuss what they have written and drawn, either with you or with their peers.

Let's write

The learners now produce an explanation and flow diagram of their own independently, having worked through a similar exercise in the previous section. Encourage them to share their work in progress with you so that, through discussion, they can improve their work.

Before writing

- Remind the learners of things they discussed in the Let's practise section.
- Encourage them to list the different activities they do in the day and then choose six of them. Acknowledge that they will not be able to include everything they do in the day – they just need to choose the key things.

- Ask them to write their sentences carefully and neatly.
- Help the learners with the spellings of words if necessary.
- Encourage the learners to look back at their explanation once they have written it and then decide which pictures best illustrate the order in which they do things in the day.

Marking criteria

Technical aspects
Look for correct use of:
• sentences that start with a capital letter • sentences that end with a full stop • sentences that use a joining word.
Content
• Do their sentences make sense? • Are their sentences written in an appropriate order? • Do the pictures in their flow diagram support the explanation they have written?

After writing

- Read through the completed explanations with the learners.
- Discuss the flow diagrams. Highlight those that have clear pictures and that flow naturally in order.

Plenary

Find other flow diagrams online or in textbooks. Show the learners how they can aid explanations. Learners may find a flow diagram showing the life cycle of a frog interesting.

Resource sheets

The resource sheets for Unit 4 provide differentiation for the writing outcome in this unit as well as further practice on using joining words.

1 A resource sheet on joining words.
2 A resource sheet on writing an explanation of a flow diagram.

Resource sheet 1: Writing an explanation: joining words

Resource sheet 1 covers further practice on recognising joining words. The learners add joining words to sentences. They then complete sentences using the sentence openers and joining words.

- Read through the resource sheet with the learners so they fully understand what is expected of them.
- Carefully read the information box with the learners.
- This resource sheet introduces an additional joining word (*so*). Say: *This resource sheet adds one more joining word. Who can tell me which joining word it is?*
- Discuss with the learners that there are a number of words that can be used as joining words.
- The learners add the missing joining words to the sentences.
- They then complete sentences that use joining words. They are also asked to identify the joining words.
- Encourage the learners to read the sentences they have written carefully.
- They can work in pairs or individually on this activity.
- Check through the learners' answers to be sure they fully understand the role of joining words in sentence construction.
- Learners who are able to work independently can complete this resource sheet for homework.

Resource sheet 2: Writing an explanation

Resource sheet 2 provides the learners with the flow diagram from Learner's Book 2 and asks them to write an explanation for it. Some learners may need support when completing the explanation; others will be able to work independently. The level of written explanation will depend on the ability of the learner.

- Use this resource sheet in conjunction with the information provided at the beginning of the unit in Learner's Book 2.
- Remind the learners what they learned. Some may be able to bring this information into their explanation; others will write a simplified explanation of what the pictures in the flow diagram are showing.
- Help them with the vocabulary they might want to use.
- Encourage them to work carefully and neatly.
- Remind them to use joining words in their explanations.
- Ask them to share their completed explanations.

Assessment

The assessment sheet for this unit, 'Explanatory writing: writing an explanation', is on page 90 of Learner's Book 2. The learners are provided with a flow diagram and asked to write a simple explanation describing what it shows.

- Read through the assessment sheet with the learners to ensure they have understood the writing task.
- Encourage them to spend some time looking carefully at the flow diagram before writing their explanation.
- Remind them that they should use joining words to extend their sentences.
- Do not penalise learners for spelling words incorrectly.

Marking criteria

Technical aspects
Look for correct use of:
• sentences that start with a capital letter
• sentences that end with a full stop
• sentences that use a joining word.
Content
• Do their sentences make sense?
• Are their sentences written in an appropriate order?
• Do the pictures in the flow diagram support the explanation they have written?

Unit 5: Instructions: writing a simple recipe

Learner's Book unit focus

This unit continues work on **writing simple instructions**. It introduces **adverbs** and also recaps previous work on **verbs**.

Progress table for Stage 2: Unit 5

Category: Instructions/advice/guidance

Writing outcome: Writing instructions

A recipe is a set of instructions for how to combine food to make a food item. It is a good example of instructions for learners of this age, introducing them to sequence, clear sentences, imperative verbs, precise language and layout.

Stage 1	Stage 2	Stage 3	Stage 4	Stage 5	Stage 6
• writing simple instructions • writing rules	• writing simple instructions	• writing simple instructions for making something	• writing simple instructions for making something • writing simple instructions for mending something • directions	• writing instructions for using something	

Cambridge Global English link: Stage 2: Unit 5: Let's count and measure

Cambridge Primary English link: Stage 2: Unit 2: How to write instructions

---

Resource list

A variety of example recipes.

Unit teaching plan

Warm up

- Ask the learners:
  - *Has anyone used a recipe to cook something?*
  - *What did you make?*
  - *Did you need to count or measure out the ingredients?*
- Highlight recipes the learners may have used in school in the past to make things.
- Show the learners examples of recipes. Look at the instructions.
- Ask the learners:
  - *Why do we need the instructions?*
  - *Why do you think the instructions need to be written in order?*

Let's read

This unit lists the recipe for mini rocky road cakes. This is a simple recipe that the learners could make, either at home or in the classroom. Following the recipe will demonstrate the importance of the order in which the instructions are written.

- First, read and discuss the recipe with the class. Be sure the learners all understand the information it conveys.
- Highlight that this is a real recipe that the children could make later.
- Ask the learners questions about the recipe:
  - *Would you like to try making these cakes?*
  - *What are your favourite ingredients?*
  - *How long does it take in total to make the cakes?*

Teacher's Resource Unit guide: Stage 2: Unit 5

- Look at the structure of the recipe with the learners. It starts with general information, gives a list of ingredients and then provides the instructions for how to make the cakes.
- Discuss whether the layout of the recipe is helpful. Ask:
  - *Do you find the information at the beginning of the recipe helpful? Why?*
  - *Is it useful to have a list of all the ingredients? Why?*
  - *Is it useful to have the instructions numbered? Why?*
- Discuss the instructions with the learners. Ask:
  - *How easy are the instructions to follow?*
  - *What makes the instructions easy to follow?*
  - *Would it matter if you changed the order of the instructions?*

Plenary

Put the learners into pairs. Ask the pairs to discuss how they might change the mini rocky road cake recipe. Are there ingredients they would add or take out to make them even tastier? Ask the pairs to share their ideas with the rest of the class.

Let's talk

This section asks the learners questions that:

- give them a greater understanding of the text
- focus on the specific writing activity covered in the unit.

Activity A: This section ensures the learners have interpreted the recipe correctly.

Answers

A *Example answers:*
1 The recipe is for mini rocky road cakes.
2 The recipe makes ten cakes.
3 Five ingredients are needed for the cakes.
4 You need 35g of butter.
5 The first instruction tells you to 'Carefully put the chocolate and butter in a bowl'.
6 The mixture needs to go in the fridge for 20 minutes or until set.

Activity B: This section focuses the learners on the instructions. It asks them to look carefully at how the instructions are written and why.

Answers

B *Example answers:*
1 We need instructions to tell us how to make the cakes.
2 There are six separate instructions.
3 It helps to have the instructions numbered so we can follow them in the correct order.
4 The order is important. When you make cakes the ingredients need to be mixed in the right order, otherwise the cakes won't work.
5 Instructions need to be short and clear. They only need to tell us the information we need to know.

Let's learn

This section:

- recaps work previously covered on *verbs (doing words)*
- introduces the role of adverbs
- gives learners the opportunity to practise what they have learned in a focused activity, before incorporating it into their own writing.

Verbs

This section revises verbs and looks specifically at the tense of the verbs. In previous units, we have looked at writing verbs in the past tense, adding -d or -ed to the verb family word. In this unit, instructions are written in the present tense, telling us that something is being done 'now'.

- Write a number of *doing words* on the board (for example, *walked*, *mixed*, *tasted*).
- Ask the learners to tell you the tense of these verbs.
- Read the information box with the learners.
- Explain to the learners that, if something has already happened, it has been done in the past. If something is happening now it is happening in the present.
- Encourage the learners to work through each exercise individually or in pairs.

Activity A: The learners identify present tense verbs.

Answers

A mix, beat, stir, make, play, put, remove, heat

Activity B: The learners add present tense verbs of their choice to given instructions.

Answers

B *Example answers:*
1 **Walk** to the shop.
2 **Count** the number of sweets.
3 **Weigh** how heavy the flour is.
4 **Pour** the water into the jug.

Adverbs

This section introduces *adverbs*. Adverbs tell us more about how something is done; they add to the verbs in sentences. Adverbs give detail of how, where or when an action is done. When adverbs are used in instructions they make them clearer.

This unit covers adverbs of manner using the *-ly* suffix, as this is the easiest concept for learners to pick up.

- Read the information box with the learners.
- Be sure the learners understand what an adverb is.
- Ask them for examples of adverbs.
- Encourage them to work through each exercise individually or in pairs.

Activity A: The learners complete word sums by adding the suffix *-ly*.

Answers

A 1 neatly   2 quickly   3 loudly
   4 sadly   5 slowly   6 carefully

Activity B: The learners add an adverb from A to each sentence.

Answers

B *Example answers:*
1 **Carefully** mix the food together.
2 Do not talk **loudly**.
3 **Neatly** write your instructions.
4 **Quickly** walk to your next lesson.

Activity C: The learners add an adverb in front of given verbs.

Answers

C *Learners add their own adverbs to two given verbs.*

Let's practise

This section allows you to model the required writing outcome with input from the learners.

Before writing

- Always encourage the learners to talk about what they are going to write.
- Discuss things that can help the learners organise their thoughts. Highlight what the pictures show.
- Look carefully at the pictures. The learners are going to write instructions on how to clean up after making the cakes. The pictures will guide what the learners write in their instructions.
- Give the learners examples of long-winded instructions and compare them with short and simple ones. Ask the learners which instructions are easier to follow.
- Remind the learners that their instructions need to be numbered and as simple and straightforward as possible.

Shared writing activity

- Organise the learners into small groups or pairs. They are going to discuss the instructions they are going to write.
- Remind them that all sentences need a capital letter and full stop. They need to write verbs in the present tense.
- Ask the learners to include adverbs in their instructions.
- Give them opportunities to discuss what they have written, either with you or with their peers.
- They can do the activity individually, in pairs or in groups.
- Share some of the learners' instructions with the class. Encourage some of them to read their instructions to the rest of the group or class.
  - *Can you make any improvements?*
- More able learners could discuss further instructions they might add.

Let's write

The learners independently produce instructions to make their favourite drink. Encourage them to share their work in progress with you so that, through discussion, they can improve their work.

Before writing

- Discuss the many different types of drink the learners could write instructions for. More able learners could create their own drinks, while less able learners could write instructions for basic drinks, even for making a glass of milk or water.
- Remind the learners of the details about writing instructions that they discussed in the Let's practise section.
- Encourage them to keep their instructions and rules simple.
- Remind them to use capital letters and full stops, and recognise when they are using present tense verbs. Where they can, they should try to add adverbs.
- Discuss the Writer's Toolbox. This provides an easy checklist to follow while they write.
- Ask them to write their instructions and rules carefully and neatly.
- Help them with spellings if necessary.

Marking criteria

Technical aspects
Look for correct use of:
• clear, simple instructions and rules that are numbered
• sentences that start with a capital letter and end with a full stop
• verbs written in their present tense
• adverbs added to some verbs.
Content
Look for correct use of:
• relevant instructions that progress in small steps.

After writing

- Read through the learners' completed instructions with them. Encourage them to share their instructions with others.
- Pick a number of drink instructions the learners have written. Make the drinks in front of the class or group, following the instructions carefully. Discuss what makes good instructions and also where improvements can be made.

Plenary

- Discuss with the learners other times instructions are important (for example, for playing a game, working equipment, getting from one place to another, etc.).
- Ask the learners to bring in other examples of instructions and display them.

Resource sheets

The resource sheets for Unit 5 provide differentiation for the writing outcome in this unit as well as further practice on capital letters, full stops and verbs.

1 A resource sheet on verbs and adverbs.

2 A resource sheet on ordering instructions.

Resource sheet 1: Writing a simple recipe: verbs and adverbs

Resource sheet 1 covers further practice of recognising verbs and adverbs and adding adverbs to sentences. Learners are given sentences and asked to identify the verbs and adverbs. They are then asked to include the given verbs and adverbs in their own sentences, finally writing a sentence of their own using a verb and adverb of their choice.

- Read through the resource sheet with the learners so they fully understand what is expected of them.
- Revise what a verb and adverb are.
- When completed, read through the sentences in Activity B with the learners to ensure they are correct. Some learners may need more support than others with this activity.
- To extend the activity, ask the learners to write further sentences that might include two verbs and two adverbs. They can then share their sentences with their peers, asking them to highlight the verbs and adverbs in each other's work.

Resource sheet 2: Writing a simple recipe: ordering instructions

Resource sheet 2 covers ordering instructions. Learners are given instructions on how to make a fruit drink, but they are in the wrong order. This resource sheet highlights the importance of ordering instructions. You can set it as a homework exercise, or use it to support those learners who are struggling with writing instructions in order.

- Explain the task and allow time for learners to ask questions so they fully understand what is required.
- Discuss the importance of reading the instructions carefully. There are hidden clues to help them order the instructions (for example, the words 'First' and 'Finally').
- Highlight that there are a couple of instructions where they can choose the order in which they would prefer to make the drink.

- Once they have written the instructions, ask them to share them with a peer. Are the instructions in a sensible order?

Assessment

The assessment sheet for this unit, 'Instructions: writing a simple recipe', is on page 91 of Learner's Book 2. The learners are provided with a series of pictures showing a bowl of fruit being assembled and asked to write instructions for them.

- Read through the assessment sheet with the learners to ensure they have understood the writing task.

- Encourage learners to spend some time looking carefully at the pictures before writing their instructions.

- Remind the learners to number and write simple, clear instructions.

- Do not penalise learners for spelling words incorrectly.

Marking criteria

Technical aspects
Look for correct use of:
• clear, simple instructions and rules that are numbered
• sentences that start with a capital letter and end with a full stop
• verbs written in their present tense
• adverbs added to some verbs.
Content
Look for correct use of:
• relevant instructions that progress in small steps.

Unit 6: Writing poems: rhyming poems and list poems

Learner's Book unit focus

This unit looks at both **rhyming** and **list poems** on the subject of bugs.

Progress table for Stage 2: Unit 6					
Category: Narrative writing					
Writing outcome: Rhyming poems and list poems					
Poems lend themselves to imaginative and expressive writing. Learners can enjoy exploring different vocabulary that creates both rhyming and list poems.					
Stage 1	**Stage 2**	**Stage 3**	**Stage 4**	**Stage 5**	**Stage 6**
• identifying rhyming words • using rhyming words	• rhyming poems • list poems	• humorous poems • rhyming poems	• acrostics • haikus	• narrative poetry	
Cambridge Global English link: **Cambridge Primary English links:**	Stage 2: Unit 6: Bugs: fact and fiction Stage 2: Unit 3: Rhymes about places and people we know Stage 2: Unit 6: Poems by famous poets Stage 2: Unit 9: All kinds of creatures				

Resource list

A selection of rhyming poems and list poems (if available).

Unit teaching plan

Warm up

- Discuss *bugs* with the learners:
  - *Name some bugs.*
  - *What are bugs?*
  - *Where do you find bugs?*
  - *Describe what some bugs look like.*
- Inform them that this unit, on the theme of bugs, will look at poems written about bugs.
- Introduce this unit on poems. Ask:
  - *Can you name some poems?*
  - *Do you enjoy listening to poems?*
- Share some familiar action poems with the learners.

- Ask the learners if they remember previous work in Stage 1: Unit 3 on rhyming words. Ask them:
  - *What is a rhyming word?*
  - *Do rhyming words have to have the same letter patterns to rhyme?*
- Ask the learners for suggestions of rhyming words.
- Ask them what a list is. Refer them to previous work covered on lists in Stage 1: Unit 1.
- Introduce the poems:
  - *We are now going to read two poems about bugs.*

Let's read

Two poems are the stimuli for this unit. The first is a rhyming poem with a humorous twist in the final line. The second, a list poem, uses the past progressive verb tense.

- Read the first poem to the class and then ask nominated learners to read it again to the class or each other. Repeat with the second poem, using different learners to read it. Be sure the learners all understand what has been read to them. Discuss any words they might not understand.
- Discuss the structure of each poem. In the first poem:
  - *Which line is repeated?*
  - *Which words rhyme?*
  - *Does the last line make you smile?*

  In the second poem:
  - *What is this poem about?*
  - *Are there any rhyming words?*
- Ask:
  - *Which poem do you think is a rhyming poem?*
  - *Which poem do you think is a list poem?*
  - *Why?*
- Discuss the learners' responses to the questions above.
- Discuss the difference between rhyming and list poems. Note that some list poems can rhyme.

Plenary

- Share further rhyming and list poems with the learners, from books or sourced on the internet.
- Put the learners into pairs. Ask each pair to read one of the poems and add actions to each verse, then ask them to perform the action poem in front of their peers.

Let's talk

This section asks the learners questions that:

- give them a greater understanding of the text
- focus on the specific writing activity covered in the unit.

Activity A: This section is to ensure learners have understood what they have read and that they have looked closely at the structure of the first poem.

Answers

A *Example answers:*
   1   You can find bugs everywhere!
   2   The bugs like to eat apples and pears.
   3   A bug buzzes in someone's hair!
   4   The line *Bugs, bugs, everywhere!* is repeated three times.
   5   The words *chair, everywhere, pear, care* and *hair* rhyme with *air*.
   6   The rhyming word is at the end of each line.

Activity B: This section is to ensure learners have understood what they have read and that they have looked closely at the structure of the second poem.

Answers

B *Example answers:*
   1   The ants were running.
   2   The crickets were jumping.
   3   The poem is called *Bugs were busy!* because it lists all the busy actions the bugs were doing before they fell asleep.
   4   The bugs stopped being busy when they fell asleep.
   5   *Learners comment on whether they think this is a list or rhyming poem.* It is a list poem because it lists the actions the bugs do.

Activity C: This section asks the learners for an opinion.

Answers

C *Learner's response on which poem they like better and why*

Let's learn

This section:

- practises work on *rhyming words*
- introduces work on *contractions*
- introduces work on the *past progressive verb tense*
- gives learners the opportunity to practise what they have learned in a focused activity, before incorporating it into their own writing.

Rhyming words

- Ask the learners: *What words rhyme with eight?* Write their answers on the board.
- Discuss with the learners how some rhyming words have the same letter pattern but some do not.
- Read the information box with the learners.
- Highlight the examples from the poems.
- Encourage the learners to work through each exercise individually or in pairs.

Activity A: The learners write rhyming words with the same letter patterns as the examples provided.

> **Answers**
>
> **A** *Example answers:*
> | | | | | |
> |---|---|---|---|---|
> | **1** | hair – pair | | **2** | boil – soil |
> | **3** | lunch – munch | | **4** | gate – late |

Activity B: The learners write rhyming words with different letter patterns from the examples provided.

> **Answers**
>
> **B** *Example answers:*
> | | | | | |
> |---|---|---|---|---|
> | **1** | date – eight | | **2** | where – share |
> | **3** | bear – care | | **5** | kite – sight |
> | **5** | light – bite | | **6** | your – shore |

Activity C: Finally, the learners write as many rhyming words as they can for the two words provided.

> **Answers**
>
> **C** *Learner's own rhyming words for* some *and* late

Contractions

- Read the information box with the learners.
- Write further examples of two word phrases and their contractions on the board. Ask the learners to tell you the missing letters of the contraction.
- Encourage the learners to give you further examples of contractions.
- Check they can clearly write an apostrophe.
- Encourage them to work through each exercise individually or in pairs.

Activity A: The learners join the given words with their contraction by drawing a line.

> **Answers**
>
> **A** | | | | |
> |---|---|---|---|
> | **1** | I am – I'm | **2** | she is – she's |
> | **3** | we are – we're | **4** | it is – it's |
> | **5** | do not – don't | **6** | they will – they'll |

Activity B: Learners complete the word sums that make contractions.

> **Answers**
>
> **B** | | | | | | |
> |---|---|---|---|---|---|
> | **1** | they're | **2** | he's | **3** | I'm |
> | **4** | we're | **5** | it's | **6** | we'll |
> | **7** | isn't | **8** | she'll | | |

Verbs

- Revise previous work on *verbs* (*doing words*).
- Beware: young learners can find it difficult to understand verbs due to their many forms and tenses.
- Discuss the past tense previously covered; the regular past simple tense is formed by adding *-d/-ed* to the verb family name, but there are also irregular verbs (for example, *went*).
- Read the information box with the learners. Introduce the term *past progressive tense*.
- Ask the learners for examples of past progressive verbs (for example, *They were running*).
- Encourage the learners to work through each exercise individually or in pairs.

Activity A: Learners underline the past tense verbs in the poem *Bugs were busy!*

> **Answers**
>
> **A** Ants <u>were running</u>,
> Bees <u>were buzzing</u>,
> Butterflies <u>were flapping</u>,
> Wasps <u>were zooming</u>,
> Crickets <u>were jumping</u>,
> Spiders <u>were spinning</u>,
> Flies <u>were flying</u>,
> Bugs <u>were</u> busy … and then they <u>went</u> to sleep!

Activity B: Learners identify and underline the past tense verbs in each sentence.

> **Answers**
>
> **B** 1 Meena and Jared <u>were running</u> to the shops.
> 2 The Sun <u>was shining</u>.
> 3 I <u>was eating</u> my lunch.
> 4 The sheep <u>were bleating</u> in the field.

Let's practise

This section allows you to model the required writing outcome with input from the learners.

Before writing

- Always encourage the learners to talk about what they are going to write. Discussing things can help the learners to organise their thoughts.
- Read through the list poem on page 51 of Learner's Book 2. Remind the learners what a list poem is (a poem that lists something). Ask the learners for examples of different things they might list about bugs (for example, movement, looks, colours, etc.).

Shared writing activity

- The learners are going to write a list poem, but first it is a good idea to help them to organise their thoughts.
- Encourage them to list the different verbs that could describe the imaginary bug.
- They should discuss in pairs the possible words they might use, to aid them in clarifying their ideas.
- The learners can do the activity individually or, if individuals need extra support, in pairs.
- Give the learners opportunities to discuss what they have written, either with you or with their peers.
- Finally, share the learners' poems. Encourage them to read their poems to the rest of the group or class.
- Ask them to add actions to their poems and perform them in front of a friend or group.

Let's write

The learners independently produce a rhyming poem of their own. Encourage them to share their work in progress with you so that, through discussion, they can improve their work.

Before writing

- Encourage the learners to think about different options and choose the best ones. The rhyming words need to work together for the poem to make sense.
- Encourage them to think about different adjectives they might use and to choose the best ones.
- Look at the structure shown in the first verse, where the adjective is used (the first line) and which two words rhyme (the last word in each line). Ask the learners to keep the same structure.

- Help the learners with spellings if necessary.
- Ask them to write their poems carefully and neatly.
- Encourage them to look back at the poem once they have written it.
  - *Could you make improvements to the rhyming words you have used?*
  - *Do the adjectives describe the imaginary bug clearly?*

Marking criteria

Technical aspects
Look for correct use of:
• verses that start with a capital letter
• verses that end with a full stop, question mark or exclamation mark
• rhyming words.
Content
• Do the learner's verses make sense?
• Have they added adjectives to improve the poem?
• Have they considered the overall poem when writing the verses?

After writing

Read through the completed poems with the learners. Encourage them to share their poems with others.

Plenary

- Discuss the different poems the learners have written.
- Encourage them to add actions to their poems and then perform them in front of a group or the class.
- Ask more able learners to write another poem using the same structure but this time writing about a real bug of their choice.

Resource sheets

The resource sheets for Unit 6 provide differentiation for the writing outcome in this unit as well as further practice on writing poems.

1 A resource sheet on rhyming words.
2 A resource sheet on writing a poem.

Resource sheet 1: Rhyming poems and list poems: rhyming words

Resource sheet 1 covers further practice on rhyming words. The learners are asked to write words that rhyme with bug names. They then have to write the pairs of rhyming words in sentences. Each sentence needs to make sense. An example is given.

- Read through the resource sheet with the learners so they fully understand what is expected of them.
- Carefully read the information box with the learners.
- Encourage the learners to write their rhyming words carefully and neatly. Ask them to identify those rhyming words with spelling patterns and those rhyming words without.
- Encourage them to read the sentences they have written carefully.
- They can work in pairs or individually on this activity.
- Check through the learners' answers to be sure they fully understand the writing of rhyming words.

Resource sheet 2: Rhyming poems and list poems: writing a poem

Resource sheet 2 provides the learners with the scaffolding on which to write a list poem. Some learners may need support when completing the different stages; others will be able to work independently on this task for homework.

- This resource sheet could be used to support those learners who find the Let's write section challenging.
- Explain the structure of a list poem.
- Ensure the learners are clear on how to build their list poem about the cricket.
- Help them with vocabulary they might want to use.
- Encourage them to work carefully and neatly.
- Ask them to share their completed poems with their peers.

Assessment

The assessment sheet for this unit, 'Writing poems: rhyming poems and list poems', is on page 92 of Learner's Book 2. The learners are provided with the structure of a poem that requires them to add animal words and verbs in the correct gaps. Animal pictures are provided as prompts.

- Read through the assessment sheet with the learners to ensure they have understood the writing task.
- If you feel it would be useful, reread the list poem on page 51 of Learner's Book 2 as a prompt.
- Encourage learners to spend some time thinking carefully about the animals they are going to choose and their related verbs.
- Do not penalise learners for spelling words incorrectly.

Marking criteria

Technical aspects
Look for correct use of:
• each line starting with a capital letter.
Content
• Do their poem lines make sense?
• Have they added appropriate verbs for each animal?
• Has they considered the overall poem when writing?

Unit 7: Factual writing: writing notes and tables

Learner's Book unit focus

This unit introduces the writing of **notes** as well as highlighting the **use of tables in non-fiction writing**. It also introduces the **use of commas in lists** as well as recapping previous work on **nouns**.

Progress table for Stage 2: Unit 7					
Category: Factual writing					
Writing outcome: Writing notes and tables					
Note-taking and organising information into tables are important skills in factual writing. In this unit, the learners are introduced to these skills.					
Stage 1	**Stage 2**	**Stage 3**	**Stage 4**	**Stage 5**	**Stage 6**
• writing simple non-fiction texts • writing facts	• writing simple non-fiction texts • writing notes • organisational devices (tables)	• writing notes • organisational devices	• organisational devices		
Cambridge Global English link: Stage 2: Unit 7: Our green Earth **Cambridge Primary English link:** Stage 2: Unit 8: Things under the sea					

Resource list

Examples of non-fiction books.

Unit teaching plan

Warm up

- Ask the learners to explain the difference between fiction and non-fiction texts. Ask:
  - *Who can find me a non-fiction book in the classroom?*
  - *Who can explain the difference between fiction and non-fiction books?*
- Explain that non-fiction books provide us with information – when we read non-fiction it often helps us to understand what the key information is.
- Show the learners examples of non-fiction texts.
- Find an example of a table in a non-fiction text. Explain how tables often simplify information.

Let's read

This unit starts with some general information about trees. It then introduces the cacao tree, the tree that provides us with the cocoa bean, which in turn is the key ingredient when making chocolate.

This non-fiction piece then goes on to describe how cocoa beans are grown.

The first paragraph has its key words highlighted. On the opposite page, these key words are written as notes and also as a table.

- Read and discuss the information on the first page of the unit with the class. Be sure the learners all understand the information it conveys.
- Ask the learners questions about the information.
  - *What do trees provide us with?*
  - *Why do you think some words are highlighted in orange?*
  - *Why are these words important?*
- Remind the learners how the key words highlight the important information in a text.
- Look at the table. Ask the learners:
  - *What does the information in this table tell us?*
  - *Is the information in this table easy to read?*
- Discuss how to pick out the key words.

- Put the learners in pairs to look at the second and third paragraphs. Ask them:
  - *Which words are the key words in the paragraph 'The cacao tree'?*
  - *Which words are the key words in the paragraph 'Where does the chocolate come from?*
- Discuss in groups the key words the pairs have identified. Ask:
  - *Has everyone picked out the same key words?*
  - *Is 'chocolate' a key word? Why?*
- Discuss why the pictures are important.
  - *Do the pictures help you to understand the information?*
  - *Do the pictures make the page more interesting to look at?*

Plenary

Ask those learners who are able to write notes highlighting the key words in the 'The cacao tree' paragraph.

Let's talk

This section asks the learners questions that:

- give them a greater understanding of the text
- focus on the specific writing activity covered in the unit.

Activity A: This section ensures the learners have interpreted the information correctly.

Answers

A *Example answers:*
  1 Trees can give us wood, food, shelter and places for animals.
  2 Trees provide some animals with food and shelter.
  3 The cacao tree gives us cocoa beans, which are used to make chocolate.
  4 It takes six months for the cacao tree pod to ripen.
  5 The cocoa beans inside the pods are white.
  6 The beans make cocoa mass, which is the main ingredient in chocolate.

Activity B: This section focuses the learners on how the information is laid out. It asks the learners for their opinion.

Answers

B *Example answers:*
  1 The notes tell us the key information in the first paragraph.

  2 We can eat fruit, seeds and leaves.
  3 The important information in the cacao tree paragraph is: they grow in hot countries, for example, West Africa; seeds = cocoa beans; they are used to make chocolate.
  4 *Learner's own suggestions for why they think writing notes might be helpful, for example, picks out important information, saves writing unnecessary information, doesn't have to be written in sentences, etc.*

Let's learn

This section:

- recaps work previously covered on *nouns*
- introduces work on *commas*
- gives learners the opportunity to practise what they have learned in a focused activity before incorporating it into their own writing.

Nouns

- The information box reminds the learners of the work they have previously covered on nouns.
- This section introduces the term *proper nouns*, previously referred to as special naming words.
- Read the information box with the learners.
- Ask the learners to give you examples of nouns and proper nouns.
- Encourage them to work through each activity individually or in pairs.

Activity A: The learners underline proper nouns in given sentences.

Answers

A 1 On <u>Wednesday</u> <u>Amil</u> flew to <u>Sri Lanka</u>.
   2 <u>Aarya</u> has her birthday in <u>September</u>.
   3 The cacao tree grows in <u>Africa</u>.

Activity B: The learners write three of their own sentences, each with a proper noun.

Answers

B *Three of the learner's own sentences, each with a proper noun.*

Commas

- The learners are introduced to commas.
- Read the information box with the learners.
- Give the learners further examples of lists using commas.

- Ask the learners to give you examples of lists, then write these lists as part of a sentence to illustrate the use of commas.
- Encourage the learners to work through each exercise individually or in pairs.

Activity A: The learners circle the commas in the given sentences.

Answers

A 1 In England some trees don't have leaves in November, December, January and February.

2 The leaves on the tree were brown, orange, red and yellow.

Activity B: The learners add the missing commas to the given sentences.

Answers

B 1 Iraz has seen monkeys, birds, spiders and lizards in the trees.

2 Edi uses a pencil, paint and a notebook to draw a picture of a tree.

3 Nanda cooks curry, rice, bread and bananas for his family.

4 Tai visits his aunt, uncle, grandma and cousins in their home.

Activity C: Finally, the learners write a sentence that includes a list with two commas.

Answers

Learner's own sentence, which includes two commas added to a list.

Let's practise

This section allows you to model the required writing outcome with input from the learners.

Before writing

- Always encourage the learners to talk about what they are going to write. Discuss things that can help the learners to organise their thoughts.
- Read through the information with the learners. It continues the journey of the cocoa beans. Be sure they understand the information.
- Remind the learners that they need to identify the 'key words'; those words that provide important information.
- Read through the information box with the learners.
- Discuss the table with the learners. Support them with filling in the information correctly.

Shared writing activity

- Organise the learners into pairs or small groups. They are going to discuss the key words in the information provided.
- Remind them that notes should not be written in sentences.
- Give them opportunities to discuss what they have written, either with you or with their peers.
- They can do the activity individually, in pairs or in groups.
- Finally, share some of the learners' notes and tables with the class. Encourage some learners to read their notes to the rest of the group or class. Have they all found the same key words and placed the actions in the table in the same order?
- You could give more able learners information on a current school topic and ask them to pick out the key words in the information.

Let's write

The learners write notes independently on some given information. Encourage them to share their work in progress with you so that, through discussion, they can improve their work.

Before writing

- Remind the learners of the details they discussed in the Let's practise section about writing notes.
- Encourage them to keep their notes simple, purely highlighting the key information.
- Ask them to write their notes carefully and neatly.
- They shouldn't need help with spellings as the key words are there to be copied from the information provided.
- Resource sheet 2 provides a follow-on activity, where learners are required to put the same information into a table, either in class or as homework.

Marking criteria

Technical aspects
Look for correct use of:
• clear, simple notes.
Content
Look for correct use of:
• key words identified
• relevant notes.

After writing

Read through the completed notes with the learners. Encourage them to share their notes with others.

Plenary

- Discuss with the learners other situations when notes can be useful.
- Ask them to make notes on some information of their choice for homework. Share the notes with others. Do they think the key words have been noted?
- Give the learners a sheet of paper with some information (for example, a description of the school copied from the internet) and invite them individually to underline the words they would use to make notes. Discuss which words everyone has underlined and others that some have perhaps underlined unnecessarily.

Resource sheets

The resource sheets for Unit 7 provide differentiation for the writing outcome in this unit as well as further practice on commas.

1 A resource sheet on commas.
2 A resource sheet on completing a table.

Resource sheet 1: Writing notes and tables: commas

This resource sheet covers further practice using commas in writing. Learners are given sentences that have missing commas. They rewrite the sentences correctly, adding the missing commas, then write a list of five of their favourite things and incorporate their list into their own sentence using commas.

- Read through the resource sheet with the learners so they fully understand what is expected of them.
- Revise the information on commas. Highlight that the final word in a list can be preceded by *or* instead of *and*.
- When completed, read through the sentences in Activity A with the learners to ensure they are correct. Some learners may need more support than others with this activity.
- To extend the activity, ask the learners to write further sentences with commas using both *and* and *or* preceding the final word in the list. They can share their sentences with their peers.

Resource sheet 2: Writing notes and tables: completing a table

This resource sheet covers completing a table using given information. It can be used independently or it can follow on from the work in the Let's write

section of Learner's Book 2. Learners are required to highlight key words in the given information. They are then asked to transfer this information into the table.

- Explain the task and allow time for learners to ask questions so they fully understand what is required.
- Revise what key words are.
- Discuss the importance of choosing the key actions when completing the table.
- Highlight that they can find all required vocabulary within the information.
- Once they have completed the table, ask them to share it with a peer. Do their tables show the same information?

Assessment

The assessment sheet for this unit, 'Factual writing: writing notes and tables', is on page 93 of Learner's Book 2. The learners are asked to write notes about the information given on 'Making chocolate'.

- Read through the assessment sheet with the learners to ensure they have understood the writing task.
- Remind the learners that notes need to highlight the important information in the extract.
- Remind them that notes need to be just words and phrases, not whole sentences.
- Do not penalise learners for spelling words incorrectly.

Marking criteria

Technical aspects
Look for correct use of:
• clear, simple notes.
Content
Look for correct use of:
• key words identified
• relevant notes.

Unit 8: Writing to communicate: interviews

Learner's Book unit focus

This unit introduces **writing questions and answers** in the form of an **interview**. It also highlights **verb tenses**.

Progress table for Stage 2: Unit 8					
Category: Writing to communicate					
Writing outcome: Interviews					
Interviews are a way of collecting information about someone or a certain topic. Questions are often prepared and then asked of someone else. Learners often enjoy collecting information in this way.					
Stage 1	**Stage 2**	**Stage 3**	**Stage 4**	**Stage 5**	**Stage 6**
	• interviews	• interviews			
Cambridge Global English link: Stage 2: Unit 8: Home, sweet home					
Cambridge Primary English link: Stage 2: Unit 5: What is my house made of?					

Unit teaching plan

Warm up

- Ask the learners if they know what an interview is. Ask:
  - *Have you ever seen an interview on television?*
  - *What happens in an interview?*
- Ask the learners to tell you about people they might like to interview:
  - *Who would you like to interview?*
  - *Is there someone famous you'd like to interview?*
  - *Why would you choose this person?*
- Discuss what happens in an interview.
- Discuss the role of the interviewer.
- Remind the learners that in this unit they will write questions. Questions need to start with a capital letter and end with a question mark.

Let's read

The learners meet Latif and his grandfather. Latif has to interview his grandfather for a school project about the homes people used to live in.

- Read the interview/conversation to the class and then ask nominated learners to do the same. Be sure the learners all understand the conversation.
- Highlight to the learners the questions Latif asks his grandfather.
- Discuss the responses Latif's grandfather gives. Ask the learners:
  - *Are the grandfather's answers interesting?*
  - *Would the answers be interesting if they were 'yes' or 'no' answers?*

- Highlight to the learners that the doing words (verbs) are written in the past tense. Ask the learners to look at the words *lived* and *shouted*:
  - *What do you notice about the ending of the words?*
- Remind the learners that by adding *-d* or *-ed* it changes the meaning of the verb to something that has happened in the past.
- Remind the learners that sentences start with a capital letter and end with a full stop, but questions (asking sentences) end with a question mark. Illustrate this with examples from the interview.

Plenary

- Use the interview as a starting point to role play a continued conversation between Latif and his grandfather.
- Discuss the similarities and differences between homes the learners live in now and those of their grandparents.

Let's talk

This section asks the learners questions that:

- give them a greater understanding of the text
- focus on the specific writing activity covered in the unit.

Introduce the term *interview*: *An interview is when someone puts questions to another person to find out more about him or her or something they know about.*

Activity A: This section is to ensure learners have understood what they have read.

Answers

A *Example answers:*

1 Latif's grandad was six in 1962.

2 Grandad didn't like his home in the town because he had to share a room with his brothers.

3 Grandad's mum wanted to move out of the town so her children had more space to play outside.

4 Grandad loved playing outside, looking after the chickens and having his own room.

5 Grandad didn't like the long walk to and from school each day.

6 Grandad was nine when he got a bike and he was pleased with it because it made the journey to school much quicker.

Activity B: This section focuses the learners on the interview itself.

Answers

B *Example answers:*

1 Latif asked Grandad five questions.

2 Latif's questions did help him get to know Grandad more because he was talking about things from his childhood that he wouldn't normally chat about.

3 Grandad's answers were helpful because they were long and detailed rather than just 'yes' or 'no' answers.

4 *The learner's suggestions of other questions Latif might have asked his Grandad.*

Let's learn

This section:

- reinforces work on *verb tenses*
- reinforces work on writing *asking sentences* and using the question mark
- gives learners the opportunity to practise what they have learned in a focused activity before incorporating it into their own writing.

Verbs – present and past tense

- Write the word *verb* on the board. Ask the learners to tell you what a verb is. Remind the learners that a verb is a *doing word*.

- Ask the learners:
  - *Using the verb family 'look', finish this sentence in the past tense.*
    I … at the sweets. [looked]
    Now finish this sentence in the present tense.
    I … … … at the sweets. [am looking]

- Give the learners further sentences to fill in, until they recognise the difference between past and present tenses.

- Read and discuss the information box with the learners.

- Encourage them to work through each exercise individually or in pairs.

Activity A: The learners add the correct tense verbs to the right columns in a given table.

Answers

A Present tense verbs – is walking, asks, are chatting, tastes
Past tense verbs – enjoyed, cried, smiled, helped

Activity B: The learners write the simple past tense of the given verb families.

Answers

B 1 liked   2 waved   3 tried
    4 hurried

Questions

- Read the information box with the learners.

- Remind the learners of the term *asking sentences*. Explain that asking sentences are questions.

- Ask the learners for some example questions.

- Encourage the learners to work through each exercise individually or in pairs.

Activity A: The learners write questions using the three words provided.

Answers

A *Example answers:*

1 What time are your friends playing cricket?

2 Have you seen the blue pen I left in the classroom?

Activity B: The learners write questions to match the answers provided.

Answers

B *Example answers:*

1 When did the cat escape?

2 Where did you live?

Let's practise

This section allows you to model the required writing outcome with input from the learners.

Before writing

- Always encourage the learners to talk about what they are going to write. Discussing things can help the learners to organise their thoughts.
- Remind the learners what an interview is.
- Discuss the different scenarios where interviews are used. Explain the scenario they are now going to prepare questions for.

Shared writing activity

- Explain to the learners that they are going to write six interview questions, but first it is a good idea to help them to organise their thoughts.
- They can discuss their question ideas in pairs to aid them in clarifying their ideas.
- Encourage them to think about the type of questions they would be interested in answering. Encourage them to list the things they like or don't like about school. This might prompt questions they might like to ask.
- Remind them about the use of capital letters and question marks.
- They can do the activity either individually or in pairs.
- The activity then asks the learners to answer the questions they have written themselves. This enables them to see how relevant and easy to answer their questions are and gives them practice in answering questions.
- Support the learners with vocabulary and spellings they might need help with.
- Remind them of the concept of improving what they have written. Ask them to check they have correctly used full stops and question marks and that they have used the correct tense for the verbs. Are their questions and answers interesting?
- Finally, share some of their interview questions and answers. Encourage some of the learners to read their questions and answers to the rest of the group.
- Give them opportunities to discuss what they have written, either with you or with their peers.

Let's write

The learners are now required to plan questions independently for an interview with their mother, father or family friend, having worked through a

similar exercise in the previous section. Encourage them to share their work in progress with you so that, through discussion, they can improve their work.

Before writing

- Remind the learners of things they discussed in the Let's practise section.
- Encourage them to think about different options for questions and to choose the best ones.
- Ask them to write their questions carefully and neatly.
- Help them with spellings if necessary.
- Encourage them to look back at the questions once they have written them and to check they have included the correct punctuation and used the correct tense for the verbs.

Marking criteria

Technical aspects
Look for correct use of:
• questions that start with a capital letter • questions that end with a question mark • verbs written in the correct tense.
Content
• Do their questions make sense? • Will the questions be interesting/engaging for the interviewee? • Is the material ordered in a logical way?

After writing

Read through the completed questions with the learners. Are there any improvements they might make?

Plenary

- Using resource sheet 2, the learner can then interview their mother, father or family friend using the questions they have prepared.
- If you send resource sheet 2 home for the learners to complete, ensure parents/friends are aware that the learners may need support when writing their answers. For some learners it may be better if the parents/friends write their own answers.
- You could create a display entitled 'What was it like back then?' You could ask the learners to bring in a photo of whoever they interviewed and display it by their questions and answers.

Teacher's Resource Unit guide: Stage 2: Unit 8

- Discuss the differences the interviews highlighted between now and what things were like when their parents were of a similar age. As a class, complete a table using the headings 'Now' and 'Then' that highlight those differences. Display it with the interviews and photos.

Resource sheets

The resource sheets for Unit 8 provide differentiation for the writing outcome in this unit as well as further practice on special naming words and writing sentences.

1 A resource sheet revising verb tenses.
2 A resource sheet on recording the prepared interview.

Resource sheet 1: Interviews: verbs tenses

This resource sheet covers further practice on identifying the past and present tenses of verbs. It asks the learners to complete a table in which they are given the verb family and asked to complete the different forms of present and past tenses.

- Read through the resource sheet with the learners so they fully understand what is expected of them.
- Encourage them to read the information supplied in the table carefully. Some learners may find this exercise tricky and will need support.
- They can work in pairs or individually on this activity.
- Check through their answers to be sure they fully understand verb tenses.
- You can use this resource sheet for homework if the learners clearly understand what is required.

Resource sheet 2: An interview

This resource sheet gives learners a structure on which to write the interview from the Let's write section of Learner's Book 2. It asks the learners to copy out their prepared questions; stick a photograph or draw a picture of the person they are interviewing in the space provided; conduct the interview; and write the answers to their questions.

- Explain the task and allow time for learners to ask questions so they fully understand what is required.
- Let the learners know that you will display their work (should you choose to).

- Encourage the learners to read carefully what they have written. Can they make any improvements?
- Help them with vocabulary they might want to use.
- In groups or as a class, discuss the differences the learners discovered from when their parents were their age.

Assessment

The assessment sheet for this unit, 'Writing to communicate: interviews', is on page 94 of Learner's Book 2. It asks the learners to write six questions they would ask in an interview with an elephant expert.

- Read through the assessment sheet with the learners to ensure they have understood the writing task.
- Discuss with the learners the types of questions they might ask:
  - *Where do elephants live?*
  - *Do elephants sleep standing up?*
  - *What is a baby elephant called?*
  - *How much does an elephant drink in one day?*
- Encourage the learners to make their questions as interesting/unusual as possible.
- Do not penalise learners for spelling words incorrectly.
- Ask the learners to read through their questions. Are there any corrections or additions they could make?

Marking criteria

Technical aspects
Look for correct use of:
• questions that start with a capital letter
• questions that end with a question mark
• verbs written in the correct tense.
Content
• Do their questions make sense?
• Will the questions be interesting/engaging for the interviewee?
• Is the material ordered in a logical way?

Unit 9: Stories: setting and characters

Learner's Book unit focus

This unit focuses on **story writing**. The learners look in detail at **settings** and **characters**. They are also reminded of previous work done on the **structure of story writing; planning the beginning, middle and end** of a story.

Progress table for Stage 2: Unit 9

Category: Narrative writing

Writing outcome: Settings and characters

Characters and settings have to be more than just names and places. Authors flesh out both characters and settings in stories by describing their appearance and revealing personalities.

Stage 1	Stage 2	Stage 3	Stage 4	Stage 5	Stage 6
• joining two sentences with *and* • characters	• sequencing sentences to form a narrative • plot – beginning, middle and end • characters • setting	• plot • story openings/ settings • continuing stories			

Cambridge Global English link: Stage 2: Unit 9: Inside and outside cities

Cambridge Primary English link: Stage 2: Unit 4: Tales from around the world

---

Unit teaching plan

Warm up

- Remind the learners of previous work they did in Unit 1 on the beginning, middle and end of stories.
- Ask the learners:
  - *Who knows what a character is?*
  - *Why are the story characters important?*
- Ask the learners:
  - *Who knows what a story setting is?*
  - *Why is the story setting important?*
- Ask the learners to think about a well-known story (that you have selected).
  - *Who are the main characters in this story?*
  - *What is the setting of the story?*
- Introduce the story from the Learner's Book Unit 9.
  - *We are now going to read a story called* Sang Kancil and Crocodile. *Listen carefully.*

Let's read

Based on an Indonesian traditional tale, Jim Carrington's adaptation of *Sang Kancil and Crocodile* (ISBN: 978-1-107-55092-6) is the stimulus for this unit. It is about a mouse deer who notices some delicious-looking water apples on the far side of a crocodile-infested river. He works out a plan to get to the other side of the river to eat the water apples without being eaten himself.

The learners are required to interpret the story, for which they might need support from you.

- First, read the extract to the class, then ask nominated learners to read it again to the class. Be sure the learners all understand what has been read to them.
- Highlight the speech marks in the extract. Explain that they show when someone is talking. To highlight this, give the characters 'voices' to distinguish between characters and narrator.

Teacher's Resource Unit guide: Stage 2: Unit 9

- Ask the learners:
  - *Did you enjoy the story?*
  - *Do you think Sang Kancil managed to eat the apples?*
- Ask the learners specifically about the setting:
  - *Is this story set in a city or outside a city?*
  - *How do we know?*
- Ask the learners specifically about the characters:
  - *How many main characters are there in this story?*
  - *Who are they?*
- Remind the learners of the difference between fact and fiction. Fact is actual information; fiction is made up.

Plenary

Put the learners into pairs. Ask each pair: *How do you think this story ends?*

Let's talk

This section asks the learners questions that:

- give them a greater understanding of the text
- focus on the specific writing activity covered in the unit.

Activity A: This section is to ensure learners have understood what they have read.

Answers

A *Example answers:*
1 Sang Kancil is a clever mouse deer.
2 Sang Kancil wanted the ripe water apples on the other side of the river.
3 Sang Kancil was worried about the crocodiles in the river.
4 The crocodiles all lined up for Sang Kancil because he said he had to count them for the king, as the king had invited them to a feast.
5 The crocodiles helped Sang Kancil across the river by positioning themselves next to each other, which meant he could walk across the river on their backs. No, the crocodiles didn't mean to help Sang Kancil across the river.
6 *Learner's own judgement on whether they think Sang Kancil's idea is clever and why.*

Activity B: This section focuses the learners on the setting and characters, while touching on previous work on the beginning, middle and end of the story.

Answers

B *Example answers:*
1 The story is set in a jungle by a river.
2 *Learner's own description of the setting. [Descriptions should include:* deep in the jungle, next to a river, a water apple tree growing on the opposite side of the bank.*]*
3 The two main characters are Sang Kancil and Crocodile.
4 *Learner's own description of Sang Kancil [a clever mouse deer].*
5 *Learner's own description of Crocodile [a bossy, unfriendly crocodile].*
6 *Learner's own suggestions about what might happen at the end of the story.*

Let's learn

This section:

- recaps work on writing sentences
- recaps work on adjectives
- recaps work on joining words
- gives learners the opportunity to practise what they have learned in a focused activity before incorporating it into their own writing.

Writing sentences

- Write the following two phrases on the board:
  the greedy crocodile
  The boy ran away from the greedy crocodile.
  Ask the learners:
  - *Are these both sentences? Why?*
  - *How do we know the second one is a sentence?* [starts with capital letter, ends with full stop, makes sense because it has a verb]
- Read the information box with the learners.
- Highlight that sentences have to make 'sense'.
- Remind the learners of the different types of punctuation used at the end of a sentence for statements, questions and exclamations.

Activity A: The learners add missing punctuation marks to given sentences.

Answers

A 1 Watch out for the crocodiles!
2 The crocodiles lined up in the river.
3 Do you think Sang Kancil is brave?

Teacher's Resource Unit guide: Stage 2: Unit 9

© Sarah Lindsay and Wendy Wren 2019

Activity B: The learners are given words to use in sentences of their own.

Answers

B *Learner's own three sentences using the given words; check each sentence ends with appropriate punctuation and makes sense*

Adjectives
- Read the information box with the learners.
- Ask the learners for examples of adjectives.
- Encourage them to be more creative in the adjectives they use.
- Check they have found every adjective in the extract.
- Encourage them to work through each exercise individually or in pairs.

Activity A: Learners add adjectives to nouns.

Answers

A *Example answers:*
1 <u>overgrown</u> jungle   2 <u>angry</u> crocodile
3 <u>old</u> apple tree   4 <u>wide</u> river

Activity B: Learners underline the adjectives in the extract from *Sang Kancil and Crocodile*.

Answers

B There was once a <u>clever</u> mouse deer named Sang Kancil, who lived deep in the jungle.

One day, Sang Kancil was walking near the river. He spotted a tree on the far bank, full of <u>ripe</u> water apples.

"Mmmm, <u>yummy</u> water apples," Sang Kancil said to himself.

But the river was full of <u>hungry</u> crocodiles and Sang Kancil knew it was impossible to cross without being eaten.

Sang Kancil thought for a while. Then he had an idea. A <u>sly</u> smile appeared on his face. He hurried back down to the water's edge.

Joining words
- Ask the learners:
  - *Who remembers what a joining word does?*
  - *Who can name a joining word?* [for example: and, but, because, so]

- Joining words were previously covered in Unit 4.
- Introduce the word *conjunction* as a term used for *joining words*.
- Discuss with the learners that other words can join sentences. Ask them if they can suggest any.
- Read the information box with the learners.
- Ask the learners in pairs to create further examples of sentences that use joining words. Share some of their examples with the class.

Activity A: The learners identify the conjunctions in the given sentences from *Sang Kancil and Crocodile*.

Answers

A **1** The king has asked me to count all the crocodiles in the river(so)he knows how many are coming.
2 I will gather all the crocodiles(and)line them up for you.

Activity B: The learners are given sentences to adapt and join together with a joining word.

Answers

B *Example answers:*
1 Sang Kancil had a good idea <u>so he</u> spoke to Crocodile.
2 Sang Kancil's idea to trick the crocodiles was a great one <u>because they</u> wanted to go to a feast with the king.

Let's practise

This section allows you to model the required writing outcome with input from the learners.

Before writing
- Always encourage the learners to talk about what they are going to write. Discussing things can help the learners to organise their thoughts.
- Remind the learners that when writing a story it helps to plan it.
- Use a story they know well to highlight the setting, the main characters and the beginning, middle and end structure of it.

Shared writing activity
- The learners are going to write a story. They are given a setting and a character, but they need to plan how best to describe them.

- Encourage the learners to list the different adjectives they might use to describe the setting and character.
- In pairs, they can discuss the different words they might use (for example, they might choose to have a shy, timid cat as their main character or a confident, grumpy cat). Support the learners as they explore the different options.
- The learners then plan the beginning, middle and end of their story.
- Give them opportunities to discuss what they have written, either with you or with their peers.

Let's write

The learners now produce a story of their own independently, having looked in detail at the setting and character and planned the story in the previous section. Encourage learners to share their work in progress with you so that, through discussion, they can improve their work.

Before writing
- The learners are given prompts in the form of a Writer's Toolbox.
- Remind the learners of things they discussed in the Let's practise section.
- The learners can start their story on the Let's write page, but they might need more paper if their story is longer than the lines provided.
- Ask them to write their sentences carefully and neatly, and to include some joining words to make their sentences more interesting.
- Help the learners with spellings if necessary.
- Encourage the learners to look back at their story once they have written it and to check they have included all punctuation correctly, as well as adjectives.

Marking criteria

Technical aspects
Look for correct use of:
• sentences written with correct punctuation
• joining words added to make longer, more interesting sentences
• adjectives included to describe both setting and character clearly.

Content
• Do their sentences make sense?
• Does their story clearly move from a beginning, to the middle and then to an appropriate ending?
• Is their description of the setting clear and detailed?
• Is their description of the character engaging?

After writing
- Read through the completed stories with the learners.
- Encourage the learners to share their stories with their peers. Read aloud the stories that impress you.

Plenary

Put the learners into groups and ask them to create a short play using the characters and setting they have written about in their stories. They could act out a chosen story or create a new story with additional characters but using the same setting.

Resource sheets

The resource sheets for Unit 9 provide differentiation for the writing outcome in this unit as well as further practice on writing adjectives and including joining words in a sentence.

1   A resource sheet on writing about a setting.

2   A resource sheet on writing about a character.

Resource sheet 1: Setting and characters: a setting

This resource sheet covers further practice on writing about a setting. The learners choose a picture of a setting from options you can provide from the internet, cut-outs from magazines or photos, or they can draw their own picture of their favourite place.

- Read through the resource sheet with the learners so they fully understand what is expected of them.
- They use their chosen picture as the stimulus to write adjectives about the setting.
- They then write a long sentence, including a joining word, describing their chosen setting.
- Help them with vocabulary they might want to use. Encourage them to work carefully and neatly.
- Encourage them to read the sentence they have written carefully.

- They can work in pairs or individually on this activity.
- You could send this activity home for homework and share the results in groups or as a class the next day.

Resource sheet 2: Setting and characters: a character

This resource sheet covers further practice on writing about a character. The learners choose a picture of a person or animal from options you can provide from the internet, cut-outs from magazines or photos, or they can draw their own picture.

- Read through the resource sheet with the learners so they fully understand what is expected of them.
- They use their chosen picture as the stimulus to write adjectives about a character they have created based on the picture.
- They then write a long sentence, including a joining word, describing their character.
- Help them with vocabulary they might want to use. Encourage them to work carefully and neatly.
- Encourage them to read the sentence they have written carefully.
- Ideally, they should work individually on this activity.
- You could send this activity home for homework and share the results in groups or as a class the next day.

Assessment

The assessment sheet for this unit, 'Stories: setting and characters', is on page 95 of Learner's Book 2. It provides the learners with a stimulus picture that they then use to write about the setting and the character.

- Read through the assessment sheet with the learners to ensure they have understood the writing task.
- Encourage them to spend some time thinking of adjectives they might choose to describe both the setting and the character.
- Remind them to punctuate their sentences correctly and to use joining words where appropriate.
- Do not penalise learners for spelling words incorrectly.

Technical aspects
Look for correct use of:
• sentences written with correct punctuation
• joining words added to make longer, more interesting sentences
• adjectives included to describe both setting and character clearly.

Content
• Do their sentences make sense?
• Is their description of the setting clear and detailed?
• Is their description of the character engaging?

Cambridge Grammar and Writing Skills

Teacher's Resource 1-3

Stage 3

Unit guides: Stage 3

Unit 1: Explanatory writing: how is it done?

Learner's Book unit focus

This unit introduces **explanatory writing** within the context of **how something happens**.

Progress table for Stage 3: Unit 1
Category: Explanatory writing
Writing outcome: Explaining how something happens
Explanatory writing explains a process. Processes that happened in the past are written in past tenses. Processes that still happen today are written in the present.

Stage 1	Stage 2	Stage 3	Stage 4	Stage 5	Stage 6
		• how something happens		• how something was done [made] in the past	• how something works

Cambridge Global English link:	Stage 3: Unit 1: Working together
Cambridge Primary English link:	Stage 2: Unit 5: What is my house made of?

Resource list

Plain sheets of A4 paper (for the assessment activity, so the learners can practise making paper aeroplanes).

Unit teaching plan

Warm up

- Discuss the difference between fiction and non-fiction. Fiction is imaginary, made-up; non-fiction is actual information, facts.
  - *In this unit we are going to write non-fiction.*
- Explain to the learners that they are going to read an explanation of how aeroplanes fly. Ask:
  - *What do you understand by the term explanation?*
  - *What is an explanation?*
  - *In which type of books would we read explanations?*
  - *Explanations tell us how something is/was made, done or happens. Can you give me an example of an explanation?*
  - *Have you ever flown in an aeroplane?*

Let's read

The text is based around two children, Mohammed and Ana, working together to prepare for a party. The theme of the party is aeroplanes, which gets them talking about how aeroplanes actually fly. Page 9 shows an example of an explanation they find in a book, called 'How do aeroplanes fly?'

- Introduce the text to the class:
  - *We are going to meet two children, Mohammed and Ana. They are working together to prepare for Mohammed's aeroplane-themed party and they get chatting about how aeroplanes actually fly.*
- The explanation can be read:
  - by you to the class
  - by learners to the class
  - individually in silence.
- Be sure the learners all understand the text.

- Elicit/explain the meaning of any unfamiliar vocabulary, for example:
  - *thrust*: a force that moves something forward
  - *lift*: a force that moves something upwards.

Plenary

- Discuss whether the learners thought the explanation was clear and easy to understand. Ask the reasons for their opinions. Discuss that different people can have different opinions, and that an opinion different from yours isn't necessarily wrong.
- Ask if any of them have flown in an aeroplane. If they have, ask them if they felt the 'thrust' and 'lift' of the aeroplane.

Let's talk

This section asks the learners questions that:

- give them a greater understanding of the text
- focus on the specific writing activity covered in the unit.

Activities A and B: These sections ensure learners have understood what they have read.

Answers

A *Example answers:*
1   Mohammed and Ana looked up how aeroplanes fly.
2   The captain is the pilot in charge of the aeroplane.
3   The pilot starts the aeroplane's engines first.
4   The pilots sit on the flight deck (in the cockpit).

B *Example answers:*
1   The aeroplane's engines create a 'thrust' that moves the aeroplane forward.
2   The plane starts to lift when it is travelling fast enough.
3   Most of the aeroplane's 'lift' comes from the wings and their shape.
4   If the aeroplane isn't moving fast enough the pilot won't be able to steer it upwards and it won't lift off.

Activity C: This section focuses the learners on the structure of an explanation, highlighting the use of pictures.

Answers

C *Example answers:*
1   How do aeroplanes fly?
2   There are four points in this explanation.
3   *For example:* starts, pushes, steers
4   *Learner's brief description of the pictures and/or diagram used in the explanation*
5   *Learner's comments on whether they find the pictures and diagram useful and why*

Let's learn

This section provides learners with the 'tools' they need. It covers the main features of grammar, style and layout appropriate to the writing outcome. It:

- revises points learners have met earlier in the course
- introduces new work
- gives learners the opportunity to become familiar with particular features of the required writing, in this case explanatory writing
- gives learners the opportunity to practise what they have learned in focused activities before incorporating it into their free writing.

Writing sentences

- Revise the terms *capital letters*, *full stops* and *question marks* with the learners.
- Ask the learners:
  - *What type of sentence ends with a full stop?* [a 'telling' sentence]
  - *What type of sentence ends with a question mark?* [an 'asking' sentence]
- Ask the learners for examples of the different types of sentence.
- Read the information box with the learners.

Activity A: The learners copy two 'telling' sentences from the explanation.

Answers

A *Example answers:*
1   The pilot starts the aeroplane's engines.
2   The captain is the pilot in charge of the aeroplane.

Activity B: The learners copy two questions/'asking' sentences from the explanation.

Answers

B **1** How do aeroplanes fly?

2 Have you ever been in an aeroplane?

Comparing words

- Remind the learners of previous work they have done on comparing words.
- Remind them of the work they previously covered in Learner's Book 2 Units 1, 3 and 9 on adjectives.
- Remind the learners of the term *adjective*. Explain that adjectives tell us more about *nouns* (*naming words*). Using adjectives makes our writing more interesting.
- Ask the learners for more examples of adjectives they can add to *the aeroplane* (for example, the *fast* aeroplane, the *huge* aeroplane, the *noisy* aeroplane, etc.).
- If appropriate, introduce the idea that it's not only adjectives that can become comparing words, but adverbs also. This is why, at this stage in Learner's Book 3, reference is made to *comparing words* rather than *adjectives* or *adverbs*.
- Read the information box with the learners.
- Illustrate comparing words by asking a small child and a tall child to stand in front of the group or class. State: [name] *is smaller than* [name]. Write the sentence on the board. Highlight how the adjective is used to compare the two children. Make further comparisons between different children, asking the learners for their suggestions.
- Spend time highlighting the changes needed when adding -*er* to words. It is important to establish these rules.
- Encourage the learners to work through each exercise individually or in pairs.
- Refer the learners to the information box to aid them in adding the correct endings to the words.

Activity A: The learners change each of the words provided into a comparing word.

Answers

A **1** higher **2** redder **3** quicker **4** wiser

5 sleepier **6** flatter **7** stronger **8** safer

Activity B: The learners complete sentences by adding comparing words.

Answers

B *Example answers:*

1 An aeroplane is <u>faster</u> than a car.

2 A car is <u>smaller</u> than an aeroplane.

Activity C: The learners write their own sentence about aeroplanes, including a comparing word.

Answers

C *Learner's own sentence about an aeroplane using a comparing word*

Headings

- Read the information box with the learners.
- Discuss why learners think pieces of writing usually have headings. [To let readers know what the piece of writing is about.]
- Encourage them to be specific when they write their headings.
- Learners should work on the task individually, either in class or as homework.

Activity A: Learners are required to write headings related to specific topics.

Answers

A *Example answers:*

1 How to organise a party

2 How do you make a paper aeroplane?

3 Different types of aeroplane

Sequences

- Read the information box with learners.
- Discuss why it is important that explanations are written in a sensible order. For example, it would be confusing to talk about an aeroplane taking off before saying that the engines have to be started!
- Learners can work individually or in pairs.

Activity A: Learners rewrite the sentences in the order they appear in the explanation.

Answers

A **1** The pilot starts the aeroplane's engines.

2 The pilot steers the aeroplane along the runway as it goes faster and faster.

3 When the aeroplane is travelling fast enough, the air moving over the wings lifts the wings and the whole aeroplane upwards.

4 Once the aeroplane is flying, it can stay at a steady speed, high above the clouds.

Pictures and diagrams

- Read the information box with learners.
- Explain the term *caption (words linked to a picture that explain what the picture is about).*
- Learners can work in pairs and report back to the class.

Activity A: Learners write their own caption for the image shown.

Answers

A *Example answer:*

Aeroplane starting to take off

Let's practise

This section allows you to model the required writing outcome with input from the learners.

Before writing

- Always encourage the learners to talk about what they are going to write. Discussing things can help them to organise their thoughts.
- Remind the learners that explanations explain how something is done.
- Remind the learners of the difference between fact and fiction.

Shared writing activity

- Explain to the learners that together you are going to write an explanation of how you learn to ride a bike.
- Learners are given illustrations and vocabulary boxes for each step in the explanation.
- Work orally, helping learners to use the vocabulary in sentences to explain what is happening in each picture. They are required to write a caption for each picture.
- Encourage them to add linking words and phrases to lead on from one step to the next.
- You may want to record the discussion on the board or ask learners to make notes.
- Finally, share the learners' captions. Do they all agree about what happens when you learn to ride a bike?
- Give the learners opportunities to discuss what they have written, either with you or with their peers.

Let's write

The learners are now required independently to produce an explanation of their own, having worked through the series of events in the previous section.

The learners are given:

- some pictures of how to ride a bike
- a Writer's Toolbox to help them edit/proofread their work.

For learners who need more support, use resource sheet 2.

Before writing

- Read through the independent writing activity with the learners.
- Allow time for learners to ask questions so they fully understand what is required.

Independent writing activity

- This section is designed for learners to work independently, putting into practice what they have learned in the unit.
- They should do the planning and writing independently, either in class or for homework.
- If, however, you feel further support is needed, encourage learners to share their work in progress with you so that, through discussion, they can improve their drafts.
- Remind learners to use the Writer's Toolbox to correct mistakes and improve their work.

Example of the finished explanation

1 First, carefully get on the bike and get balanced with the help of an adult.
2 Place one foot on a pedal and one on the ground.
3 Start riding the bike at a steady speed with an adult supporting the back of the bike.
4 Then ride the bike without an adult holding the bike but running alongside to support if needed.
5 When you are ready you can ride the bike without any help.

Marking criteria

Technical aspects – 10 marks
Look for correct use of:
• sentence structure
• verb tenses
• linking words and phrases.

Resource sheets

The resource sheets for Unit 1 provide practice and reinforcement for:

1 sentences
2 writing an explanation.

Resource sheet 1: How is it done? sentences

Resource sheet 1 provides learners with practice in identifying the features and words found in sentences.

Answers

A 1 I learned to ride my bike when I was five years old**.**

2 Why did it take me so long to learn how to ride my bike**?**

3 Did you fall off your bike many times**?**

4 I remember how it felt to ride by myself for the first time**.**

B 1 Barney's bike is <u>faster</u> than my scooter.

2 I was <u>braver</u> than my brother when I fell off my bike.

3 The roads are <u>icier</u> than yesterday so I have to be <u>careful</u> while riding my bike.

4 My bike is <u>older</u> than all my friends' bikes but I still love it.

C *Learners write two sentences using the correct punctuation and including a verb and comparative adjective.*

Resource sheet 2: How is it done? writing an explanation

Resource sheet 2 provides the learner with support for the Let's write activity in the Learner's Book. The sheet provides a series of incomplete sentences for an explanation, which learners complete using the vocabulary provided.

Answers

1 First you need to <u>get on</u> your bike <u>carefully</u>. An adult can help <u>support</u> the bike.

2 Then place one <u>foot</u> on the <u>ground</u> and one on a <u>pedal</u>.

3 Start <u>riding</u> your bike at a steady <u>speed</u> with an <u>adult</u> helping.

4 Then try to <u>ride</u> your bike without the adult <u>helping</u> but <u>running</u> alongside just in case your bike wobbles.

5 When you are <u>ready</u>, you can <u>ride</u> your bike <u>without</u> any help.

Assessment

The assessment sheet for this unit, 'Explanatory writing: how is it done?', is on page 99 of Learner's Book 3. Learners are given the scenario of brushing their teeth when getting ready for Mohammed's party and a Writer's Toolbox of grammar and style features to include.

- Read the scenario box with the learners to ensure they have understood the writing task.
- Encourage them to spend some time planning, i.e. thinking carefully about *everything* they do when brushing their teeth.
- Before they write their first draft, read through the Writer's Toolbox to remind them what they need to include in their explanation.
- After they have produced a first draft, they should go back to the Writer's Toolbox and tick the 'tools' they have used.
- Encourage them to do further work on their draft to include more 'tools'.
- They should then produce a final copy.
- Use the marking criteria on pages 104–105 of this Teacher's Resource.

Unit 2: Writing to communicate: writing a letter

Learner's Book unit focus

This unit introduces **letter writing**. It looks in detail at **personal letter writing**.

Progress table for Stage 3: Unit 2

Category: Personal writing

Writing outcome: Writing a letter

Letters are a way of communicating. Letters can be written for many different reasons:

- to ask something
- to congratulate someone
- to tell someone something
- to explain something
- to complain about something.

Stage 1	Stage 2	Stage 3	Stage 4	Stage 5	Stage 6
	• interview questions	• personal letter	• book blurbs		• business/formal letter

Cambridge Global English link: Stage 3: Unit 2: Family and memories

Cambridge Primary English link: Stage 3: Unit 5: Letters

Resource list

Examples of different letters.

Unit teaching plan

Warm up

- Explain to the learners that they are going to read a personal letter written by Grandma to her two grandchildren, Aanya and Arjun.
- The stimulus will look in more detail at the purposes of letter writing, including a letter's layout and paragraphing.
- Ask the learners:
  - *Have you ever received a letter?*
  - *Who was the letter from?*
  - *Have you written a letter?*
  - *Who was it to?*
  - *Why do we write letters?*
- Letter writing is a form of communication. Discuss other ways of communicating (for example, email, telephone, texts, etc.).
- Share examples of different types of letter (for example, personal, complaint, business, invite, bill). Ask:
  - *What types of letter might adults receive that you may not?*

Let's read

The letter is based on a memory Grandma has of her two grandchildren, Aanya and Arjun. They were eating ice creams and arguing over who had the biggest ice cream when out of nowhere a big, colourful bird swooped down and grabbed the ice creams from their hands, causing them to slip into the rock pool they were sitting beside.

- Introduce the letter to the class.
  - *We are going to read a letter Grandma has written to her grandchildren Aanya and Arjun. She is writing about a memory she has.*

- The letter can be read:
  - by you to the class
  - by learners to the class
  - individually in silence.
- Be sure the learners all understand what they have read.
- Discuss:
  - the address and date – why they are included
  - the content – why the letter was written
  - the layout – the letter uses three paragraphs
  - the beginning – who the letter is written to
  - the ending – how the letter ends.
- Elicit/explain the meaning of any unfamiliar vocabulary, for example:
  - *attic*: a room in the roof of a house
  - *rock pool*: a pool of water surrounded by rocks left when a tide has retreated
  - *chuckle*: a quiet laugh to oneself.
- You are in the best position to determine the vocabulary that will be unfamiliar to the learners.

Plenary

- Ask whether the learners would appreciate receiving a letter like this one.
- Discuss how they might respond if they were Aanya or Arjun.
- Discuss how writing emails differs from writing letters. What are the similarities and differences?
- Consider why many people still appreciate and value receiving letters.

Let's talk

This section asks the learners questions that:

- give them a greater understanding of the text
- focus on the specific writing activity covered in the unit.

Activities A and B: These sections are to ensure learners have understood what they have read.

Answers

A *Example answers:*
1 The letter is to Aanya and Arjun and from Grandma.
2 The letter is about a memory Grandma has of her grandchildren when they were younger.

3 The children were arguing about the size of their ice creams.
4 The children toppled into the rock pool because they were surprised when a bird stole their ice creams.

B *Example answers:*
1 We know this letter is about something that happened in the past because it describes a memory and is written in the past tense.
2 The beach is described as sandy and with beautiful views.
3 Grandma still 'chuckles to this day' because it made her laugh when the children fell into the rock pool.
4 Would you like to come to stay again?

Activity C: This section focuses the learners on the structure of a letter.

Answers

C *Example answers:*
1 Grandma's address is at the top of the letter.
2 The date is written just below the address.
3 The letter is finished 'Lots of love, Grandma'.
4 We know Grandma knows the children very well because she ends the letter with 'Lots of love'.

Let's learn

This section provides learners with the 'tools' they need. It covers the main features of grammar, style and layout appropriate to the writing outcome. It:

- revises points the learners have met earlier in the course
- introduces new work
- gives learners the opportunity to become familiar with particular features of the required writing, in this case letter writing
- gives learners the opportunity to practise what they have learned in focused activities before incorporating it into their free writing.

Pronouns

Young writers have a tendency to repeat the names of characters rather than using the appropriate pronouns. This can make a piece of writing repetitious and dull.

- Read through the information box with the learners.
- Point to a boy in the class. Name him. Ask:
  - *What pronoun could I use instead of* [name]? [he]
- Point to a girl in the class. Name her. Ask:
  - *What pronoun could I use instead of* [name]? [she]
- Ask two learners to stand up. Name them. Ask:
  - *What pronoun could I use instead of* [name and name]? [they]
- Point to yourself. Name yourself. Ask:
  - *What pronoun could I use instead of* [name]? [I]
- Ask a learner to come and stand beside you. Name yourself and the learner. Ask:
  - *What pronoun could I use instead of* [name and name]? [we]
- Revise what a proper noun is before the learners start Activity A. In this activity all the proper nouns are names of people.
- The learners should work individually on this task either in class or as homework.

Activity A: The learners copy the sentences and replace the proper nouns with pronouns.

Answers

A 1 <u>They</u> visited Grandma.
  2 <u>She</u> thought she had the biggest ice cream.
  3 <u>He</u> thought he had the biggest ice cream.
  4 Grandma smiles when she thinks about <u>them</u> in the water.

Activity B: The learners write a sentence with a first person pronoun.

Answers

B *Learner's own sentence that includes a first person pronoun*

Address and date
- First, look at an example of a real letter. Ask the learners where the address is.
- Discuss the position of the address and date in a letter.
- Spend time discussing the details of an address; how, if the number or name of a house on a street isn't stated, the letter might get to the street but not to the right home, etc.
- Discuss why letters are dated (so it is recorded when they are written, should they need to be referred back to, just as emails are dated).

- Read the information box with the learners.
- The learners should work individually.

Activity A: The learners write their own address and the date.

Answers

A *Learner's own address and the date*

Paragraphs
- Read the information box with the learners.
- Look back at the letter and highlight how it is broken into chunks of writing. Explain that these are paragraphs.
- Highlight how each paragraph is indented.
- Be sure the learners understand the scenario given within the activity before they begin writing.
- Learners can do this individually, or as a class on the board.

Activity A: Learners are required to write the opening paragraph of a letter from Grandma.

Answers

A *Example answer:*
  I would love to have Aanya and Arjun come and stay with me during their next holiday. There are many things we could do and I really enjoy their company.

Activity B: Learners are required to write the closing paragraph of a letter from Grandma.

Answers

B *Example answer:*
  I hope the children would like to come to see me. We could all go to the beach on the day you bring them here. I look forward to hearing from you.

Letter endings
- Read the information box with learners.
- Discuss the different ways letters are finished.
- Although not relevant to a personal letter, discuss the more formal letter endings of 'Yours sincerely' (when you know the name of the person to whom you are writing), 'Yours faithfully' (when you don't know the name of the person to whom you are writing), etc. Ask the learners when these letter endings might be used.
- Learners can work individually or in pairs.

Activity A: The learners write three ways you can finish a letter.

Answers

A *Example answers:*

Best wishes

Kind regards

With love

From

Let's practise

This section allows you to model the required writing outcome with input from the learners.

Before writing

- Always encourage the learners to talk about what they are going to write. Discussing things can help them to organise their thoughts.
- Read through the letter from Grandma again.
- Discuss the letter, highlighting how it starts with the address, the date and the name of the person they are writing to. Clearly show where these things need to be positioned on the page.
- Highlight how paragraphing breaks up the different subjects in a letter. Look in detail at the letter on page 18, discussing the content of each paragraph.
- Finally, discuss how a letter is finished. The conclusion of a letter is very much dependent on how well you know the person to whom you are writing.

Shared writing activity

- Explain to the learners that, together, you are going to write a letter from Aanya and Arjun to their grandmother.
- Learners are asked questions to help them plan their letter.
- Introduce the activity. Be sure the learners fully understand each stage of letter writing and the correct layout of a letter.
- Give the learners opportunities to discuss what they have written, either with you or with their peers.
- Finally, the learners write their letter. Encourage them to edit and proofread their work, correcting mistakes in spelling, punctuation and grammar.

Let's write

The learners are now required to produce a letter of their own independently, having worked through the previous section. The learners are given

- questions that pinpoint the content and structure of their letter
- a Writer's Toolbox to help them edit/proofread their work.

For learners who need more support, use resource sheet 2 as a letter scaffold. It gives the structure for the letter they are asked to write. It could be used as a template for a first draft of the letter.

Before writing

- Read through the independent writing activity with the learners.
- Allow time for learners to ask questions so they fully understand what is required.

Independent writing activity

- This section is designed for learners to work independently, putting into practice what they have learned in the unit.
- They should do the planning and writing independently, either in class or for homework.
- If, however, you feel further support is needed, encourage learners to share their work in progress with you so that, through discussion, they can improve their drafts.
- Remind learners to use the Writer's Toolbox to correct mistakes and improve their work.

Marking criteria

Technical aspects – 10 marks
Look for correct use of:
<ul><li>an address</li><li>a date</li><li>first person pronouns</li><li>paragraphs</li><li>an appropriate letter ending.</li></ul>
Content – 10 marks
<ul><li>Does the first paragraph explain why the letter is being written?</li><li>Is the main part of the letter relevant?</li><li>Does the final paragraph conclude the letter in an interesting way?</li></ul>
Award a higher mark for a letter that:
<ul><li>includes interesting adjectives</li><li>flows from one paragraph to the next.</li></ul>

Resource sheets

The resource sheets for Unit 2 provide practice and reinforcement for:

1 pronouns
2 writing a letter.

Resource sheet 1: Writing a letter: pronouns

Resource sheet 1 provides learners with practice in identifying and writing pronouns.

Answers

A 1 <u>I</u> am looking forward to going to Grandma's house.

2 <u>He</u> always wants to have a bigger ice cream!

3 <u>You</u> made <u>me</u> laugh.

4 <u>We</u> will not fall in a rock pool again.

B *Learner's own sentences using the pronouns provided*

C 1 <u>It</u> was watching <u>them</u> eating their ice creams.

2 <u>Their</u> clothes were soaking wet and <u>they</u> needed to change.

Resource sheet 2: Writing a letter

Resource sheet 2 provides the learner with scaffolding for the Let's practise and Let's write activities. It gives the structure for the letter they are asked to write. It could be used as a first draft of the letter.

Assessment

The assessment sheet for this unit, 'Writing to communicate: writing a letter', is on page 100 of Learner's Book 3. Learners are given the scenario of writing a letter to a friend in a different town and a Writer's Toolbox of grammar and style features to include.

- Read the scenario with learners to ensure they have understood the writing task. Discuss the suggestions.

- Encourage learners to spend some time planning what will go in each paragraph of their letter.

- Before they write their first draft, read through the Writer's Toolbox with the learners to remind them what they need to include in their letter.

- After they have produced a first draft, learners should go back to the Writer's Toolbox and tick the 'tools' they have used.

- Encourage them to do further work on their draft to include more 'tools'.

- They should then produce a final copy.

- Use the marking criteria on page 109 of this Teacher's Resource.

Unit 3: Narrative writing: dialogue in stories

Learner's Book unit focus

This unit introduces **dialogue in stories**. It moves learners on from looking at speech in speech bubbles to writing dialogue in stories.

Progress table for Stage 3: Unit 3					
Category: Stories					
Writing outcome: Dialogue in stories					
Dialogue is the conversation between characters. It can move the plot along and give insight into the personality of each character.					
Stage 1	**Stage 2**	**Stage 3**	**Stage 4**	**Stage 5**	**Stage 6**
	• speech bubbles	• adding speech marks when speaker is at the end • dividing spoken words from non-spoken words by a comma, question mark and exclamation mark • capital letter for first spoken word • different words for *said*	• paragraphing in dialogue • contractions • synonyms for *said* • split direct speech		• business/formal letter
Cambridge Global English link: Stage 3: Unit 3: The desert **Cambridge Primary English link:** Stage 3: Unit 8: Wonderful world					

Resource list

A range of comics and class reading books with examples of conversation.

Unit teaching plan

Warm up

- Explain to the learners that they are going to read a story about two jerboas. Jerboas are small desert animals who hop like kangaroos and are eaten by fennec foxes.
- For further information about jerboas, fennec foxes and camels, look up the animals on the internet.
- Ask the learners:
  - *Who can tell me where a camel lives?*
  - *Who can tell me what a jerboa is?*
  - *Who can tell me what a fennec fox is?*
- Remind the learners that previously, in Stage 2 Unit 2, we looked at speech when it was written in speech bubbles. Remind the learners by showing them examples of comics.
- Introduce the term direct speech. Explain that this is when punctuation marks signify when someone is speaking.
- Introduce speech marks. Show learners how to write speech marks (" ").

111

- Write the sentence, *We are going to play outside said Adie.* on the board.
- Ask the learners which part of the sentence is spoken. Clearly mark the spoken words with speech marks.
- Draw the marks clearly on the board for the learners to see.
- Ask the learners to look carefully at the story's layout.
- Share examples of different familiar reading books. Ask the learners to work in pairs to identify examples of direct speech.
  - *Find me an example of when someone says something.*
  - *What punctuation is used?*

Let's read

The story is about two brother jerboas who get lost, meet a camel and get chased by a fennec fox before safely finding their way home to their mother.

- Introduce the story to the class.
  - *We are going to read a story about a race between two brothers.*
- The story can be read:
  - by you to the class
  - by learners to the class
  - individually in silence.
- Be sure the learners all understand what they have read.
- Elicit/explain the meaning of any unfamiliar vocabulary, for example:
  - *jerboa*: a small, mouse-like creature with long legs that hops like a kangaroo
  - *fennec fox*: a small fox with large ears, and thick fur under its feet so it can walk on the hot sand; it eats jerboas
  - *skidded to a halt*: stopped very quickly
  - *toppled*: tipped over.
- You are in the best position to determine the vocabulary that will be unfamiliar to the learners.

Plenary

- To help learners understand which words are said and which words aid the flow of the story, split the learners into groups of five. Four of the learners take on the roles of Mum, Fabio, Jac and the camel and read their spoken words. The fifth learner is the narrator, who reads everything but the spoken words.

- If learners are confident enough, they can perform the reading in front of the rest of the class.

Let's talk

This section asks the learners questions that:

- give them a greater understanding of the text
- focus on the specific writing activity covered in the unit.

Activity A: This section ensures learners have understood what they have read.

Answers

A *Example answers:*
1 The story is set in a desert.
2 Mum asks them to come home in ten minutes.
3 The brothers decide to race to a faraway tree.
4 Fabio was scared because he couldn't see his home; they were lost.
5 The strange grumbling sound was a sleeping camel.
6 A fennec fox chased Fabio and Jac.

Activity B: This section looks in more detail at the characters in the story.

Answers

B *Example answers:*
1 Fabio and Jac are jerboas. They are brothers.
2 The boys are racing and want to continue, which suggests they are having fun.
3 We know Fabio is the more cautious brother because he is worried about being lost and the strange noise they hear.
4 We know Jac is the braver brother because he takes the lead when Fabio is scared, and is reassuring about things.

Activity C: This section focuses the learners on the dialogue in the story.

Answers

C *Example answers:*
1 *An example of something Fabio says:* "I'm scared."
2 *An example of something Jac says:* "It's OK, let's hop this way."

Teacher's Resource Unit guide: Stage 3: Unit 3

© Sarah Lindsay and Wendy Wren 2019

3 *An example of something the camel says:*
"Can I help you two?"

4 The speaker's name comes after the spoken words.

Let's learn

This section provides learners with the 'tools' they need. It covers the main features of grammar, style and layout appropriate to the writing outcome. It:

- revises points learners have met earlier in the course
- introduces new work
- gives learners the opportunity to become familiar with particular features of the required writing, in this case dialogue in stories
- gives learners the opportunity to practise what they have learned in focused activities, before incorporating it into their free writing.

Dialogue

- Read the first information box with the learners.
- Reinforce previous examples of writing speech marks (see the Warm up section).
- Go through the list, asking learners to point to an example in the extract of:
  - speech marks
  - the name of a speaker
  - a comma to divide spoken and non-spoken words (highlight how this punctuation mark is written within the speech marks)
  - a capital letter for the first word spoken.
- Read through the second information box with the learners, either before or after they have attempted Activity A.
- Write a large *question mark* and a large *exclamation mark* on the board and ask the learners to name them and explain when they should be used.
- Write a variety of direct speech sentences on the board, omitting the punctuation at the end of the spoken words, for example:

  "When is your birthday…" said Jacob.

  "Watch out, the tree is falling…" exclaimed Tia.

  "It is time to walk to school…" said Harry.

  Ask learners to volunteer to add the missing punctuation.

Activity A: This focuses purely on the addition of speech marks to given sentences. Learners should work individually.

Answers

A 1 "I'm not sure Jac," said Fabio.

2 "I'm scared," said Fabio.

3 "It's OK, let's hop this way," said Jac.

4 "We are sorry, Mum," said the brothers.

Activity B: This focuses purely on the addition of punctuation at the end of spoken words. Learners should work individually.

Answers

B 1 "Where could my boys have hopped to**?**" wondered Mum.

2 "We really should go home**,**" said Fabio.

3 "Quick, hop this way**!**" called Jac.

4 "Is this the right way**?**" asked Fabio.

5 "I think so**,**" said Jac.

Activity C: In this activity the learners write their own sentences with speech marks and specified end punctuation.

Answers

C 1 *Learner's own sentence with speech marks and a comma*

2 *Learner's own sentence with speech marks and a question mark*

3 *Learner's own sentence with speech marks and an exclamation mark*

Plenary

- Check the learners' answers to the activities.
- Ensure learners have put the punctuation at the end of the direct speech *before* the closing speech marks.
- Give more able learners resource sheet 1, which challenges them to recognise all the skills in writing direct speech.

Contractions

- Write *is not* and *isn't* on the board.
- Elicit/explain the difference, that *isn't* is a short form of *is not*. An *apostrophe* (') is used instead of the missing letter (*o*).
- Ask the learners for other examples. If one gives a shortened form, ask another learner to 'expand' it.
- If all the examples are *not/n't*, suggest a few of your own to include examples such as:

    they are/they're

    she is/she's   etc.

- Read the information box with the learners.
- Check the learners can clearly write an apostrophe.
- Encourage them to work through each exercise individually or in pairs.
- One common problem is that learners put the apostrophe in the wrong place, for example, *could'nt/was'nt*, etc. If this occurs, spend some time reinforcing that the apostrophe comes in place of the missing letter(s), for example:

    *could n**o**t*   *couldn**'**t*

    *was n**o**t*   *wasn**'**t*

    *it **i**s*   *it**'**s*

Activity A: Learners complete word sums that specify the words used in contractions.

Answers

A	1	she will	2	it is	3	they are
	4	should have	5	you are	6	I am
	7	he is	8	you will

Activity B: Learners copy sentences, replacing underlined words with contractions.

Answers

B	1	"<u>I'm</u> very tired," said Fabio.
	2	"We <u>mustn't</u> stop hopping," said Jac.
	3	"<u>I've</u> been so worried," said Mum.

Other words for *said*

- Read the information box with the learners.
- Can the learners think of other words that can be used for *said*?

- For those learners who are able, introduce the word *synonym*. Explain that synonyms are words that *mean the same or nearly the same* (for example, *chatted*, *discussed*). This is formally introduced in Stage 4 Unit 5. Ask the learners for some examples.

Activity A: Learners find three words in the story that are used in place of the word *said*.

Answers

A   shouted, whispered, asked

Activity B: Learners write two words that replace the word *said* in given sentences.

Answers

B	*Example answers:*
	1 laughed, joked, moaned
	2 complained, pleaded, whispered
	3 exclaimed, replied, shouted

Activity C: Learners write their own sentences that include the dialogue words provided.

Answers

C   *Learner's own sentences using the dialogue words provided*

Let's practise

This section allows you to model the required writing outcome with input from the learners – the next part of the story with dialogue.

Before writing

- Ask the learners to retell the story extract.
    - *Can you name the characters?*
    - *What happened in the story?*
    - *How did the story end?*
- Explain to the learners that together you are going to write the next part of the story.

Shared writing activity

- Read the information box with the learners to introduce the writing activity.
- Read each question with the learners. Write the questions on the board. Note down their suggestions. Build up the dialogue.

Teacher's Resource Unit guide: Stage 3: Unit 3

© Sarah Lindsay and Wendy Wren 2019

- The learners can then copy the dialogue, adding capital letters for the first word spoken, speech marks and other punctuation under your supervision.
- When the dialogue is complete, ask the learners to read through the Writer's Toolbox, correcting any mistakes or omissions in their work.

Plenary
- In groups, the learners prepare a reading of the dialogue for the class.
- This activity helps them to understand that words such as *said* and the *characters' names* are **not** spoken.

Let's write

The learners are given:

- a scenario as the basis for their writing
- question prompts
- suggested alternative words for *said*
- a Writer's Toolbox to help them edit/proofread their work.

For learners who need more support, use resource sheet 2.

Before writing
- Read through the writing activity with the learners.
- Allow time for learners to ask questions so they fully understand what is required.

Independent writing activity
- This section is designed for learners to work through independently, putting into practice what they have learned in the unit.
- The learners should do the planning and writing either in class or for homework.
- If, however, you feel further support is needed, encourage learners to share their work in progress with you so that, through discussion, they can improve their drafts.
- Remind learners to use the Writer's Toolbox to correct mistakes and improve their work.

Marking criteria

Technical aspects – 10 marks
Look for correct use of:
• speech marks
• speaker's name
• commas
• capital letters
• question marks
• exclamation marks
• contractions.

Content – 10 marks
• Does the dialogue make sense?
• Is the dialogue relevant to the scenario?
• Have interesting dialogue words been used?
Award a higher mark if the learner has:
• attempted longer sections of dialogue rather than a series of very short sentences.

Resource sheets

The resource sheets for Unit 3 provide practice and reinforcement for:

1 writing dialogue
2 using speech bubbles.

Resource sheet 1: Dialogue in stories: writing dialogue

Resource sheet 1 gives learners further practice in identifying spoken words and adding missing punctuation and capital letters to dialogue correctly.

Answers

A 1 **"W**hat are we going to eat for tea tonight**?"** asked Jac**.**

2 **"W**e will go and hunt for insects as soon as the sun goes down**,"** said Mum**.**

3 **"I** was hoping you were going to say that**!"** laughed Fabio**.**

4 **"I** love chasing insects**,"** giggled Jac**.**

B *Learner's own sentence to continue the conversation, written with correct punctuation and capital letters*

Resource sheet 2: Dialogue in stories: using speech bubbles

Resource sheet 2 provides additional support for those learners struggling to identify the 'spoken' words in dialogue. They write a speech bubble conversation and then identify one scene to write as direct speech. Encourage discussion about the conversation between Fabio and Jac before learners start writing.

Answers

Learner's own conversation between Fabio and Jac, initially written in speech bubbles but with one scene written as direct speech

Assessment

The assessment sheet for this unit, 'Narrative writing: dialogue in stories', is on page 101 of Learner's Book 3. The learners are asked to write a conversation and are provided with a scenario on which to base the conversation.

- Read the scenario box with learners to ensure they have understood the writing task.
- Encourage them to spend some time planning, i.e. thinking about what they would say about their chosen topic.
- Before they write their first draft, read through the Writer's toolbox with the learners to remind them what they need to include in their conversation.
- After they have produced a first draft, learners should go back to the toolbox and tick the 'tools' they have used.
- Encourage learners to do further work on their draft to include more 'tools'.
- They should then produce a final copy.
- Use the marking criteria on page 115 of this Teacher's Resource.

Unit 4: Poems: humorous poems

Learner's Book unit focus

This unit consolidates previous work on **rhyming poems** in the form of **humorous poems**.

Progress table for Stage 3: Unit 4

Category: Poems

Writing outcome: Humorous poems

Humorous poems are often popular with learners. In this unit, a rhyming poem has been chosen to consolidate previous work in Stage 1: Unit 3 and Stage 2: Unit 6.

Stage 1	Stage 2	Stage 3	Stage 4	Stage 5	Stage 6
• identifying rhyming/ patterned words • using rhyming/ patterned words	• rhyming poems • list poems	• humorous poems • rhyming poems	• acrostics • haikus	• narrative poetry	

Cambridge Global English link:	Stage 3: Unit 4: Look again
Cambridge Primary English links:	Stage 3: Unit 9: Laughing allowed
	Stage 3: Unit 3: See, hear, feel, enjoy
	Stage 3: Unit 6: Poems from around the world

Resource list

A selection of humorous poems (if available).

Unit teaching plan

Warm up

- Introduce this unit on poems. Ask:
  - *Can you name some poems?*
  - *Do you enjoy listening to poems?*
- Share some familiar action poems with the learners.
- Ask the learners if they remember previous work in Stage 1: Unit 3 and Stage 2: Unit 6 on rhyming words. Ask them:
  - *What is a rhyming word?*
  - *Do rhyming words have to have the same letter patterns to rhyme?*
- Ask the learners for suggestions of rhyming words.
- Discuss the word *humorous* (causing laughter and amusement).
  - *What makes you laugh or smile?*

- Introduce the poem.
  - *We are now going to read a humorous poem. If you were to see this in real life it would make you 'look again'!*

Let's read

The stimulus for this unit is a rhyming poem.

- The poem can be read:
  - by you to the class
  - by learners to the class
  - individually in silence.
- Elicit/explain the meaning of any unfamiliar vocabulary, for example:
  - *icicle*: a long narrow strip of ice formed by the freezing of dripping water
  - *skyscraper*: a very tall building
- You are in the best position to determine the vocabulary that will be unfamiliar to the learners.

- Discuss the structure of the poem.
  - *How many verses are there?*
  - *Where do the rhyming words appear in each verse?*
  - *Does the poem make you smile?*
- Discuss the learners' responses to the questions above.
- Discuss what makes this a humorous poem. If the learners saw this for real, would it make them 'look again'?

Plenary

- Share further rhyming poems with the learners, either from books or sourced on the internet.
- Put the learners into pairs. Ask each pair to read one of the poems and add actions to each verse. Then ask the learners to perform the action poem in front of their peers.

Let's talk

This section asks the learners questions that:

- give them a greater understanding of the text
- focus on the specific writing activity covered in the unit.

Activity A: This section is to ensure learners have understood what they have read.

Answers

A *Example answers:*
   1 The poem describes the imaginative journey of a rhyme.
   2 The rhyme ran out the door.
   3 The rhyme turned into a cat after being put in a hat.
   4 The rhyme was caught by the tail before it stretched into a whale.
   5 The rhyme was fed tin and paper.
   6 The rhyme eventually flew out of sight.

Activity B: This section highlights the features of this humorous poem.

Answers

B *Example answers:*
   1 We know it is a rhyming poem because the last words in each line of a verse rhyme.
   2 For example: goat/boat
   3 For example: caught, ran, melted
   4 Eight verses

Activity C: This section asks the learners for an opinion.

Answers

C 1 *Learner's own comments on whether the poem makes them laugh or smile*
   2 *Learner's own comments on the fact that this is a nonsense poem*
   3 *Learner's own comments on whether they like the poem and why*

Let's learn

This section provides learners with the 'tools' they need. It covers the main features of grammar, style and layout appropriate to the writing outcome. It:

- practises work on *rhyming words*
- practises work on *pronouns*
- introduces work on *irregular past simple tense verbs*
- introduces work on *prepositions*
- gives learners the opportunity to practise what they have learned in a focused activity before incorporating it into their free writing.

Rhyme

- Remind the learners how some rhyming words have the same letter pattern but some do not.
- Ask the learners:
  - *What word rhymes with eight?*
- Write their answers on the board.
- Highlight words that don't end with the same *-ight* letter pattern.
- Read the information box with the learners.
- Encourage them to work through each exercise individually or in pairs.

Activity A: The learners list the pairs of rhyming words in the poem.

Answers

A time – rhyme   floor – door
   bicycle – icicle   hat – cat
   tail – whale   boat – goat
   paper – skyscraper kite – sight

Activity B: The learners write as many rhyming words as they can for the words provided.

Answers

B *Learner's own rhyming words for cage, stair, kite and list, for example:*

1 cage – page, stage, rage
2 stair – share, bear, mare
3 kite – height, sight, flight
4 list – fist, missed, mist

Pronouns

Learners will be familiar with the term *pronoun* from earlier in the course.

- Read the information box with the learners.
- Explain that we use *I* when writing about ourselves rather than using our name. Say:
  - *We use* we *when there is a group of us doing/experiencing the same thing.*
- Encourage the learners to work through each exercise individually or in pairs.

Activity A: The learners underline the pronouns in the sentences provided.

Answers

A 1 Meena grabbed <u>her</u> rhyme and put <u>it</u> in a box.
2 Jacob caught <u>his</u> rhyme in a bag.
3 <u>He</u> struggled to keep hold of <u>it</u>.
4 "<u>We</u> are never going to get <u>them</u> under control," said Jacob to Meena.
5 "<u>You</u> are right!" <u>she</u> replied.

Activity B: Learners write sentences using chosen pronouns.

Answers

B *Learners write five of their own sentences, each including a chosen pronoun.*

Verbs

- Revise previous work on past tense *verbs* (*doing words*).
- Beware: young learners can find understanding verbs tricky due to their many forms and tenses.
- Discuss the past tense previously covered. The regular past simple tense is formed by adding *-d/-ed* to the verb family name.

- Read the information box with the learners.
- Ask the learners for examples of other irregular verb families.
- Encourage them to work through each exercise individually or in pairs.

Activity A: Learners underline the past tense verbs in the poem *Catch a Little Rhyme*.

Answers

A Once upon a time
I <u>caught</u> a little rhyme

I <u>set</u> it on the floor
but it <u>ran</u> right out the door

I <u>chased</u> it on my bicycle
but it <u>melted</u> to an icicle

I <u>scooped</u> it up in my hat
but it <u>turned</u> into a cat

I <u>caught</u> it by the tail
but it <u>stretched</u> into a whale

I <u>followed</u> it in a boat
but it <u>changed</u> into a goat

When I <u>fed</u> it tin and paper
it <u>became</u> a tall skyscraper

Then it <u>grew</u> into a kite
and <u>flew</u> far out of sight…

Activity B: Learners identify past tense verbs that don't have *-d* or *-ed* added to them.

Activity C: Learners write the family names of the verbs listed in B.

Answers

B and C *Example answers:*

fed – to feed
became – to become
grew – to grow
flew – to fly
caught – to catch

Teacher's Resource Unit guide: Stage 3: Unit 4

Prepositions

- Introduce the term *preposition* to the learners. A preposition tells us the 'position' of something.
- Highlight the word 'position' within the word *preposition*.
- Ask the learners for examples of prepositions before they start the activities.
- Read the information box with the learners.
- Encourage them to work through each exercise individually or in pairs.

Activity A: The learners underline the prepositions in given sentences.

Answers

A 1 I skidded <u>on</u> my bicycle.
    2 I put it <u>in</u> my hat.
    3 I hid <u>behind</u> a tree.
    4 I lay <u>upon</u> a bench.
    5 I jumped <u>over</u> the fence.
    6 I put the food <u>inside</u> the box.

Activity B: Learners identify prepositions among a number of words.

Answers

B inside, under, in, on, out, over, off, outside, down

Activity C: Learners write sentences using chosen prepositions.

Answers

C *Learners write four of their own sentences, each including a chosen preposition.*

Let's practise

This section allows you to model the required writing outcome with input from the learners.

Before writing

- Always encourage the learners to talk about what they are going to write. Discussing things can help them to organise their thoughts.
- Read through the humorous poem on pages 38 and 39 with the learners.

Shared writing activity

- The learners are going to write a humorous poem using the same structure as the poem they have read, but first it is a good idea to help them to organise their thoughts.

- The learners list nine different pairs of rhyming words in preparation.
- They then list nine different past tense verbs that could be used in their poem.
- Finally, they list possible prepositions they might use.
- In pairs, they can discuss the possible words they might use to aid them in clarifying their ideas.
- Give them opportunities to discuss what they have written, either with you or with their peers.
- When the verses are complete, ask the learners to read through the Writer's Toolbox, correcting any mistakes or omissions in their work.
- Finally, share some of the learners' verses with the class. Encourage some of the learners to read their verses to the rest of the group or class.
- Ask the learners to add actions to their poems and perform them in front of a friend or group.

Let's write

The learners are now required to complete the humorous poem independently. Encourage learners to share their work in progress with you so that, through discussion, they can improve their work.

Before writing

- Read through the writing activity with the learners.
- Allow time for learners to ask questions so they fully understand what is required.

Independent writing activity

- Encourage the learners to think about different options of rhyming, verb and preposition combinations, as discussed in the previous section.
- Ask the learners to keep the same structure as in the original poem.
- Help them with spellings if necessary.
- Explain to learners that they may need to rewrite their poem, just as real poets do, to create the best poem they possibly can.
- Encourage the learners to look back at the poem once they have written it:
  - *Could you make improvements to the rhyming words you have used?*
  - *Is there a sense of humour running throughout the poem?*
- Ask them to write their poems carefully and neatly.

Teacher's Resource Unit guide: Stage 3: Unit 4

Marking criteria

Technical aspects – 10 marks
Look for correct use of:
• verses that start with a capital letter
• rhyming words
• past tense verbs
• prepositions.
Content – 10 marks
• Do their verses make sense?
• Is their poem humorous?
• Has the learner considered the overall poem when writing the verses?
Award a higher mark if the learner has:
• conveyed humour without it being based on silliness.

After writing

Read through the completed poems with the learners. Encourage them to share their poems with others.

Plenary

- Discuss the different poems they have written.
- If appropriate, encourage the learners to add actions to their poems and then perform them in front of a group or the class.

Resource sheets

The resource sheets for Unit 4 provide differentiation for the writing outcome in this unit as well as further practice on prepositions.

1   A resource sheet on prepositions.
2   A resource sheet on rhyming words.

Resource sheet 1: Humorous poems: prepositions

Resource sheet 1 covers further practice on prepositions.

- The learners can complete this resource sheet as homework, to reinforce work covered in school.
- Read through the resource sheet with them so they fully understand what is expected of them.
- Carefully read the information box with the learners.
- Encourage them to read the sentences they have written carefully.
- Check through the learners' answers to be sure they fully understand prepositions.

Answers

A **1** below **2** outside **3** off **4** over
  5 to   **6** in   **7** down **8** in front

B *Learner's completed sentences, each including a preposition*

C *Learner's own sentence, including a pair of opposite prepositions from Activity A*

Resource sheet 2: Humorous poems: linking rhyming words

Resource sheet 2 provides the learner with a bank of rhyming words that can be used for the Let's practise and Let's write activities.

- This resource sheet could be used to support those learners who find the Let's practise and Let's write sections challenging. It supports them in building the rhyming word bank ahead of writing the poem.
- Explain that the resource sheet has pairs of rhyming words; however, these are all muddled up and need to be linked.
- Three words don't have a linking rhyming word. The learners are required to write one.
- Encourage the learners to work carefully and neatly.
- They can complete this resource sheet at home.

Assessment

The assessment sheet for this unit, 'Poems: humorous poems', is on page 102 of Learner's Book 3. The learners are asked to write a humorous poem and given suggestions of things to think about.

- Read the information with the learners to ensure they have understood the writing task.
- Encourage learners to spend some time planning, i.e. thinking about words they might use and trying out different words within different lines in their poem.
- Before they write their first draft, read through the toolbox with the learners to remind them what they need to include in their poem.
- After they have produced a first draft, they should go back to the toolbox and tick the 'tools' they have used.
- Encourage them to do further work on their draft to include more 'tools'.
- They should then produce a final copy.
- Use the marking criteria above.

Unit 5: Instructions: writing instructions and rules

Learner's Book unit focus

This unit continues work on **writing instructions**. It introduces the term **imperative verb** and looks at **number and colour adjectives**.

Progress table for Stage 3: Unit 5					
Category: Instructions/advice/guidance					
Writing outcome: Writing instructions and rules					
Sequence, clear sentences, imperative verbs, precise language and layout are important features of instructions.					
Stage 1	**Stage 2**	**Stage 3**	**Stage 4**	**Stage 5**	**Stage 6**
• writing simple instructions • writing rules	• writing simple instructions	• writing instructions • writing rules	• recipes	• directions	• leaflets with instructions/ advice/guidance
Cambridge Global English link: Stage 3: Unit 5: Inventors and inventions **Cambridge Primary English link:** Stage 2: Unit 2: How to write instructions					

Unit teaching plan

Warm up

- Ask the learners:
  - *What is an invention?*
  - *Has anyone ever invented something?*
  - *What did you make?*
- Highlight the everyday things the learners use that were invented in the past (for example, televisions, mobile phones, etc.).
- Ask the learners:
  - *Why do we need instructions?*
  - *Why do you think instructions need to be written in order?*

Let's read

This unit looks at the instructions for an imaginary invention. The instructions and rules are based on an invention for feeding cats.

- The instructions and rules can be read:
  - by you to the class
  - by learners to the class
  - individually in silence.

- Elicit/explain the meaning of any unfamiliar vocabulary, for example:
  - *conveyor belt*: a moving belt that transports things from one place to another
  - *lever*: a bar that moves up and down
  - *magnet*: an object that attracts iron or steel
  - *recycle*: to use again.
- You are in the best position to determine the vocabulary that will be unfamiliar to the learners.
- Ask the learners questions about the invention.
  - *Would you like to try using this invention?*
  - *How could you improve the invention?*
  - *Do you think the rules are important?*
  - *Which rule is the most important?*
  - *Could this invention be used to feed other animals?*
- Look at the structure of the instructions with the learners. It starts with what needs to be done first and continues by giving a step-by-step guide of how to use the machine.
- Discuss the instructions with the learners. Ask:
  - *How easy are the instructions to follow?*
  - *What makes the instructions easy to follow?*

- *Would it matter if you changed the order of the instructions?*
- Discuss the rules with the learners. Ask:
  - *Do rules need to be written in order?*
  - *Can you change the order of these rules? Would it matter?*

Plenary

- Put the learners into pairs. Ask the pairs to discuss how they might change the cat-feeding invention. Ask the pairs to share their ideas with the rest of the class.
- Use the recycling rule on page 49 of the Learner's Book to discuss why recycling is important for society now. Ask the learners if they recycle any items.

Let's talk

This section asks the learners questions that:
- give them a greater understanding of the text
- focus on the specific writing activity covered in the unit.

Activity A: This section ensures the learners have understood what they have read.

Answers

A *Example answers:*
1 The instructions tell you how to use the cat-feeding invention.
2 First, you should place your cat to the side of the conveyor belt.
3 We know the machine is ready to use when the yellow light comes on.
4 The levers control the movement of the cans and the pouring of the cat crunchies.
5 The first and third rules are about safety.
6 Recycling materials is important and that is why Nasar has included a rule about it.

Activity B: This section focuses the learners on the instructions. It asks the learners to look carefully at how the instructions are written and why.

Answers

B *Example answers:*
1 We need instructions to tell us how to use things.
2 We need to remember to write instructions in order.

3 The sentences are short and simple. Instructions need to be short and simple. They need to tell us only the information we need to know.
4 For example: place, press, use, hold, lift, watch, twist, lower, deliver, turn

Activity C: This section focuses the learners on the rules. It asks the learners to look carefully at how the rules are written and why.

Answers

C 1 Rules tell us what must or must not be done.
2 Rules don't need to be written in order because they stand alone with the information they provide.
3 Nasar has emphasised the word 'ALWAYS' to get the message across that each rule is very important.
4 *Learner's own choice of most important rule and why they think it is the most important*

Let's learn

This section provides learners with the 'tools' they need. It covers the main features of grammar, style and layout appropriate to the writing outcome. It:
- revises points learners have met earlier in the course
- introduces new work
- gives learners the opportunity to become familiar with particular features of the required writing
- gives learners the opportunity to practise what they have learned in focused activities before incorporating it into their free writing.

Imperative verbs

- Read the information box with the learners.
- Explain that *imperative verbs* tell you what you should do. They are 'bossy' verbs.
- They are the *infinitive form* (*family name*) of the verb without the *to*.
- Write these infinitives on the board:
     to walk   to jump   to press
- Ask learners to say the imperative form of each verb:
     walk   jump   press
- Ask them to use these imperative verbs in sentences of their own. For example:
     Walk to the bus stop.

Jump on your bike.
Press the button.

Activity A: The learners identify imperative verbs in the instructions.

Activity B: The learners write the imperative verb that is used three times.

Answers

A place, press, wait, take, lift, watch, twist, lower, press, press

B press

Activity C: The learners add an imperative verb to each given sentence.

Answers

C *Example answers:*
1 Pour some cleaner on to a cloth.
2 Wipe the cloth over the dirty areas.
3 Rinse the cloth in water.
4 Get a dry cloth.
5 Rub the cloth over all the areas of the machine to make it shine.

Activity D: The learners write their own instruction that includes an imperative verb.

Answers

D *Learner's own instruction that includes an imperative verb (underlined).*

Adjectives

Learners will be familiar with the term *adjective* from earlier in the course.

- Read the information box with the learners.
- Be sure the learners understand what an *adjective* is.
- Ask them for examples of colour, number or order adjectives.
- Encourage them to work through each exercise individually or in pairs.

Activity A: The learners add the number and number order adjectives to the correct columns in the table.

Answers

A

Number adjectives	Number order adjectives
two	thirtieth
seven	fifth
twenty-nine	eightieth
fifteen	tenth
six	seventeenth
ninety-nine	third

Activity B: The learners add a different colour and number adjective to each of the given nouns.

Answers

B *Learner's own number and colour adjectives added to given nouns*

Sentences

Learners will be familiar with the term *sentence* from earlier in the course. They will have come across *short sentences* before. In instructions and rules, short sentences are used for clarity.

- Read the information box with the learners.
- Learners can work in pairs or individually.
- Highlight the differences and similarities between instruction sentences and rules.

Activity A: The learners read the instructions. They then order and rewrite the instructions.

Answers

A *Example answers:*
1 Plug the television into the wall.
2 Press the green button at the top of the remote control to turn the television on.
3 Press the red button on the remote control to turn the television off.

Activity B: The learners read the rules. They then rewrite the rules.

Answers

B *Example answers:*

Don't have water near a television.

Don't lose the television handset.

Let's practise

This section allows you to model the required writing outcome with input from the learners.

Before writing

- Ask the learners what they can remember about how to write instructions and rules.

- Explain that they have a picture of a machine that can make a variety of drinks. It is their job to write instructions and rules for how to use it.

- Discuss the picture with the learners. Encourage them to look carefully at it.

- Always encourage them to talk about what they are going to write.

- Explain that they are going to begin their planning by writing a number of imperative verbs that they might use in their instructions.

- Give them examples of long-winded instructions and compare them with short and simple ones. Ask the learners which instructions are easier to follow.

- Remind them that their instructions need to be numbered and as simple and straightforward as possible.

Shared writing activity

- Organise the learners into small groups or pairs. They are going to discuss the answers to the questions.

- Ask the learners to include, if appropriate, number, order and colour adjectives in their instructions.

- Give them opportunities to discuss what they have written, either with you or with their peers.

- They can do the activity individually, in pairs or in groups.

- When the instructions and rules are complete, ask the learners to read through the Writer's Toolbox, correcting any mistakes or omissions in their work.

- Share some of the learners' instructions with the class. Encourage some of the learners to read their instructions and rules to the rest of the group or class. Can they make any improvements?

- More able learners could discuss further instructions that might be added.

Let's write

The learners are required to produce instructions and rules independently for their own invention. Encourage them to share their work in progress with you so that, through discussion, they can improve their work.

Before writing

- Remind the learners of the details they discussed about writing instructions and rules in the Let's practise section.

- Read through the writing activity with the learners.

Independent writing activity

- This section is designed for learners to work independently, putting into practice what they have learned in the unit.

- The planning and writing should be done independently, either in class or for homework.

- If, however, you feel further support is needed, encourage learners to share their work in progress with you so that, through discussion, they can improve their drafts.

- Remind learners to use the Writer's Toolbox to correct mistakes and improve their work.

- Encourage them to keep their instructions and rules simple.

- Discuss the Writer's Toolbox. This provides an easy-to-use checklist to follow while they write.

- Ask them to write their instructions and rules carefully and neatly.

- They can use resource sheet 2 as the scaffolding for the first draft, before they copy it neatly.

- Help the learners with spellings if necessary.

Marking criteria

Technical aspects – 10 marks
Look for use of: • imperative verbs • short sentences • the correct layout • colour, number or order adjectives.
Content – 10 marks
Look for correct use of: • relevant instructions that progress in small steps • clear, simple instructions that are numbered • rules that are short and to the point.

After writing

- Read through the completed instructions and rules with the learners. Encourage them to share them and their invention designs with others.
- Within small groups, discuss where potential improvements can be made to some instructions or rules.

Plenary

- Display the learners' pictures of their inventions alongside their instructions and rules.
- Discuss with the learners other situations in which instructions are important (for example, for a game, working equipment, getting from one place to another, etc.).
- Ask the learners to bring in other examples of instructions and display them.

Resource sheets

The resource sheets for Unit 5 provide practice and reinforcement for:

1 imperative verbs
2 writing instructions and rules.

Resource sheet 1: Writing instructions and rules: imperative verbs

Resource sheet 1 covers the identification of imperative verbs. It asks learners to write given imperative verbs into sentences and write a sentence using an imperative verb of their choice. They can do this as homework or as further practice during class time.

Answers

A 1 (Stop) before you cross a road.
   2 (Look) carefully at the directions.
   3 (Watch) the time.
   4 (Catch) the ball before it lands on the ground.
   5 (Turn) the steering wheel so the car moves straight ahead.

B *Learner's own sentences using five given imperative verbs*

C *Learner's own sentence with an imperative verb of their choice*

Resource sheet 2: Writing instructions and rules

Resource sheet 2 provides a template for the Let's write activity. It can be used for the learners' first draft, or final draft for those who need support with the layout of their instructions and rules.

Assessment

The assessment sheet for this unit, 'Instructions: writing instructions and rules', is on page 103 of Learner's Book 3. It asks learners to write instructions and rules for a given invention.

- Read the prompts with learners to ensure they have understood the writing task and the thought they need to put in to it.
- Encourage them to spend some time planning, i.e. thinking about the important instructions and rules they need to include.
- Before they write their first draft, read through the Writer's Toolbox with them to remind them what they need to include in their instructions and rules.
- After they have produced a first draft, they should go back to the toolbox and tick the 'tools' they have used.
- Encourage learners to do further work on their draft to include more 'tools'.
- They should then produce a final copy.
- Use the marking criteria above.

Unit 6: Writing to persuade: posters and leaflets

Learner's Book unit focus

This unit looks at the category of **writing to persuade**, in the form of **posters** and **leaflets**.

Progress table for Stage 3: Unit 6					
Category: Writing to persuade					
Writing outcome: Posters and leaflets					
Posters and leaflets surround us in our daily lives. They are often carefully crafted to persuade readers to buy or join something or visit somewhere. Persuasion is an attempt to alter the way a person thinks. Posters and leaflets use persuasive language and attractive layouts to grab the readers' attention. Rhymes, alliteration and quotations can also be used when persuading the reader and these are looked at in Stage 4 Unit 7 and Stage 5 Unit 4.					
Stage 1	**Stage 2**	**Stage 3**	**Stage 4**	**Stage 5**	**Stage 6**
		• posters • leaflets	• advertisements	• leaflets	• film/book review
Cambridge Global English link: Stage 3: Unit 6: Dinosaurs **Cambridge Primary English link:** Stage 3: Unit 8: Wonderful world					

Resource list

- A variety of posters and leaflets advertising different things
- Large sheets of plain paper.

Unit teaching plan

Warm up

- Discuss posters with the learners. Ask:
  - *Where have you seen posters?*
  - *Why are the posters there?*
  - *What are the posters telling you about?*
  - *Which posters do you remember the best?*
  - *Are the posters trying to persuade you to do or buy something?*
- Have a variety of posters to show the learners.
- Let the learners discuss which posters they like/find most persuasive/don't like.
- Repeat these activities with leaflets.

Let's read

'Dinosaurs' Den' is an example of a poster and leaflet advertising a new play area.

- The poster and leaflet can be read:
  - by you to the class
  - by learners to the class
  - individually in silence.
- Elicit/explain the meaning of any unfamiliar vocabulary, for example:
  - *brand-new*: completely new
  - *series*: a number of things coming one after another
  - *if you dare*: if you have the courage, are brave enough.
- You are in the best position to determine the vocabulary that will be unfamiliar to the learners.

Plenary

- Discuss with the learners whether they would be persuaded by the poster to go to Dinosaurs' Den.

— *What areas would you enjoy the most?*

— *What would you not enjoy?*

- Encourage learners to give reasons.

Let's talk

This section asks the learners questions that:

- give them a greater understanding of the text
- focus on the specific writing activity covered in the unit.

Activity A: This section looks in detail at the poster.

Answers

A *Example answers:*

1 People use posters to let others know about things they can buy, places they can go to or things they can do.

2 *Learner's own opinions on who would like the poster more: adults or children.*

3 The pictures show children having fun to encourage others to go to a place that is fun and which children enjoy.

4 *Learner's own responses on whether they have ever looked at a poster and been persuaded to go somewhere*

Activity B: This section looks in detail at the leaflet.

Answers

B *Example answers:*

1 The leaflet is about a new dinosaur play area.

2 Children of all ages will enjoy the play area.

3 Climb on, get a fright from, ride on and watch dinosaurs

4 The Dangerous Dinosaur Den might be a little scary.

5 You will find the cuddly dinosaurs in the soft play area.

6 If you want a dinosaur snack you go to the café and picnic area.

Activity C: This section draws learners' attention to features of posters and leaflets.

Answers

C *Example answers:*

1 A poster gives the basic information about something in an attractive way. Leaflets tend to give more information than posters, but they still aim to inform and persuade.

2 A catchy title is important to encourage people to read more.

3 For example: new, exciting (dinosaur play area), slippery (slide), Dangerous (Dinosaur Den)

4 Pictures are used so people can see what it might be like and imagine the fun they could have.

5 The poster and leaflet include a web address so people can access more information, for example, where it is, how much it costs, what hours it is open, etc.

Let's learn

This section provides learners with the 'tools' they need. It covers the main features of grammar, style and layout appropriate to the writing outcome. It:

- revises points learners have met earlier in the course
- introduces new work
- gives learners the opportunity to become familiar with particular features of the required writing, i.e. posters and leaflets
- gives learners the opportunity to practise what they have learned in focused activities before incorporating it into their free writing.

Adjectives

Learners will be familiar with the term *adjective* from earlier in the course.

Adjectives perform the same function in posters and leaflets, i.e. description, but the emphasis here is on *more interesting adjectives* that show what is being written about in the best possible light.

- Read the information box with the learners.
- Start a display board of interesting adjectives, so at a glance learners can see a bank of adjectives they could use in their own writing.

- Give them a noun and challenge them, in pairs, to come up with the most interesting adjective they can to describe it.

Activity A: The learners need to come up with adjectives to complete sentences. They can do this in pairs, with learners reporting back to the class.

Answers

A *Example answers:*
1 Come to the <u>exciting</u>, <u>daring</u> play area.
2 Ride on the <u>scary</u> dinosaur rides.
3 Buy some <u>delicious</u> dinosaur snacks.
4 Be careful as you walk around the <u>frightening</u> *Dinosaur Den*.
5 Slide down Rexus's <u>slippery</u>, <u>bumpy</u> tail.

Activity B: The learners work independently to write their own sentence about a dinosaur that includes two interesting adjectives.

Answers

B *Learner's own sentence about a dinosaur that includes two interesting adjectives*

Plenary
- Discuss learners' suggestions for Activity A.
- Share the learners' sentences in Activity B.

Conjunctions
Conjunctions were previously covered in Stage 2 Unit 4.

- Ask the learners:
  - *Who remembers what a joining word does?*
  - *What is another name for joining words?* [conjunctions]
  - *Who can name a conjunction?* [and, but, or, because]
- Discuss with the learners that other words can join sentences. Ask them if they can suggest any.
- Read the information box with the learners.
- Highlight the words that join the sentences and are to do with 'time', for example, *before*, *when*, *after*, *while*.
- Ask the learners, in pairs, to create further examples of sentences that use these 'time' conjunctions. Share their examples with the class.

Activity A: The learners identify the conjunctions in the sentences provided.

Answers

A 1 Some dinosaurs had wings, (but) they could not fly.
2 Scientists now believe birds are living relatives of dinosaurs (because) they believe small dinosaurs became birds.
3 The dinosaur hunters dug very carefully (after) one of them found a small bird-like fossil.
4 Dead creatures and plants become fossils (when) they are buried in mud for thousands of years.

Activities B and C: The learners write their own sentences using the words *before* and *after* as conjunctions.

Answers

B and C *Learner's own sentences using the given conjunctions.*

Sentences
This section reminds the learners about the different types of sentence that can be written.

- Revise the terms *capital letters*, *full stops*, *question marks* and *exclamation marks* with the learners.
- Ask the learners:
  - *What type of sentence ends with a full stop?* [a telling sentence]
  - *What type of sentence ends with a question mark?* [an asking sentence]
  - *What type of sentence ends with an exclamation mark?* [an exclamation]
- Ask the learners for examples of the different types of sentence.
- Read the information box with the learners.
- Highlight that sometimes telling sentences can end with an exclamation mark. Adding an exclamation mark allows expression in the written word (for example, compare 'Quick, we must go' with 'Quick, we must go!').

Activity A: The learners are asked to find an example of each type of sentence in the leaflet on page 59 of the Learner's Book.

Answers

A *Example answers:*

1   A question: What will you enjoy at Dinosaurs' Den?

2   A statement: You will be entertained for hours with this new, exciting dinosaur play area.

3   An exclamation: Walk through, if you dare, before you are caught by the dinosaurs!

Information

Learners will be familiar with the term *information* from earlier in the course.

- Read the information box with the learners.
- What other types of writing have they done that need information/facts?

Activity A: Learners are asked what other information would be useful to know if the website hadn't been provided. Learners can work in groups and report back to the class.

Answers

A *Example answers:*

telephone number, address, directions, cost, opening times, etc.

Layout

- Read the information box with the learners.
- Discuss the different aspects of layout with the learners.

Activity A: This section includes questions regarding the layout of the poster. Learners can work in pairs or small groups and report back to the class.

Answers

A 1   font size, colour, artwork

2   Green is the main colour, but other bright colours have been used.

3   The title is written in a large size and is yellow. The information is in black or white and smaller than the title. The different colours and sizes are used to stand out and help the reader notice information.

4   The pictures add interest and colour, allowing the reader to imagine being there.

Plenary

Ask the learners if they would change anything on the poster to make it look better and more appealing.

Let's practise

This section allows you to model the required writing outcome (advertisement) with input from the learners.

Before writing

- Ask the learners to summarise what they have learned about creating a poster.
- Explain that, together, you are going to create a poster about a new dinosaur book.
- Discuss each point in the Planning section with the learners.
- Help them make notes to answer the questions.
- Learners can work individually and use the notes when they come to make a rough drawing of the poster. Explain that they do not have to write every word in their rough drawing; just plan where the heading, text and illustrations will go. It is to give them a feel for what the poster will look like.

Shared writing activity

- Give each learner a large sheet of plain paper.
- The learners can use the notes and their rough layout to create their own poster under your supervision.
- Advise them to work in pencil at first to ensure everything they want in the poster will fit.
- They can then introduce colour when they are confident nothing will change.
- When the poster is complete, ask the learners to read through the Writer's Toolbox, correcting any mistakes or omissions in their work.

Plenary

Learners can make neat copies of their posters for display.

Let's write

The learners are asked to create a short leaflet for a film on dinosaurs. The learners are given:

- prompts to help them focus on the writing features
- a space to make a rough layout
- a Writer's Toolbox to help them edit/proofread their work.

Before writing

- Read through the writing activity with the learners.
- Allow time for learners to ask questions so they fully understand what is required.
- Highlight the differences between posters and leaflets. Leaflets give more information than posters.
- Encourage the learners to look back at the poster and leaflet on pages 58 and 59 of the Learner's Book.

Independent writing activity

- This section is designed for learners to work independently, putting into practice what they have learned in the unit.
- They should do the planning and writing independently, either in class or for homework.
- If, however, you feel further support is needed, encourage learners to share their work in progress with you so that, through discussion, they can improve their drafts.
- Remind learners to use the Writer's Toolbox to correct mistakes and improve their work. Resource sheet 2 provides further guidance on what the learners might write on their leaflet.

After writing

Encourage the learners to share their leaflets with others.

Marking criteria

Technical aspects – 10 marks
Look for correct use of:
• interesting adjectives
• information.
Content – 10 marks
• Does the message of the poster or leaflet stand out?
• Is the poster or leaflet attractive?
• Are the picture(s) relevant?
• Does the poster or leaflet give useful information?
Award a higher mark if the learner has:
• created an attractive poster or leaflet with careful thought about the vocabulary used to persuade the reader to watch the film.

Plenary

- Discuss the different leaflets. Encourage the learners to discuss what they might improve.
- Display the finished leaflets around the classroom.

Resource sheets

The resource sheets for Unit 6 provide differentiation for the writing outcome in this unit as well as further practice on adjectives.

1 A resource sheet on adjectives.
2 A resource sheet on planning the writing for a leaflet.

Resource sheet 1: Posters and leaflets: adjectives

Resource sheet 1 covers further practice on writing and using adjectives in sentences.

- Read through the resource sheet with the learners so they fully understand what is expected of them.
- Carefully read the information box with the learners.
- Encourage them to write their adjectives carefully and neatly.
- Encourage them to read the sentences they have written carefully.
- They can work in pairs or individually on this activity.
- This resource sheet is suitable as a homework task.
- Check through the learners' answers to be sure they fully understand adjectives.

Resource sheet 2: Posters and leaflets: planning the writing for a leaflet

Resource sheet 2 provides the learners with questions that will help prompt what they write on their leaflet.

- This resource sheet could be used to support those learners who find the Let's write section challenging.
- It would also be appropriate to send home as homework, so the learners come back into school prepared for the Let's write task.
- Help them with vocabulary they might want to use.
- Encourage them to work thoughtfully.

Assessment

The assessment sheet for this unit, 'Writing to persuade: posters and leaflets', is on page 104 of Learner's Book 3.

- Learners are given:
    - information about caves where a dinosaur fossil has been found
    - instructions to name the cave tour
    - instructions to think about what they might write on the poster or leaflet to persuade people to go on the tour
    - a Writer's Toolbox of grammar and style features to include.
- Read the scenario with the learners to ensure they have understood the writing task.
- Encourage them to spend some time planning.
- Before the learners write their first draft, read through the Writer's Toolbox with them to remind them what they need to include in their poster or leaflet.
- After they have produced a first draft, they should go back to the Writer's Toolbox and tick the 'tools' they have used.
- Encourage them to do further work on their draft to include more 'tools'.
- They should then produce a final copy.
- Use the marking criteria on page 131 of this Teacher's Resource.

Unit 7: Narrative writing: play scripts

Learner's Book unit focus

This unit continues the category of **narrative writing** by introducing **play scripts**.

Progress table for Stage 3: Unit 7

Category: Narrative writing

Writing outcome: Play scripts

A play script contains:

- a list of characters
- a description of the scene where the action takes place
- the dialogue spoken by the actors
- stage directions indicating tone of voice and actions.

Some short plays can be one scene. Longer plays can be divided into acts that each have several scenes. A scene change usually occurs when the action of the play has moved location, or some time has passed.

Stage 1	Stage 2	Stage 3	Stage 4	Stage 5	Stage 6

		• prose into play script	• play scenes
			  – plot
			  – setting
			  – characters
				• writing a play script with two scenes	• prose into play script

Cambridge Global English link:	Stage 3: Unit 7: Puzzles and codes
Cambridge Primary English link:	Stage 3: Unit 3: See, hear, feel, enjoy

Resource list

Examples of simple play scripts.

Unit teaching plan

Warm up

- Explain to learners that they are going to read a play script called *The Code of the Trees*.
- Ask the learners about their experience of plays:
  - *What do they understand by the term 'a play'?*
  - *Have they been to a play?*
  - *Where are plays often watched?*
  - *Have they acted in a play?*

Let's read

The text is an example of a play script.

- The play can be read:
  - by you to the class
  - by learners to the class
  - individually in silence.

- Elicit/explain the meaning of any unfamiliar vocabulary, for example:
  - *glances*: quickly looks at
  - *ridiculous*: silly/unreasonable
- You are in the best position to determine the vocabulary that will be unfamiliar to the learners.
- Ask the learners to look carefully at the layout of the play script.

Plenary

With guidance, in groups of three, the learners can practise and perform the play.

Let's talk

This section asks the learners questions that:

- give them a greater understanding of the text
- focus on the specific writing activity covered in the unit.

Activity A: This section ensures the learners have interpreted the play script correctly.

Answers

A *Example answers:*

1 The children are among some trees.
2 The children are looking for the next clue.
3 Mo finds the red book.
4 The numbers are carved into the tree trunks.
5 The clue is solved by linking the numbers on the trees with the ordered letters in the alphabet.

Activity B: This section focuses the learners on the characters and the roles they play.

Answers

B *Example answers:*

1 Mo, Anil, Ama
2 Anil finds the numbers on the trees.
3 Mo gets frustrated when they can't solve the clue.
4 Ama solves the clue.

Activity C: This section is to draw learners' attention to features of the play script. Point out the bracketed, italic words and explain that these are *stage directions*.

Answers

C *Example answers:*

1 You know where the play is taking place because the beginning of the play script introduces what is happening and where it is happening.
2 It is useful to know who the characters are so you can get the right number of people when preparing for the play.
3 The character name is written on the left-hand side of the script, next to the words they say.
4 The words in italics are the stage directions, detailing how things are said, where they are said, etc.

Let's learn

This section provides learners with the 'tools' they need. It covers the main features of grammar, style and layout appropriate to the writing outcome. It:

- revises points learners have met earlier in the course
- introduces new work
- gives learners the opportunity to become familiar with particular features of the required writing, in this case play scripts
- gives learners the opportunity to practise what they have learned in focused activities before incorporating it into their free writing.

Layout of play scripts

- Read the information box with the learners.
- Go through the list, ensuring learners are comfortable with the terminology.
- Learners can work individually or in pairs.

Activity A: This section asks the learner to add the missing labels to complete the play script.

Answers

A From top to bottom, the labels are:

title
characters
scene information
actors' words
stage directions
actors' words

Dialogue in play scripts

- Revise/introduce the term *dialogue* (a conversation between two or more people).
- Ask the learners how they know when someone is speaking in a story. Spoken words are in speech marks with *said* and [character's name].
- Read the information box with the learners.
- Ask learners to point out the differences on the page between a character speaking in a story and a character speaking in a play.
- These activities can be done in class or as homework.

Activity A: This section asks the learner to identify who has said what in the play script.

Answers

A 1 Ama   2 Anil   3 Anil   4 Ama

Activity B: This section asks the learner to correctly lay out the play script.

Answers

B **Anil:** Do you think we go this way?

Mo: Yes I do.

Ama: I'm not sure. The map looks confusing!

Anil: I agree but shall we try it anyway?

Adverbs

- Read the information box with the learners.
- Walk across the room very slowly. Ask:
  - *How am I walking?* [slowly]
- Talk loudly:
  - *How am I speaking?* [loudly]
- Ask learners to supply the adverbs from these adjectives to extend their vocabulary:
  - bright [brightly]   sharp [sharply]
    tight [tightly]
- Can the learners suggest other interesting adverbs of their own?
- Keep an adverb book in the classroom for learners to write in interesting adverbs that they discover in their reading.
- Resource sheet 1 provides further practice on adverbs for more able learners. They can complete it in class or take it home as homework.

Activity A: This section asks the learner to complete word sums.

Answers

A	**1**	clear	**2**	neat	**3**	serious
	4	patient	**5**	honest	**6**	tuneful

Activity B: This section asks the learner to add an adverb before or after each given verb.

Answers

B *Learner's own adverbs, for example:*

1	peacefully	**2**	quickly
3	slowly	**4**	excitedly
5	gently	**6**	sternly
7	quietly	**8**	messily

Activity C: This section asks the learner to think of an adverb to tell us more about 'how' each scenario happens.

Answers

C *Learner's own adverbs, for example:*

1	seriously	**2**	quickly
3	impatiently	**4**	grumpily

Let's practise

This section allows you to model the required writing outcome with input from the learners.

Before writing

- Ask the learners to summarise what happened in the play script on pages 68 and 69.
- Always encourage the learners to talk about what they are going to write. Discussing things can help the learners to organise their thoughts.
- Read through the information with the learners. It continues the search for the hidden treasure with Mo, Ama and Anil.
- Explain that together you are going to write the next part of the play.

Shared writing activity

- Discuss each question in turn with the learners, making notes on the majority decisions.
- Learners can use the notes to continue the play under your supervision.
- When the writing is complete, ask the learners to read through the Writer's Toolbox, correcting any mistakes or omissions in their work.

Let's write

- The learners are asked to write the ending to the play.
- A summary of what happens is given: the children hunt all around the bridge and can't find the treasure anywhere, then suddenly they notice something under the bridge, just below the water.
- The learners are given:
  - questions to help them focus on the dialogue and stage directions
  - a Writer's Toolbox to help them edit/ proofread their work.
- Resource sheet 2 provides the structure for the play script for those learners who need the support. More able learners can write their section of the play on a blank piece of paper.

Before writing

- Read through the writing activity with the learners.
- Allow time for learners to ask questions so they fully understand what is required.

Independent writing activity

- This section is designed for learners to work independently, putting into practice what they have learned in the unit.
- They should do the planning and writing independently, either in class or for homework.
- If, however, you feel further support is needed, encourage learners to share their work in progress with you so that, through discussion, they can improve their drafts.
- Remind the learners to use the Writer's Toolbox to correct mistakes and improve their work.

Marking criteria

Technical aspects – 10 marks
Look for correct use of:
• a short description of where the scene is set
• a character list
• correct layout, with names on the left, dialogue on the right, stage directions in brackets.

Content – 10 marks
Look for correct use of:
• dialogue that flows
• appropriate stage directions reflecting what is said and what the children are doing.

After writing

Read through the completed plays, asking some learners to read them aloud.

Plenary

- Discuss with the learners the different ways the plays finished. Did anyone introduce a new character?
- Ask the learners what would happen if the play continued.
- Give the learners, in groups of three, the opportunity to practise and perform the parts of the play they wrote in the Let's practise and Let's write activities.

Resource sheets

The resource sheets for Unit 7 provide practice and reinforcement for:

1. adverbs
2. the layout of a play.

Resource sheet 1: Play scripts: adverbs

Resource sheet 1 covers further practice using adverbs.

- Read through the resource sheet with the learners so they fully understand what is expected of them.
- Revise the information on adverbs.
- When completed, read through the sentences in Activity C with the learners to ensure they have correctly inserted an adverb. Some learners may need more support than others with this activity.

Resource sheet 2: Play scripts: the layout of a play

Resource sheet 2 covers how to lay out a play. It provides scaffolding for the correct way to lay out a play. You could use it in conjunction with the Let's practise section to guide the learners. Explain the layout and allow time for learners to ask questions so they fully understand what they should write where.

Assessment

The assessment sheet for this unit, 'Narrative writing: play scripts', is on page 105 of Learner's Book 3.

- Learners are given:
  - the scenario
  - the number of characters
  - what the characters are talking about.
- Read the scenario box with the learners to ensure they have understood the writing task.
- Encourage them to spend some time planning, for example, thinking about what the characters will say.
- Before the learners write their first draft, read through the Writer's Toolbox with them to remind them what they need to include in their play script.
- After they have produced a first draft, they should go back to the Writer's Toolbox and tick the 'tools' they have used.
- Encourage them to do further work on their draft to include more 'tools'.
- They should then produce a final copy.
- Use the marking criteria on this page.

Unit 8: Alphabetic texts: a glossary

Learner's Book unit focus

This unit introduces **glossaries** while revisiting **dictionaries** at a more advanced level than that previously covered.

Progress table for Stage 3: Unit 8					
Category: Factual writing					
Writing outcome: A glossary					
There are a number of alphabetic texts the learners will be familiar with. Stage 1: Unit 6 introduced a simple dictionary. This unit looks at a more sophisticated dictionary that links the information needed in a dictionary with that provided in a glossary.					
Stage 1	**Stage 2**	**Stage 3**	**Stage 4**	**Stage 5**	**Stage 6**
• alphabetic texts (simple dictionary)		• alphabetic texts (dictionary, glossary)			
Cambridge Global English link: Stage 3: Unit 8: Our amazing body					
Cambridge Primary English links: Stage 3: Unit 8: Let's have a party! Stage 3: Unit 8: Wonderful world					

Resource list

A variety of dictionaries, and examples of glossaries and indexes.

Unit teaching plan

Warm up

- Recite the alphabet with the learners.
- Ask the learners questions about the alphabet. Ask:
  - *How many letters are in the alphabet?*
  - *What are the vowel letters?*
  - *What is a consonant?*
- Hold up a dictionary and ask the learners if they know what it is and what it can be used for.

Let's read

This unit starts with a more advanced dictionary page than that found in Stage 1 Unit 6. It then introduces an example of a glossary based on a book entitled *Our Amazing Body*.

- The dictionary page and glossary can be read:
  - by you to the class
  - by learners to the class
  - individually in silence.

- Elicit/explain the meaning of any unfamiliar vocabulary, though most words are detailed in the dictionary page or glossary.
- You are in the best position to determine the vocabulary that will be unfamiliar to the learners.
- Introduce the term *alphabetical order*.
- Work through the information carefully. Make sure all learners are able to appreciate why words are found in the order they are in dictionaries and glossaries.
- Discuss in detail how the dictionary and glossary pages are laid out.
- Discuss the role of a dictionary and compare it with the role of a glossary.
- Discuss the importance of spelling the words correctly.

Plenary

- Look at a dictionary with small groups of learners. Do some exercises that will familiarise them with the dictionary (for example, ask them to find a word in the dictionary to tell the rest of the group about). Ask them to find specific words on a page.

- Discuss other texts that are also written in alphabetical order (for example, indexes and address books).

Let's talk

This section asks the learners questions that:

- give them a greater understanding of the text
- focus on the specific writing activity covered in the unit.

Activity A: This section is to ensure learners appreciate the layout and content of a dictionary page.

Answers

A 1 s and t   2 small, soft   3 six nouns
   4 soft   5 soft and ticket

Activity B: This section is to ensure learners appreciate the layout and content of a glossary page.

Answers

B 1 the body
   2 Ribs protect the heart and lungs.
   3 the lungs
   4 Glossaries help to explain words readers might not be familiar with.
   5 eyes and heart

Activity C: This section compares the dictionary and glossary pages.

Answers

C 1 The dictionary page has more information about the words than the glossary.
   2 A glossary has words that are on a theme linked to a subject; dictionaries have every word.
   3 Alphabetical order is the order in which the letters are found in the alphabet. Putting words in alphabetical order helps readers to access them quickly and easily.

Let's learn

This section provides learners with the 'tools' they need. It covers the main features of grammar, style and layout appropriate to the writing outcome. It:

- revises points learners have met earlier in the course
- introduces new work

- gives learners the opportunity to become familiar with particular features of the required writing, in this case glossaries
- gives learners the opportunity to practise what they have learned in focused activities before incorporating it into their free writing.

Alphabetical order

Alphabetical order is the order in which the letters are placed in the alphabet.

- Place three items in front of a group and ask them to rearrange them in alphabetical order, according to their first letter, as quickly as possible.
- Read the information box with the learners.
- Practise ordering words that start with the same letter. Encourage the learners to look at the second and third letters in the word to help them order them correctly.
- Encourage the learners, individually, to order the given letters. More able learners will be able to do this without referring to the alphabet provided.
- Encourage the learners to work through the exercises individually or, if individuals need extra support, in pairs.
- Remind the learners that when they order words alphabetically they need to use the first letter of the words.
- They can do Activity C as a challenge in pairs, one learner writing six body words and their partner ordering them alphabetically.
- Resource sheet 1 provides further support and practice for those learners who need it.

Activity A: The learners are asked to order random letters alphabetically.

Answers

A 1 a d k m r z   2 b k l q s x
   3 a c h i p t

Activity B: The learners are required to order words alphabetically, some using the first letter, others the second and third letters in the words.

Answers

B 1 arm   teeth   waist
   2 bone   head   skeleton
   3 shoulder   spine   stomach
   4 shin   skin   skull
   5 back   body   brain
   6 toenail   tongue   tooth

Activity C: Finally, the learners are asked to choose six words and write them in alphabetical order.

Answers

C **1** *Six of the learner's own words for body parts*
   2 *Learner's six words for body parts written in alphabetical order*

Parts of speech

- Read the information box with the learners.
- Discuss other parts of speech they know (for example, adverbs).
- Encourage the learners to work through the exercises individually or, if individuals need extra support, in pairs.
- Ask the learners for further examples of words that can be found in more than one column of the table, for example, rock can be either a verb (*to rock*) or a noun (*a rock*).

Activity A: The learners are asked to write the given words (nouns, verbs or adjectives) into the correct column(s) of the table.

Answers

A **nouns:** hand, stomach, arm, elbow, nose, fingers (also smell)
   verbs: push, chew, grab, smell, hold, write (also hand)
   adjectives: long, soft, smooth, shiny, slippery, tall

Activity B: The learners are asked to fill the gaps in the table with their own nouns, verbs or adjectives.

Answers

B *Further words of learner's own choice, added to gaps in the table*

Definitions

- Read the information box with the learners.
- Highlight the differences between the two definitions provided in the information box.
- The learners can work independently or in pairs on these activities.
- If learners need added support, give them a long, wordy definition of a word and ask them to cut it down to a short and clear definition.

Activity A: The learners are asked to write definitions for some given words.

Activity B: The learners are asked to rewrite the definitions from Activity A using no more than seven words.

Answers

A and B *The learner's own definitions for the words* arm, foot *and* smell. *Their rewritten definitions should use no more than seven words each.*

Let's practise

This section allows you to model the required writing outcome with input from the learners.

Before writing

- Look again at the dictionary and glossary pages at the beginning of the unit.
- Ask the learners to summarise what they have learned about glossaries.
- Explain that, together, you are going to create a glossary page for a book on sport.
- Discuss each point in the Planning section with the learners.
- Help them make notes to answer the questions.
- Highlight while working through the given activities that the learners are eventually going to write their own glossary.

Shared writing activity

- Organise the learners into pairs. Explain that they can discuss each activity with their partner, though the final glossary page will be their own work.
- Carefully work through each activity with the learners, clearly illustrating how each one builds towards the final outcome.
- Talk to them about writing a sentence for each word. They need to get the essence of the word in one sentence. They may well need support with this, either from you or from their peers.
- Resource sheet 2 provides the structure for the glossary.
- When the learners have completed their glossary components, ask them to read through the Writer's Toolbox, correcting any mistakes or omissions in their work.

Plenary

Learners can compare the words they have included in their glossaries. Did everyone choose the same words? Did the words chosen depend on which sports the learners enjoy the most?

Let's write

The learners are asked to create a glossary for a book of their choice. The learners are given:

- prompts to help them focus on the writing features
- a Writer's Toolbox to help them edit/proofread their work.

Before writing

- Read through the writing activity with the learners.
- Allow time for them to ask questions so they fully understand what is required.

Independent writing activity

- This section is designed for learners to work independently, putting into practice what they have learned in the unit.
- They should do the planning and writing independently, either in class or for homework.
- If, however, you feel they need further support, encourage learners to share their work in progress with you so that, through discussion, they can improve their drafts.
- Remind them to use the Writer's Toolbox to correct mistakes and improve their work.
- Resource sheet 2 provides the structure for the learners' glossary.

Marking criteria

Technical aspects – 10 marks
Look for correct use of:
• words written in alphabetical order
• words spelled correctly.
Content – 10 marks
Look for correct use of:
• appropriately chosen words that relate to the chosen subject
• short, clear definitions.

After writing

Read through the completed glossaries with the learners. Encourage them to share their glossaries with others.

Plenary

Discuss what problems would occur if the entries in a glossary were not in alphabetical order.

Resource sheets

The resource sheets for Unit 8 provide differentiation for the writing outcome in this unit as well as further practice.

1 A resource sheet on alphabetical order.
2 A resource sheet on writing a glossary.

Resource sheet 1: A glossary: alphabetical order

Resource sheet 1 covers further practice on alphabetical order.

- Read through the resource sheet with the learners so they fully understand what is expected of them.
- Revise the alphabet.
- Encourage the learners to think carefully about the order in which the letters are found in the alphabet.
- When completed, check the order of the words in Activity C with each learner to ensure they are correct. Some learners may need more support with this activity than others.
- To extend the activity, give the learners five words instead of three to order alphabetically.

Answers

A a b c d e f g h i j k l m n o p q r s t u v w x y z

B 1 lake leaf lizard

2 sea square star

3 hand horse hug

4 berry bottle bridge

C *Further words of learner's choice for the three subjects listed, written in alphabetical order*

Resource sheet 2: Writing a glossary

Resource sheet 2 provides a framework for the practice and writing activities in the Learner's Book.

- Discuss the importance of working with care and consideration so the words are put correctly in alphabetical order and the sentences are clear.
- Help them with vocabulary they might want to use.

Assessment

The assessment sheet for this unit, 'Alphabetic texts: a glossary', is on page 106 of Learner's Book 3. Learners are given the title of a non-fiction book for which they need to write a glossary.

- Read the information with the learners to ensure they have understood the writing task.
- Encourage them to spend some time planning, thinking about which words will be most suitable.
- Before the learners write their first draft, read through the Writer's Toolbox with them to remind them what they need to include in their glossary.
- After they have produced a first draft, learners should go back to the Writer's Toolbox and tick the 'tools' they have used.
- Encourage learners to do further work on their draft to include more 'tools'.
- They should then produce a final copy.
- Use the marking criteria on page 140 of this Teacher's Resource.

Unit 9: Narrative writing: story settings and endings

Learner's Book unit focus

This unit consolidates and extends the work done on **narrative story writing** in the previous stages. This unit looks closely at the **description of a setting used to open a story** and **how stories might end**.

Progress table for Stage 3: Unit 9						
Category: Narrative writing						
Writing outcome: Story settings and endings						
Story settings set the scene for a story or part of a story. They require description that builds a picture in the reader's mind of the scene in which the story is set. Story endings can vary; however, they must be interesting and tie up any loose ends.						
Stage 1	**Stage 2**	**Stage 3**	**Stage 4**	**Stage 5**	**Stage 6**

• captions
 • sentences
	• sequencing narrative
	 • speech bubbles
	 • characters
	 • setting
		• dialogue
		 • plot: beginning/ middle/end
		 • story openings
		 • continuing a story/story endings
			• characters
			   – physical appearance
			   – personality
				• stories teaching lessons	• story endings

Cambridge Global English link: Stage 3: Unit 9: Big and little **Cambridge Primary English link:** Stage 3: Unit 1: Ordinary days						

Unit teaching plan

Warm up

- Remind the learners of previous work they have done on the beginning, middle and end of stories.
- Ask the learners:
  - *Who knows what a story setting is?*
  - *Why is the story setting important?*
- Ask them to think about a well-known story (selected by you). Ask:
  - *What is the setting of the story?*
  - *What picture does the setting conjure up in your mind?*
  - *How does the story end?*
  - *How else could this story end?*
- Introduce the story.
  - *We are now going to read a story called 'Too small… too big!' Listen carefully.*

Let's read

The extract is an example of a setting, in this case used as the opening of a story. The story is unfinished, encouraging the learners to think of possible story endings.

- The extract can be read:
  - by you to the class
  - by learners to the class
  - individually in silence.
- Elicit/explain the meaning of any unfamiliar vocabulary, for example:
  - *competitive*: competing against each other
  - *slow motion*: where action appears to happen at a slower rate
  - *slumped*: sunk heavily.
- You are in the best position to determine the vocabulary that will be unfamiliar to the learners.

Plenary

- Put the learners into pairs. Ask each pair to predict how the story ends:
  - *How do you think this story ends?*
- Discuss the layout of the conversations in the story, referring back to previous work in Unit 3. Highlight the positioning of speech marks and associated punctuation.
- Highlight where new paragraphs start.

Let's talk

This section asks the learners questions that:

- give them a greater understanding of the text
- focus on the specific writing activity covered in the unit.

Activity A: This section is to ensure learners have understood what they have read.

Answers

A *Example answers:*

1 The story opens by describing a busy school playground, with children playing and teachers watching.
2 The main characters are three friends: Tony, Seline and Sophie.
3 The story begins with the children playing catch with Tony's ball.
4 Seline and Sophie comfort Tony.
5 Seline and Tony's brother try to reach the ball.
6 Seline was too small; Tony's brother was too big.

Activity B: This section focuses the learners on the setting described.

Answers

B *Example answers:*

1 The story is set in a school playground.
2 This is a good way to start the story as it enables the reader to picture the surroundings in which the story is set.
3 The opening focuses on the senses of sight and hearing: it describes things that are seen and heard.
4 It might also have included the sense of smell.

Activity C: This section focuses the learners on what might happen at the end of the story.

Answers

C *Example answers:*

1 We don't know how the story ends.
2 *Learner's own predictions about what they think Tony's idea is*
3 *The learners state whether they think the three friends reach the ball.*
4 *The learners comment on what they think makes a good story ending.*

Let's learn

This section provides learners with the 'tools' they need. It covers the main features of grammar, style and layout appropriate to the writing outcome. It:

- revises points learners have met earlier in the course
- introduces new work
- gives learners the opportunity to become familiar with particular features of the required writing, in this case story endings
- gives learners the opportunity to practise what they have learned in focused activities, before incorporating it into their free writing.

Past tenses

- Read the information box with the learners.
- Learners should be familiar with the *past simple* and *past progressive* tenses.
- Use examples of regular verbs from the story for learners to put into different tenses, for example:

  to shout   *he shouts/he is shouting/he shouted/he was shouting/he will shout*

- Choose an irregular verb and repeat, for example:

  to take   *she takes/she is taking/she took/she was taking/she will take*

- Classify the verbs they note for Activity A as regular and irregular verbs.

Activity A: The learners copy examples of past tense verbs in the story.

Answers

A *Example answers:*

were running, were chatting, kicked, were playing, shouted, caught, threw, reached, smiled

Activity B: The learners are given verbs to use as past tense verbs in sentences of their own.

Answers

B *Learner's own three sentences in the past tense using the verbs provided*

Adjectives

- Read the information box with the learners.
- Ask the learners for examples of adjectives.
- Encourage them to be more creative with the adjectives they use.
- Check they have found every adjective in the paragraph provided.
- Encourage them to work through each exercise individually or in pairs.

Activity A: Learners identify adjectives in the opening paragraph of the story.

Answers

A The <u>school</u> playground was <u>busy</u>. <u>Hot</u> children were running, shouting, laughing and smiling. Teachers were chatting and sipping their <u>cold</u> drinks as they watched the <u>excited</u> children at playtime. Balls were being kicked back and forth in <u>competitive</u> games of football and cricket. <u>Other</u> groups of children were playing with skipping ropes or sitting in the <u>cool</u> corners of the playground quietly chatting and eating fruit.

Activity B: Learners write two adjectives they could use to describe the nouns provided.

Answers

B *Example answers:*
  1 the tree: bushy, leafy
  2 Tony's brother: tall, kind
  3 the fence: old, wooden

Story structure

- Read the information box with the learners.
- Remind them of previous work on the beginning, middle and end of stories covered in Stage 2 Unit 1.
- Ask them to detail the beginning, middle and end of a familiar story in note form.
- They can work in pairs and compare their answers.

- Discuss why this story structure is important.
- Encourage the learners to discuss with others what they think might happen at the end of the story. Encourage them to choose an unexpected ending for 'Too small… too big!' to make the story more interesting.

Activity A: The learners identify, in note form, the beginning and middle of 'Too small… too big!'

Answers

A *Example answers:*

  Beginning: Tony, Seline and Sophie play catch.

    Seline misses the ball.

    The ball gets stuck in a tree near the playground fence.

  Middle: Seline tries to climb up and get the ball; she is too small.

    They ask Tony's brother to try.

    He thinks he will break the fence because he is too big.

Activity B: The learners write in note form what they think happens at the end of the story.

Answers

B *Learner writes in note form what they think will happen at the end of the story*

Writing an opening

- Read the information box with the learners.
- Discuss what a setting describes.
- Discuss why using a setting as the opening of a story can be a good idea.
- Emphasise the importance of building a picture with words for the reader.

Activity A: The learners talk about the setting described in the story opening.

Answers

A 1 A school playground
  2 The children are running, shouting, laughing, smiling, playing with balls and skipping ropes, sitting, chatting and eating fruit.
  3 *Example answers:*
    Sounds: shouting, laughing, talking, calling, screaming
    Smells: teachers' drinks (for example, coffee), fruit being eaten (for example, banana)

Writing an ending

- Read the information box with the learners.
- It is important the learners appreciate that stories can end in many different ways. How a story ends is vital for ensuring the reader enjoys the story. A boring story can leave the reader feeling flat and uninterested, whereas a story that ends with something unexpected can leave the reader satisfied with what they have just read.
- Discuss the three types of story ending:
  - happy ending – when everything in the story reaches a conclusion and the outcome is happy
  - twist – when everything in the story reaches a conclusion but there is one unexpected surprise element
  - cliffhanger – when at least one element of the story remains unsolved.
- The learners can work in pairs to plan their story endings.

Activity A: The learners write three different endings to the story 'Too small… too big!', one reflecting a happy ending, one an ending with a twist and finally one with a cliffhanger.

Answers

A *Learner writes three different endings to the story 'Too small…too big!', one happy, one with a twist and one with a cliffhanger*

Let's practise

This section allows you to model the required writing outcome with input from the learners.

Before writing

- Read through the scenario provided with the learners. Explain that this is just a skeleton of a story and that they can adapt it in any way they would like.
- Always encourage them to talk about what they are going to write. Discussing things can help the learners to organise their thoughts.
- Encourage the learners, in their pairs, to discuss many different options.
- Explain that, together, you are going to write the opening setting and ending to the story.

Shared writing activity

- Discuss each question in turn with learners, making notes on the majority decisions.

- Remind the learners to use correct punctuation when writing, including the correct use of speech marks.
- They can then use the notes to write the setting and ending to the story under your supervision.
- When the learners have completed the writing, ask them to read through the Writer's Toolbox, correcting any mistakes or omissions in their work.

Let's write

The learners are asked to write the opening setting and ending of the story from the perspective of the cat. They are given:

- questions to help them focus on the opening setting and the beginning, middle and end of the story
- a Writer's Toolbox to help them edit/proofread their work.

Before writing

- Read through the writing activity with the learners.
- Allow time for learners to ask questions so they fully understand what is required.
- Remind the learners to use correct punctuation when writing, including the correct use of speech marks.

Independent writing activity

- This section is designed for learners to work independently, putting into practice what they have learned in the unit.
- They should do the planning and writing independently, either in class or for homework.
- If, however, you feel further support is needed, encourage learners to share their work in progress with you so that, through discussion, they can improve their drafts.
- Remind them to use the Writer's Toolbox to correct mistakes and improve their work.

Marking criteria

Technical aspects – 10 marks
Look for correct use of:
• verbs written in the past tense
• sentences written with correct punctuation, including the correct use of speech marks
• adjectives included to describe both the opening setting and story ending clearly.

Content – 10 marks
Look for correct use of:
• an opening setting that paints a picture for the reader
• an appropriate ending to the story, with either a happy ending, a twist or a cliffhanger.
Award a higher mark for:
• a story setting and ending that engage the reader.

After writing

Read through the completed story settings and story endings, asking some learners to read them aloud.

Plenary

- Discuss with the learners the different ways the story settings are described and the story ends.
- Ask the learners what might happen if the story was to continue.

Resource sheets

The resource sheets for Unit 9 provide practice and reinforcement for:

1 verb tenses
2 writing a story setting.

Resource sheet 1: Story settings and endings: verb tenses

Resource sheet 1 provides an extension activity that looks in more detail at verb tenses. This will help learners to recognise the tense in which verbs have been written. They can do it in class or as homework.

Answers

A

Verb family name	Past (simple) tense	Present (simple) tense	Future tense
to sleep	I slept	I sleep	I shall sleep
to run	he ran	he runs	he will run
to climb	we climbed	we climb	we shall climb
to eat	she ate	she eats	she will eat
to drink	I drank	I drink	I shall drink
to believe	he believed	he believes	he will believe

B 1 future   2 past   3 present
    4 past   5 future   6 past

Resource sheet 2: Story settings and endings: writing a story setting

The learners are given a picture stimulus. They are required to write about the setting they see, describing it in as much detail as possible.

Assessment

The assessment sheet for this unit, 'Narrative writing: story settings and endings', is on page 107 of Learner's Book 3. The learners are asked to write a story setting and story ending. They are provided with a scenario on which to base the story sections.

- Read the scenario box with learners to ensure they have understood the writing task.
- Encourage them to spend some time planning, thinking about what will happen in their story.
- Before they write their first draft, read through the Writer's Toolbox with the learners to remind them what they need to include in their story setting and story ending.
- After they have produced a first draft, they should go back to the Writer's Toolbox and tick the 'tools' they have used.
- Encourage them to do further work on their draft to include more 'tools'.
- They should then produce a final copy.
- Use the marking criteria on pages 145–146.

Stage 1: Unit 1: resource sheet 1
Writing words, lists and captions: write a list

Make a list of presents you would like for your next birthday.

Teacher's Resource Stage 1: Unit 1: resource sheet 1

Stage 1: Unit 1: resource sheet 2
Writing words, lists and captions: write captions

A Colour each of the things in the pictures.

B Then write a caption for each thing. You can use the colour words in the box below. Some you have seen before, some are new.

Word box

red	yellow	blue	green
brown	purple	orange	pink

1

_____

2

_____

3

_____

4

_____

5

_____

6

_____

7

_____

8

_____

Stage 1: Unit 1: resource sheet 3
Writing words, lists and captions: use naming and describing words

A Sort the naming and describing words in the box into the correct lists.

Word box

red	pen	book	green
cat	blue	hat	yellow

Naming words

_____

_____

_____

_____

_____

Describing words

_____

_____

_____

_____

_____

B Add two more words to each list.
   Make sure they are naming and describing words.

Teacher's Resource Stage 1: Unit 1: resource sheet 3

Stage 1: Unit 2: resource sheet 1
Special naming words and writing sentences

A Look very carefully at these sentences.
Copy the sentences.
Add all the missing capital letters and full stops.

1 the car is fast

_____

2 jess likes reading

_____

3 today tuhil is going to the park

_____

4 it is time to go

_____

B Write two sentences about this picture.

1 _____

2 _____

Stage 1: Unit 2: resource sheet 2
Writing names and simple sentences: write about your family

A Draw and colour a picture of someone in your family.

B Write three sentences about the person.

_____

_____

_____

Teacher's Resource Stage 1: Unit 2: resource sheet 2

Stage 1: Unit 3: resource sheet 1
Writing poems: rhyming words

A Draw a line to the rhyming words.

1 log   smell   dig

2 net   hose   dog

3 duck   spoon

4 nose   Sun
                                        jump

5 Moon   luck
                                              clock

6 bell   pet

**B Copy the four words in A that don't have a rhyming word.
Write a rhyming word for each one.**

1 _____   _____

2 _____   _____

3 _____   _____

4 _____   _____

**C Many words rhyme with *bat*.
Write as many rhyming words as you can.**

bat

Stage 1: Unit 3: resource sheet 2
Write a poem

Add the missing lines to the poem.
The last word in the line must rhyme with the word above.

Word box

on a mat	and listen to a band	and have fun
in a hut	and count to ten	

Having fun

I love to run

_____.

I love to hold a hen

_____.

I love to eat a nut

_____.

I love to stroke a cat

_____.

I love to stand in sand

_____.

Stage 1: Unit 4: resource sheet 1
Writing sentences: naming words and describing words

A **Read these sentences.**
Copy the naming words.
Copy the describing words.

    1 She has long hair.   Naming word: _____

                                          Describing word: _____

    2 They love the sandy beach.   Naming word: _____

                                          Describing word: _____

    3 He rides the fast horse.   Naming word: _____

                                          Describing word: _____

    4 I love the cold snow.   Naming word: _____

                                          Describing word: _____

B **Write three naming words.**
Write three describing words.

Naming words: _____ _____ _____

Describing words: _____ _____ _____

C **Write two sentences, each with a naming word and a describing word.**

    1 _____

    2 _____

Stage 1: Unit 4: resource sheet 2
Writing sentences: write about a friend

A Write phrases describing someone in your class.

_____   _____

_____   _____

_____   _____

_____   _____

B Write a description of the person.

_____

_____

_____

_____

_____

_____

C Ask someone to guess who the person is.

Teacher's Resource Stage 1: Unit 4: resource sheet 2

Stage 1: Unit 5: resource sheet 1
Writing labels and captions: more than one

Top Tip

Remember, if a word means *more than one* it is a *plural word*.

A Sort these words into the table.

Word box

kites	book	vans	cakes	bike
log	hands	desk	apples	spoon

one	more than one

B Write these words so they are plural words.

1 hat _____

2 farm _____

3 sock _____

4 clip _____

C Write a sentence using these plural words.

1 horses _____

2 cars _____

Teacher's Resource Stage 1: Unit 5: resource sheet 1

Stage 1: Unit 5: resource sheet 2
Writing labels and captions: write about a day out

Think about a day out you have had.

- **Did you go to a park?**   • **Did you go to a friend's house?**   • **Did you go to a zoo?**

A Draw four pictures showing things you did on your day out.

B Write a caption for each picture.

Teacher's Resource Stage 1: Unit 5: resource sheet 2

Stage 1: Unit 6: resource sheet 1
Alphabetic texts: alphabetical order

a b c d e f g h i j k l m n o p q r s t u v w x y z

A Copy the alphabet.

____ ____ ____ ____ ____ ____ ____ ____ ____ ____ ____ ____ ____

____ ____ ____ ____ ____ ____ ____ ____ ____ ____ ____ ____ ____

B Sort these letters into alphabetical order.

1 b a c ____ ____ ____   2 G V U ____ ____ ____

3 L P N ____ ____ ____   4 s o n ____ ____ ____

C Write three words on these subjects.
Each word must start with a different letter.
Now write the words in alphabetical order.

1 transport

_____ _____ _____

_____ _____ _____

2 animals

_____ _____ _____

_____ _____ _____

3 countries

_____ _____ _____

_____ _____ _____

Stage 1: Unit 6: resource sheet 2
Alphabetic texts: plan a dictionary page

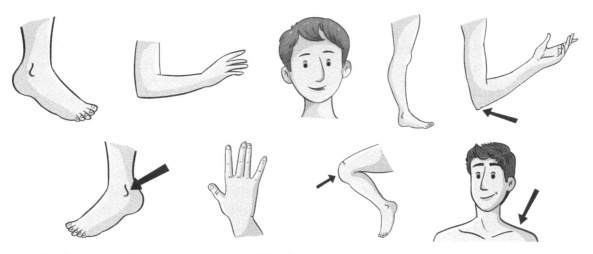

A Write four words that are parts of the human body.
Circle the first letter in each word.

_____ _____ _____ _____

B Circle the letters in the alphabet. This will help you write the words in the correct order.

a b c d e f g h i j k l m n o p q r s t u v w x y z

C Copy the words from Activity A in alphabetical order.
Write a sentence about each word.

_____

_____

_____

_____

_____

_____

_____

_____

Teacher's Resource Stage 1: Unit 6: resource sheet 2

Stage 1: Unit 6: resource sheet 3
Alphabetic texts: write a dictionary page

Write a dictionary page.
For each word:
A Neatly write the word.
B Draw a picture for the word.
C Write a sentence about the word.

Stage 1: Unit 7: resource sheet 1
Writing instructions and rules: write sentences and look for doing words

A Use these words to make a sentence. The first one has been done for you.

1 dog   walk

I walk my dog in the morning. _____

2 swim   sea

_____

3 run   school

_____

4 cake   cook

_____

5 play   game

_____

B Circle all the doing words (verbs) in Activity A.

C Write two of your own sentences. Underline the verb in each one.

1 _____

2 _____

Stage 1: Unit 7: resource sheet 2
Writing instructions and rules: write instructions

Top Tip

Remember, *instructions* need to be:
- numbered
- clearly written.

Think carefully about how you get from home to school.

Write instructions for your journey to school.
Start at home.
Finish at school.

_____

_____

_____

_____

_____

_____

_____

_____

_____

Stage 1: Unit 7: resource sheet 3
Writing instructions and rules: write rules

Top Tip

Remember, *rules* give us important information we need to know. They need to be:
- short
- easily understood.

You have to be very careful when crossing a road.

Write four rules you need to remember when crossing a road safely.

1 _____

_____

2 _____

_____

3 _____

_____

4 _____

_____

Teacher's Resource Stage 1: Unit 7: resource sheet 3

Stage 1: Unit 8: resource sheet 1
Writing recounts: doing words and describing words

Read the recount carefully.
Underline the doing words.
Circle the describing words.

A trip to Ben's house

I went to Ben's house today.

We walked to his house after school.

I didn't like the walk. It was a long walk.

When we got there we had a cold drink and some cake.

Then we played with Ben's new kitten.

I loved playing with her.

She chased the string.

After tea we watched a good game of football.

Then I went home.

Stage 1: Unit 8: resource sheet 2
Writing recounts: rewrite a recount

A Read the recount carefully.

Out with my dad

dad and I watch_____ a football match

it was a _____ game

we had a _____ drink and some food

then we walk_____ home

I really enjoy_____ the day

B Copy the recount.
Add the missing capital letters and full stops.
Write the doing words in the past tense.
Add some describing words.

Out with my dad

_____

_____

_____

_____

_____

_____

Teacher's Resource Stage 1: Unit 8: resource sheet 2

Stage 1: Unit 9: resource sheet 1
Writing a fact file: writing questions

A Look at the question words in the box.
What two letters does each word start with? _____

B Add a question word from the Top Tip box to each of these questions.

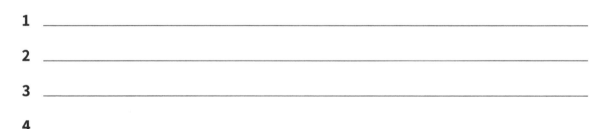

1 _____ time will you get here?

2 _____ are you late?

3 _____ shall we meet?

4 _____ is coming with you?

5 _____ does school start?

C Choose four of the question words from the Top Tip box.
Write a question using each one.

1 _____

2 _____

3 _____

4 _____

Teacher's Resource Stage 1: Unit 9: resource sheet 1   © Sarah Lindsay and Wendy Wren 2019

Stage 1: Unit 9: resource sheet 2
Writing a fact file: fact file layout

Fact file: _____

• _____

_____

_____

• _____

_____

_____

• _____

_____

_____

• _____

_____

_____

Stage 2: Unit 1: resource sheet 1
Plot: exclamation marks

If a sentence shows someone who is surprised or angry or is shouting, it ends with an *exclamation mark (!)*.

surprised	I don't believe it!
shouting	Quick, or we will be late!
angry	Come here, now!

A Sort these exclamations into the table.

Word box

Watch out!   You are late!

              Here I am!   Go to bed, now!

That can't be true!   Time to go!

Exclamations		
Surprised	**Shouting**	**Angry**

B Write your own exclamation.

_____

_____

Stage 2: Unit 1: resource sheet 2
Plot: ordering a story

A Look at the pictures.

B Sort these sentences into the right order.

Pep and Lin help Seagull.   Seagull is stuck in the bin.   Seagull looks in the bin.

Seagull flies off.   Seagull eats ice cream.

_____

_____

_____

_____

_____

C Write two sentences in the beginning, the middle and the end boxes.

The beginning of the story

_____

_____

The middle of the story

_____

_____

The end of the story

_____

_____

Teacher's Resource Stage 2: Unit 1: resource sheet 2   © Sarah Lindsay and Wendy Wren 2019

Stage 2: Unit 2: resource sheet 1
Dialogue in stories: speech bubbles

Copy the sentences into the speech bubbles. Make sure the comic strip makes sense.

Teacher's Resource Stage 2: Unit 2: resource sheet 1

Stage 2: Unit 2: resource sheet 2
Dialogue in stories: what happens next?

What happens next? Continue the comic strip story.

Draw your own pictures and add two speech bubbles in each scene.

Stage 2: Unit 3: resource sheet 1
Writing a recount: verbs and adjectives

A Sort these verbs into the table.

Word box

| grab | jumped | kick | lift |
| saved | munched | stop | licked |

Present tense verbs	Past tense verbs

B Sort these adjectives into the table.

Word box

| longer | tight | fuller | new |
| warm | old | kinder | deeper |

Adjectives	Comparative adjectives

Teacher's Resource Stage 2: Unit 3: resource sheet 1

Stage 2: Unit 3: resource sheet 2
Writing a recount

Write a recount about something exciting that happened to you.

Add a photo or draw a picture showing what happened.

<u>Something exciting happened!</u>

Stage 2: Unit 4: resource sheet 1
Writing an explanation: joining words

Sometimes we can join short sentences to make one long sentence.

A *joining word* (conjunction) is used to join the sentences.

The words *and*, *but*, *so* and *because* can be joining words.

Sometimes we look into the sky *and* it is light.

Sometimes we look into the sky *but* it is dark.

A Add the missing joining word from the box to finish each sentence.

Word box

| so | because | and | but |

1 I like waking up early _____ watching the sun rise.

2 I am very tired _____ I went to bed very late.

3 We must walk home now _____ we are not walking when it gets dark.

4 The Sun is shining _____ it is still cold in the wind.

B Finish these sentences. Underline the joining word.

1 I love to go swimming but _____

_____

2 I woke up early so _____

_____

3 I ran to school because _____

_____

Teacher's Resource Stage 2: Unit 4: resource sheet 1

Stage 2: Unit 4: resource sheet 2
Writing an explanation

Look carefully at this flow diagram.

Write an explanation describing what happens to the Sun during the day and the night.

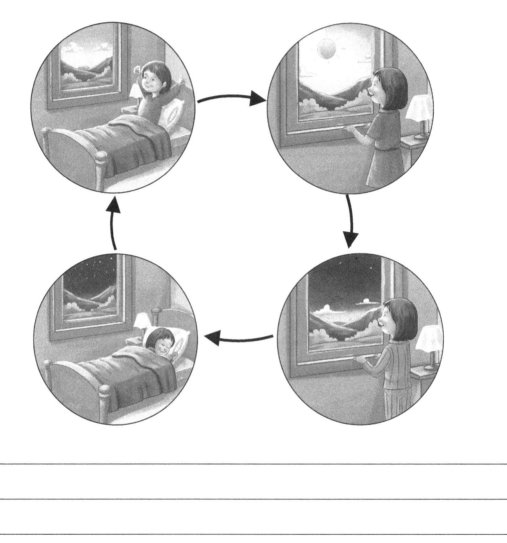

_____

_____

_____

_____

_____

_____

_____

Stage 2: Unit 5: resource sheet 1
Writing a simple recipe: verbs and adverbs

Top Tip

Remember, a *verb* is a doing word.
An *adverb* adds to the verb.
It tells us more about how something is done.

A Circle the verbs and underline the adverbs in each sentence.

  1 Tayla happily walked to her friend's house.

  2 The cow can suddenly moo if it wants some food.

  3 Mum quickly cleans before the visitors arrive.

  4 The water slowly ran into the bucket.

B Use these words to make a sentence.

  1 greedily   ate

  _____

  2 works   quickly

  _____

  3 neatly   laid

  _____

  4 shouted   angrily

  _____

C Write your own sentence adding an adverb.

  _____

  _____

Teacher's Resource Stage 2: Unit 5: resource sheet 1

Stage 2: Unit 5: resource sheet 2
Writing a simple recipe: ordering instructions

Top Tip

Remember, *instructions* need to be:
- numbered
- clearly written.

These instructions tell you how to make a drink, but they have been written in the wrong order.

Copy the instructions in the right order.

Add a piece of fruit.

Now fill the glass with water.

Finally, drink your fruit drink.

Take a glass from the cupboard.

Add some ice cubes.

First, add some fruit juice to the glass.

_____

_____

_____

_____

_____

_____

Teacher's Resource Stage 2: Unit 5: resource sheet 2　　　　© Sarah Lindsay and Wendy Wren 2019

Stage 2: Unit 6: resource sheet 1
Rhyming poems and list poems:
rhyming words

Top Tip

Remember, sometimes rhyming words end in the *same letter pattern*. Sometimes rhyming words *sound the same but are spelled differently*.

A Write a rhyming word for each of these bug names. The first one has been done for you.

1 ant _____pant_____   **2** bee _____

3 cricket _____   **4** beetle _____

5 moth _____   **6** spider _____

7 hornet _____   **8** snail _____

B Write each pair of rhyming words from Activity A in a sentence. The first one has been done for you.

1 The ant had to pant as it dragged the fallen leaf. _____

2 _____

3 _____

4 _____

5 _____

6 _____

7 _____

8 _____

Teacher's Resource Stage 2: Unit 6: resource sheet 1

Stage 2: Unit 6: resource sheet 2
Rhyming poems and list poems: writing a poem

Write a list poem about the cricket in the pictures below.

Describe exactly what this cricket looks like.
Think about the adjectives you can use to make your poem interesting.
Start by writing words and phrases about the cricket.

Word box

long legs   bright eyes

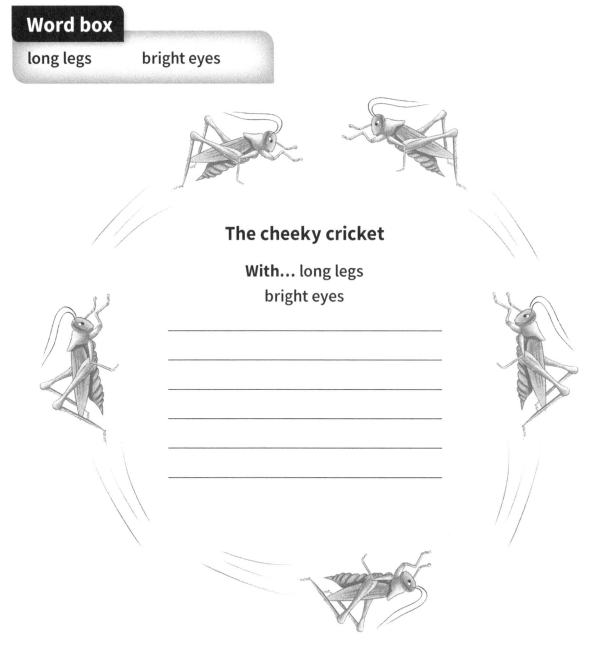

The cheeky cricket

With... long legs
bright eyes

_____

_____

_____

_____

_____

_____

Stage 2: Unit 7: resource sheet 1
Writing notes and tables: commas

We use *commas* when we write a **list** in a sentence.

We can join the last two things in the list with *and* or *or*.

Trees also give us fruits such as oranges, apples, lemons *and* olives.

A **Copy these sentences. Add the missing commas.**

1 I like the colours red yellow green and blue.

_____

2 Shall I go to the pool park shops or cinema?

_____

3 We went on a car train plane and bus to see my grandmother.

_____

4 I like to eat fish rice corn bread and honey.

_____

B **Write a list of five of your favourite things.**

_____

_____

_____

_____

_____

C **Write your favourite things in a sentence using commas.**

_____

_____

_____

Teacher's Resource Stage 2: Unit 7: resource sheet 1

Stage 2: Unit 7: resource sheet 2
Writing notes and tables: completing a table

At the factory

When the beans arrive at the factory, they are sorted and cleaned. Next they are roasted in a very hot oven, which cooks them. The beans are then crushed, which helps the shells fall off. After that, they are ground to make a thick, fatty cream called cocoa mass. Finally, the cocoa mass is squeezed very hard until all the fat comes out, leaving a dry powder called cocoa powder. This powder is used to make the chocolate bars we eat.

A Underline the key words in the information.

B Complete the table with the key information.

What happens to the beans in the factory	
Order	**Action**
1	sorted and cleaned
2	
3	
4	
5	

Stage 2: Unit 8: resource sheet 1
Interviews: verb tenses

A Add the missing verbs to this table. The first one has been done for you.

Verb family name	present tenses	past tense
to wave	she __waves__ I am __waving__	he __waved__
to cry	we _____ they _____ _____	I _____
to walk	you _____ he _____ _____	they _____
to shout	he _____ they _____ _____	we _____
to hurry	I _____ we _____ _____	you _____
to glide	it _____ you _____ _____	she _____

B Choose one of the verb families in the table.

Write three sentences, each sentence using one of the different verb tenses from the verb family.

1 _____

2 _____

3 _____

Stage 2: Unit 8: resource sheet 2
An interview

After writing your questions, you will be ready to do the interview.

A Write your questions neatly.

B Add a photograph or draw a picture of the person you are interviewing.

C Have the interview. Write the answers.

What was it like back then?

I am interviewing _____

Question 1 _____

_____

_____

_____

Teacher's Resource Stage 2: Unit 8: resource sheet 2

© Sarah Lindsay and Wendy Wren 2019

Question 2

_____

_____

_____

_____

_____

Question 3

_____

_____

_____

_____

_____

Question 4

_____

_____

_____

_____

_____

Question 5

_____

_____

_____

_____

Question 6

_____

_____

_____

_____

Teacher's Resource Stage 2: Unit 8: resource sheet 2

Stage 2: Unit 9: resource sheet 1
Setting and characters: a setting

A Cut out and stick a picture of a setting or draw a picture of your favourite place in the box.

B Write as many adjectives as you can to describe the setting.

C Write a long sentence describing the setting. Include a joining word.

_____

_____

Stage 2: Unit 9: resource sheet 2
Setting and characters: a character

A Draw or cut out a picture of a person or animal. Stick it on the page.

B Create a character for the person or animal in this picture.
   Write as many adjectives as you can to describe the character.

C Write a long sentence describing your character. Include a joining word.

_____

_____

Stage 3: Unit 1: resource sheet 1
'How is it done?' sentences

Top Tip

Remember, every sentence needs:
- a capital letter
- a verb
- punctuation at the end of the sentence.

Adjectives can make our sentences more interesting.

A Add the correct punctuation at the end of each of these sentences.

   1 I learned to ride my bike when I was five years old

   2 Why did it take me so long to learn how to ride my bike

   3 Did you fall off your bike many times

   4 I remember how it felt to ride by myself for the first time

B Circle the nouns and underline the adjective in each of these sentences.

   1 Barney's bike is faster than my scooter.

   2 I was braver than my brother when I fell off my bike.

   3 The roads are icier than yesterday so I have to be careful while riding my bike.

   4 My bike is older than all my friends' bikes but I still love it.

C Write two of your own sentences.

Use the correct punctuation and make sure you have a verb and comparative adjective in each sentence.

   1 _____

      _____

   2 _____

      _____

Teacher's Resource Stage 3: Unit 1: resource sheet 1

Stage 3: Unit 1: resource sheet 2
'How is it done?': writing an explanation

Use the words in the box to add to each step of the explanation on learning to ride a bike.

1
Word box		
carefully	support	get on

First you need to _____ _____ your bike _____.
An adult can help _____ the bike.

2
Word box		
ground	foot	pedal

Then place one _____ on the _____ and one on a _____.

3
Word box		
riding	adult	speed

Start _____ your bike at a steady _____ with an _____ helping.

4
Word box		
running	helping	ride

Then try to _____ your bike without the adult _____ but _____
alongside just in case your bike wobbles.

5
Word box		
without	ready	ride

When you are _____, you can _____ your bike _____ any help.

Stage 3: Unit 2: resource sheet 1
Writing a letter: pronouns

Remember, we can use *pronouns* in place of nouns. For example:

Noun	Pronoun
the boy	he
the girl	she
the boy and girl	they

People often write *letters* using the pronouns *I* and *we* because the writer is writing about something they experienced. These are known as *first person pronouns*.

> *I* was sorting through some old photos…
> … *we* went to the sandy beach…

A Underline the pronouns in these sentences.

1 I am looking forward to going to Grandma's house.

2 He always wants to have a bigger ice cream!

3 You made me laugh.

B Write your own sentences using these pronouns.

1 It _____

2 she _____

3 we _____

C Copy these sentences and add pronouns instead of the underlined words.

1 The bird was watching the children eating their ice creams.

_____

2 Aanya and Arjun's clothes were wet and Aanya and Arjun needed to change.

_____

Stage 3: Unit 2: resource sheet 2
Writing a letter

Address   _____

_____

_____

_____

Date   _____

Dear _____ name of who you are writing to

Paragraph 1: saying why you are writing the letter

_____

_____

_____

_____

Paragraph 2: the main part of the letter

_____

_____

_____

_____

Paragraph 3: an interesting ending to the letter

_____

_____

_____

_____

_____ A friendly ending

_____ Your name

     Teacher's Resource Stage 3: Unit 2: resource sheet 2

Stage 3: Unit 3: resource sheet 1
Dialogue in stories: writing dialogue

Top Tip

Remember, you know who is speaking because the writer puts *speech marks* ("…") *around the words that are spoken*.

The writer also:
- uses a *capital letter* for the first word spoken
- uses a *comma* between the spoken words and the non-spoken words
- names the *speaker*.

A Copy the sentences. Write them correctly, adding all missing punctuation and capital letters.

1 what are we going to eat for tea tonight asked Jac

_____

_____

2 we will go and hunt for insects as soon as the sun goes down said mum

_____

_____

3 i was hoping you were going to say that laughed Fabio

_____

_____

4 i love chasing insects giggled Jac

_____

_____

B Write one final sentence showing Mum's response to Fabio and Jac.

_____

_____

Stage 3: Unit 3: resource sheet 2
Dialogue in stories: using speech bubbles

The next day Fabio and Jac are playing in the sand dunes again.

Jac wants to go exploring, but Fabio reminds him of what happened the day before.

Fabio gets cross with Jac and says he won't go with him.

A Add the conversation Fabio and Jac are having to these speech bubbles. Look carefully at the pictures.

B Choose one picture. Write the conversation in a sentence using capital letters, speech marks and other punctuation properly.

_____

_____

_____

Teacher's Resource Stage 3: Unit 3: resource sheet 2

Stage 3: Unit 4: resource sheet 1
Humorous poems: prepositions

Top Tip

Remember, *prepositions* are words that tell us where something is, the 'position' of something.

The word pre<u>position</u> even has the word *position* in it!

It describes the relationship of a noun or pronoun to another word in a sentence.

A **Write a preposition that is the *opposite* of each of these words. The first one has been done for you.**

1 above   <u>below</u>

2 inside   _____

3 on   _____

4 under   _____

5 from   _____

6 out   _____

7 up   _____

8 behind   _____

B **Complete each sentence. Include a preposition.**

1 The sun came out from _____

2 The chicken scratched _____

3 The duck landed _____

4 We hid _____

5 Tuhil jumped _____

6 The horse cantered _____

C **Choose a pair of opposite prepositions from Activity A.**

  Write both prepositions in the same sentence.

_____

_____

Stage 3: Unit 4: resource sheet 2
Humorous poems: linking rhyming words

Link the rhyming words with a line.

Three words don't have a rhyming word to link with.

Write a rhyming word for each one in an empty box and join them with a line.

camel

pen

treat

rain

hall

coat

picture

vet

phone

track

dirt

straw

chair

queue

screw

den

street

land

meat

house

bear

channel

sack

fork

mixture

band

bone

mane

pet

ewe

shirt

sheet

shoe

floor

stork

hair

pear

Teacher's Resource Stage 3: Unit 4: resource sheet 2

Stage 3: Unit 5: resource sheet 1
Writing instructions and rules: imperative verbs

Top Tip

Remember, we can think of *imperative verbs* as 'bossy' verbs.
They are *present tense verbs* that tell us what to do.
First, *place* your cat to the side of the conveyor belt.

A Circle the imperative verb in each sentence.

1 Stop before you cross a road.

2 Look carefully at the directions.

3 Watch the time.

4 Catch the ball before it lands on the ground.

5 Turn the steering wheel so the car moves straight ahead.

B Use these verbs in a sentence.

1 drop

_____

2 cook

_____

3 hide

_____

4 mix

_____

5 throw

_____

C Write your own sentence using an imperative verb.

_____

© Sarah Lindsay and Wendy Wren 2019

Stage 3: Unit 5: resource sheet 2
Writing instructions and rules

Instructions for: _____

Instructions

1 _____

   _____

2 _____

   _____

3 _____

   _____

4 _____

   _____

5 _____

   _____

Rules

• _____

• _____

Teacher's Resource Stage 3: Unit 5: resource sheet 2

Stage 3: Unit 6: resource sheet 1
Posters and leaflets: adjectives

Adjectives are describing words.

Interesting adjectives can be used in posters to *persuade* the reader.

You will be entertained for hours with this *new, exciting* dinosaur play area.

A Write three interesting adjectives to describe each of these nouns.

    1 dinosaur

    _____ _____ _____

    2 book

    _____ _____ _____

    3 your friend

    _____ _____ _____

B Choose an interesting adjective that you have written in each question in Activity A. Write it into an interesting sentence you might use on a poster.

    1 _____

    _____

    2 _____

    _____

    3 _____

    _____

C Write each of these phrases into an interesting sentence.

    1 the terrified boy

    _____

    2 the chatty girl

    _____

Stage 3: Unit 6: resource sheet 2
Posters and leaflets: planning the writing for a leaflet

Spend a bit of time thinking about your film on dinosaurs.

Answer the questions below.

1 What is the name of your film?

_____

2 Describe the main characters.

_____

_____

_____

3 Write a few sentences about what happens in the film.

_____

_____

_____

_____

_____

4 Why should people come and see the film?

_____

_____

_____

_____

5 Where can people see the film?

_____

_____

Stage 3: Unit 7: resource sheet 1
Play scripts: adverbs

Adverbs tell us more about verbs.

We use adverbs in play scripts to show how something is done.

    The children walk *anxiously* through the trees.

How did the children walk?   *anxiously*

    Yes, open it *quickly* Ama!

How was Ama asked to open it?   *quickly*

Many adverbs are made by adding *-ly* to an adjective: *careful* + *ly* = carefully

A Write an adverb using each of these adjectives.

    1 quiet _____   **2** sad   _____

    3 bright _____   **4** nice   _____

B List six more adverbs.

_____   _____   _____

_____   _____   _____

C Copy these stage directions. Add an adverb to each one.

    1 The children ran over to the bridge.

    _____

    2 The children talked among themselves.

    _____

    3 The children climbed down to the water's edge.

    _____

    4 The children dragged the treasure out of the water.

    _____

Stage 3: Unit 7: resource sheet 2
Play scripts: the layout of a play

[Title] _____

Characters: _____   _____   _____

[Scene information] _____

_____

_____

[Stage direction] _____

_____

[Actor's name]   [Actor's words and stage direction]

_____ : _____

_____

_____ : _____

_____

_____ : _____

_____

_____ : _____

_____

_____ : _____

_____

_____ : _____

_____

Continue on a blank sheet of paper if there isn't enough space on this page.

Teacher's Resource Stage 3: Unit 7: resource sheet 2

Stage 3: Unit 8: resource sheet 1
A glossary: alphabetical order

Alphabetical order is the order in which you find letters in the alphabet.

These words are written in alphabetical order:

     *a*nkle   *k*nee   *t*high

If words start with the same letter you then need to look at the following letters and place those in alphabetical order. For example:

     h*a*nd   h*e*art   h*i*p

A Write the alphabet.

____ ____ ____ ____ ____ ____ ____ ____ ____ ____ ____ ____ ____

____ ____ ____ ____ ____ ____ ____ ____ ____ ____ ____ ____ ____

B Sort these words into alphabetical order. Each word starts with the same letter so you need to look at the second letter to place the words in alphabetical order.

1 lake   lizard   leaf   _____ _____ _____

2 square   sea   star   _____ _____ _____

3 horse   hug   hand   _____ _____ _____

4 bottle   berry   bridge   _____ _____ _____

C Write three words on these subjects. Each word must start with the same letter.

   Now write the words in alphabetical order.

1 sports   _____ _____ _____

                  _____ _____ _____

2 animals   _____ _____ _____

                  _____ _____ _____

3 names   _____ _____ _____

                  _____ _____ _____

Stage 3: Unit 8: resource sheet 2
Writing a glossary

Book title _____

Glossary

_____   _____

                   _____

_____   _____

                   _____

_____   _____

                   _____

_____   _____

                   _____

_____   _____

                   _____

_____   _____

                   _____

Teacher's Resource Stage 3: Unit 8: resource sheet 2

Stage 3: Unit 9: resource sheet 1
Story settings and endings: verb tenses

Verbs are written in the *past*, the *present* or the *future* tense.

Past = something that has already happened

She *jumped* in the water. She *was jumping* in the water.

Present = something that is happening now

She *jumps* in the water. She *is jumping* in the water.

Future = something that will happen

She *will jump* in the water.

A Complete the table with the correct verb tenses. The first one has been done for you.

Verb family name	Past (simple) tense	Present (simple) tense	Future tense
to sleep	I ___slept___	I ___sleep___	I shall ___sleep___
to run	he _____	he _____	he will _____
to climb	we _____	we _____	we shall _____
to eat	she _____	she _____	she will _____
to drink	I _____	I _____	I shall _____
to believe	he _____	he _____	he will _____

B Write whether each sentence is written in the past, present or future tense.

1 The cows will come in to be milked this afternoon. _____

2 I washed my dirty feet in the river. _____

3 Miss Patel's class work hard at their times tables. _____

4 The strong wind blew the tree over. _____

5 I shall run to school tomorrow. _____

6 I swam six lengths of the pool in record time. _____

Teacher's Resource Stage 3: Unit 9: resource sheet 1   © Sarah Lindsay and Wendy Wren 2019

Stage 3: Unit 9: resource sheet 2
Story settings and endings: writing a story setting

A Spend some time looking carefully at this picture.

B Write words and phrases you would use to describe the scene you are looking at.

```



```

C Write a detailed description of the setting, as if it was an opening to a story.

_____

_____

_____

_____

_____

_____

Teacher's Resource Stage 3: Unit 9: resource sheet 2

Glossary: Stages 1–3

The first use of each glossary term is indicated by the stage number in brackets.

adjective (S1)

describing word (S1)

describes a noun or pronoun:

the **fierce** lion; a **bright** moon

comparative adjective (S2)

compares two things, for example:

He is tall. She is **taller**.

adverb (S2)

gives extra information about a verb

manner (S2)

an adverb of manner

- tells us how something is done
- usually ends in -ly, for example:

He wrote **quickly**.

She sang **beautifully**.

alphabetical order (S1)

the order in which you find the letters in the alphabet

apostrophe (S2)

a punctuation mark indicating omission or possession

contraction (S2)

an apostrophe replaces missing letters when words are contracted, for example:

he is   he's

did not   didn't

capital letter (S1)

upper-case alphabet letter used to begin a sentence and proper nouns

captioned picture (S1)

a picture/illustration that has writing to explain what it is about

character (S2)

person or animal in a story, poem or play

comma (S2)

a punctuation mark indicating a short pause

in a list (S2)

a comma is used to separate words in a list within a sentence:

My favourite colours are red, blue, green and yellow.

in dialogue (S3)

a comma is used to separate spoken and non-spoken words, for example:

"I'm hungry," he said.

She said, "What is there to eat?"

contraction (S2)

shortened form of a word, most usually used in dialogue; an apostrophe replaces the missing letter(s), for example:

"**Where's** he going?" she asked.

"I **don't** know," he replied.

conjunction (S1)

word used to join sentences (also known as a *joining word*), for example:

I met a cat. I don't know where it lives.

I met a cat **but** I don't know where it lives.

definition (S3)

an explanation of what a word means

dialogue/direct speech (S3)

the actual words a character says

in prose (S3)

punctuated using speech marks for the spoken words; commas, question marks, exclamation marks and full stops are used, for example:

"I've finished my homework," he said.

He said, "I've finished my homework."

"Have you finished your homework?" she asked.

"Finish your homework!" she shouted.

in a play script (S3)

does not use speech marks; the dialogue is set out after the character's name, for example:

TOM: We visited an art gallery.

edit (S3)

to improve/correct a piece of writing

exclamation (S2)

speech that indicates, surprise, anger, fear, etc., for example:

I hate spiders!

exclamation mark (S2)

punctuation used to show surprise, anger, fear, etc., for example:

That's really scary**!**

explanatory writing (S3)

writing that explains how something is/was done; the stages in a process

fact (S1)

information considered to be true

fiction (S2)

pieces of writing based on the imagination

final copy (S3)

a piece of work that has been edited and proofread

first draft (S3)

a first attempt at a piece of work

flow diagram (S2)

a way of illustrating information in a specific order

glossary (S3)

a list of words, with their definitions, written in alphabetical order; glossaries explain the meaning of words that may be unfamiliar to readers

heading (S3)

the title of a piece of work, indicating what it is about

humorous poem (S3)

poem that makes the reader smile or laugh

illustration (S3)

drawing, photograph, diagram, chart, etc. that illustrates a piece of work

imperative verb (S3)

the form of a verb indicating an order or command; the imperative form is the infinitive of the verb without the **to**, for example:

Stop that!

Stir the mixture.

information (S3)

facts, statistics, measurements, etc. considered to be true

instructional writing (S1)

a form of writing that instructs, directs, advises and guides

interview (S1)

where one person asks questions of another

joining word (S1)

see *conjunction*

label (S1)

text to highlight information in a picture/illustration/diagram

layout (S3)

the way a piece of writing is arranged on the page

list (S1)

a group of words that are linked

list poem (S2)

poetry that is written as a list

non-fiction (S2)

writing that deals with information and is based in fact

notes (S2)

facts relevant to the writing task using phrases, abbreviations, etc.

noun (S1)

the name of a thing (also known as a *naming word*)

paragraph (S3)

   non-fiction (S3)

   a group of sentences within a longer piece of writing that deals with one aspect of a topic

past tense verb (S1)

indicates that actions have happened in the past

   past simple (S1)

   a regular verb forms the past simple with -*ed*/-*d*:

      I laugh**ed**

      I smil**ed**

   some verbs have irregular past simple forms, for example:

      I **ate**

      I **bought**

   past progressive (S2)

   formed with the past simple of the verb *to be* + *ing*, for example:

      I **was singing**.

      They **were clapping**.

persuasive writing (S3)

a form of writing that attempts to persuade the reader to buy something, visit somewhere or agree with the writer's opinion, for example, advertising

207

play script (S3)

the text of a play which includes the scene number, cast, setting, characters' names, dialogue and stage directions

plural (S1)

more than one of something

preposition (S3)

a word within a sentence that tells us the position of something; it describes the relationship of a noun or pronoun to another word in a sentence, for example:

    I hid **behind** a tree.

present tense verb (S1)

indicates that actions are happening now

    present simple (S1)

    I/you **read**

    he/she/it **reads**

    we/they **read**

pronoun (S3)

stands in place of a noun

    personal (S3)

    I/you/he/she/it/we/they

    first person (S3)

    I/we

proofread (S3)

check work for spelling, grammar and punctuation mistakes

proper noun (S1)

a noun with a capital letter

    name of a person (S1)

    Len/Himil/Ali

    day of the week (S2)

    Monday/Tuesday/Wednesday

    name of a place (S2)

    Mount Everest/Malaysia/Bank Street

question (S1)

used to indicate an enquiry, for example:

    What time is it?

question mark (S1)

a punctuation mark used with a question, for example:

    Where are you going**?**

recount (S1)

a form of writing that is based on the writer's experience

rhyme (S1)

words with similar sound, for example:

    cat   mat

    sea   bee

    bough   now

rule (S1)

a statement of something that must or must not be done

sentence (S1)

a group of words that:

- begins with a capital letter
- ends with a full stop, question mark or exclamation mark
- makes sense

    The box is empty.

    Is the box empty?

    The box is empty!

sequence (S3)

the way in which information, plot, etc. is ordered within a piece of writing

setting (S2)

a description of where a story or poem takes place

scene (S3)

where the action of part of a play takes place

singular (S1)

one of something

special naming word (S1)

see *proper noun*

speech bubble (S2)

a bubble coming from the mouth of a character showing what they are saying

speech mark (S3)

punctuation mark used to indicate spoken words, for example:

    "I have followed the recipe carefully," he said.

stage direction (S3)

instruction in a play script indicating how an actor says the lines or describes what they should do, for example:

    [*anxiously*]   Are we trapped?

    [*banging on the door*]   We have to get out of here.

title (S3)

the heading of a piece of writing